# THE
# CRAFT
## OF
# BAKING

# THE
# CRAFT
## OF
# BAKING

Cakes, Cookies & Other Sweets
**WITH IDEAS FOR INVENTING YOUR OWN**

**KAREN DeMASCO** & mindy fox

PHOTOGRAPHS BY ELLEN SILVERMAN

Clarkson Potter/Publishers
New York

Copyright © 2009 by Karen DeMasco and Mindy Fox
Photographs copyright © 2009 by Ellen Silverman

Library of Congress Cataloging-in-Publication Data
is available upon request.

ISBN 978-0-307-40810-5

Printed in China

Design by Amy Sly
Prop styling by Bette Blau
Food styling by Karen DeMasco and Mindy Fox

10  9  8  7  6  5  4  3  2  1

First Edition

To the loving memory of my grandparents
Leroy and Charlotte Parham and to the two most
talented craftswomen I know, my mother, Nancy Parham,
and my grandmother Edna Rankin

# CONTENTS

# INTRODUCTION

Growing up in Cleveland, Ohio, I was lucky to have family nearby. And I don't mean just a set of grandparents—we're talking several aunts and uncles and loads of cousins. We'd see each other throughout the year, but it was our Christmas supper together at my Grandma Rankin's house that I loved most.

Coming out of the cold winter air and into the warmth of Grandma Rankin's, I'd stop in the doorway just long enough for one slow, deep inhalation of simmering savory dishes and the toasted butter and caramelized sugar of sweets—scents that hung heavy in the air, having accumulated over days as my grandmother busily prepared for our arrival.

Inside, amid the twinkling lights and colored balls, was a table spread with freshly baked ham and all the fixings. And piled high on pretty plates and three-tiered cookie trays were pecan puffs, rugalach, cinnamon rolls, sugar cookies, popcorn balls, and linzer tarts, awaiting eager hands small and large. Tucked under the tree, there were toys and books wrapped in colorful holiday paper for the kids, and for the grown-ups, there was Grandma Rankin's coveted perfectly sweet and slightly salty cashew brittle, packed into cellophane bags tied with ribbon and adorned with gift tags. The year I turned thirteen, I found a bag of the brittle with my own name on the tag. It was a sign that I was growing up.

Today, Grandma Rankin—all five foot two of her, and still going strong at ninety-five—is still quite famous for her brittle. Her way with freshly roasted nuts, sugar, butter, and just the right amount of salt proved more than an inspiration for me, both as a simple home baker and as a professional pastry chef. In fact, learning how my grandmother cooked her butter and sugar together to just the right amber tone, carefully whisked in the baking soda and salt as the caramel rose up and bubbled, gingerly folded in the cashews until they were lovingly coated, spread the mixture onto a baking pan to achieve just the right thinness, and finally broke the cooled candy into crunchy shards of sweet, nutty goodness not only taught me how to make great candy, it set the foundation for my style as a pastry chef.

## THE LONG, SWEET PATH TO THE CRAFT OF BAKING

Like many chefs, bakers, wine professionals, restaurant managers and owners, and even waiters, my career in food was not at first an obvious path. Having graduated from college with a degree in English, I went out into the

world in pursuit of that elusive "creative career," a craft to which I could devote myself. Leads and instincts steered me to the publishing world and a solid first job at Simon & Schuster, where I managed the production of book jackets and covers.

Working in a fast-paced environment, complete with inventive colleagues, ever-looming deadlines, last-minute requests, and late nights, was exciting. But it took just one volunteer catering job—a favor to a friend in need—to realize that working with food contained all of those elements and, for me, much more. It was where I belonged.

I enrolled at New York Restaurant School, taking evening and weekend courses to learn the fundamentals of cooking. Upon graduation, I did an internship at Alison on Dominick—a cozy French restaurant tucked away on a secluded side street in Tribeca. There my garde manger responsibilities included preparing salads and appetizers and plating desserts. The sweets were simple and delicious; one has especially stuck with me for all of these years since. It was a rustic caramelized apple tart, served warm with a dollop of tangy crème fraîche—the perfect illustration that to be spot-on, a dessert does not require dozens of components or fussy preparations. Just keep it simple and do it well.

Over time, I realized that of all my tasks, I was most drawn to making the tarts, cookies, caramels, custards, and other delights of the pastry station. So I made it my goal to become a pastry chef and pursued it voraciously,

seeking to learn from professionals I admired at restaurants I loved. From New York's Chanterelle and Gramercy Tavern to Fore Street in Portland, Maine, I found exceptional mentors who shared their passion for quality and purity with me.

Chanterelle was a perfect jumping-off point. Preparing classic French desserts like vacherin, its crisp meringue disks layered with whipped cream and fruit; crunchy cream puffs filled with pastry cream and then dipped into sweet caramel; delicate mille-feuille made with endless layers of puff pastry; and homemade chocolates filled with cherry cordial or hazelnut praline gave me a good education in traditional European pastry technique.

From Chanterelle, I went to Gramercy Tavern, where I was fortunate to work for Claudia Fleming. Like Tom Colicchio, the former chef at Gramercy and now chef-proprietor at Craft, Claudia is a master at drawing intense flavor from seasonal ingredients. Under Claudia's tutelage, I came to think about pastry the same way that Tom and his crew think about cooking. Seasonal ingredients became the basis for my inspiration to try something new. I learned that applying just the proper cooking technique to an individual ingredient allows its primary flavor elements to shine.

At Gramercy Tavern I also learned flexibility. For example, with such a variety of local fruit coming from the Union Square Greenmarket, it was beneficial to understand how to substitute plums for apples in a crisp, or to replace cherries with a combination of figs and Concord grapes for a clafouti as the seasons changed. This was useful when I later found myself landing the pastry chef position at Sam Hayward's Fore Street. Sam's dedication to using fresh local ingredients is fierce. Farmers show up at the restaurant in the morning with basketfuls of ingredients for cooks to use that night. Having little idea what and how much would arrive, there was no time for planning ahead. I turned to rustic, homey desserts, folding the edges of cornmeal sablé dough, for example, over wild blueberries tossed with sugar to make a wood oven–baked free-form tart. Desserts like these recalled both the formal French fruit tarts of my Chanterelle days and the fresh flavor elements of Claudia's approach. By adding cornmeal to my sablé dough, I was also returning to the classic American traditions that Grandma Rankin often followed. A style all my own, built step-by-step, was coming together.

## BAKING IS A TRUE CRAFT

I refer to baking as a craft because it's about making things with care and ingenuity, using artistic skill, dexterity, and the purest ingredients. To hone a craft requires grace, commitment, and a deep personal interest. To excel at the craft of baking means being inventive while retaining a recipe's original integrity.

I have become known for a simple approach—building upon traditional recipes and familiar home baking techniques to create new modern-day treats. Grandma Rankin's Cashew Brittle, for example, inspired my Pumpkin Seed, Cacao Nib, Honeycomb, and Pink Peppercorn brittles.

These recipes, and others you'll find in this book, will feel familiar to you by the nature of their simple techniques and straightforward ingredients. At the same time, you'll notice a unique flair in how those ingredients are used or combined—an unexpected pairing of pear and fresh ginger in a crisp; a creamy, grown-up butterscotch pudding with a hint of salt; white chocolate cupcakes frosted with a decadent white chocolate cream cheese buttercream.

For me it feels natural to sprinkle a Milk Chocolate Hazelnut Panna Cotta with crushed shards of bittersweet Cacao Nib Brittle. Sorbets made from sour cherries or almond milk may sound complex but are just as easy to prepare as ordinary raspberry or lemon ones.

*The Craft of Baking* is a book that satisfies a wide range of moods and needs. Little Lemon Bars are ideal for a relaxed afternoon lunch; dark, rich Devil's Food Cupcakes with Cream Filling will be a hit at a children's party; and Pine Nut Tart with Rosemary Cream adds the final touch to a grown-up dinner. Whatever your occasion or whim, I hope you'll enjoy these recipes and use them as jumping-off points to explore your own flavors and combinations.

# THE CRAFT OF BAKING
# PANTRY

The key to making great desserts is using fresh, high-quality ingredients. I like to keep my pantry stocked with basics and to purchase any items I might use less often as I need them. Though not an exhaustive baking pantry list, this section includes the ingredients I use most and that are found in the recipes in this book. See Sources (page 249) for purchasing information.

## FLOURS AND GRAINS

For long-lasting freshness, store flours in airtight containers, preferably in containers that do not allow light to penetrate or in a light-free pantry, in a cool place. King Arthur is my go-to brand for all flours, including organic.

### UNBLEACHED ALL-PURPOSE FLOUR

From biscuits, scones, and muffins to cookies, cakes, and pie dough, all-purpose flour is the most common flour used in baking. Look specifically for *unbleached* flour, which is free of bitter-tasting chemicals and potentially harmful additives.

### CAKE FLOUR

A finely milled flour made with a softer wheat than all-purpose flour and with a lower protein level, cake flour produces tender cakes and pastry and is often used in conjunction with other flours, such as all-purpose.

### HIGH-GLUTEN FLOUR (BREAD FLOUR)

As its name suggests, this flour is high in gluten, or protein, giving elasticity to breads.

### NUT FLOURS AND NUT MEALS

Nut flour is ground from the cake that remains after the oils are pressed out of nuts. Nut meal is made from finely ground nuts. You can purchase nut flours or meals, or you can finely grind your own (see page 157). For example, for ¾ cup almond flour, finely grind ¾ cup sliced blanched almonds with 1 tablespoon unbleached all-purpose flour. Nut flour and meal can be used interchangeably. Best when fresh, nut flours and meals should be stored in an airtight container in the freezer for up to 1 month.

### POLENTA AND CORNMEAL

I love the gritty texture that polenta, or coarsely ground cornmeal, gives to cookies and tart crusts. The most flavorful cornmeal comes from artisanal mills. My all-time favorite is Anson

Mills' yellow Artisan Fine Polenta. Keep cornmeal well sealed in an airtight container in the freezer. It will last for up to a year.

## SWEETENERS

### GRANULATED SUGAR

The most common sugar, granulated sugar can be purchased in either refined or natural states. I prefer the natural version, which, less refined and unbleached, retains both a rich flavor and some color from the molasses of the sugarcane. Ranging in color from pale blond to golden, natural cane sugar can be used in any recipe that calls for granulated sugar, in a one-to-one substitution.

### DEMERARA SUGAR

This unrefined cane sugar has large crystals that retain their ragged texture through the baking process. I use it liberally to create a crunchy topping for cookies and cakes.

### MAPLE SUGAR

This sugar is what's produced when the water has been boiled out of the sap from a sugar maple tree. It can be used in conjunction with cane sugar when you want a little added maple flavor, and is great incorporated into ice cream, cookies, whipped cream, and more.

### HONEY

One of my favorite ingredients, for both its sweetness and its incredible range of flavor, honey can be used simply as a sweetener or as the major flavor component of a dessert. My good friends from Tremblay Apiaries in Van Etten, New York, first taught me about honey

and its many varieties, from the gentle floral notes of a mild linden honey to the deep, earthy tones of an intense bamboo honey. Experiment with honeys of various flavors as you bake, and see what you like best.

### BROWN SUGAR

Brown sugar comes in light and dark varieties. Conventional brown sugar is granulated sugar with molasses added to deepen its color and flavor. If you're using conventional brown sugar, I recommend dark. Conventional light brown sugar has very little flavor. Overall, however, I prefer the organic versions, which retain their natural molasses. Both light and dark organic varieties are much more flavorful than their conventional counterparts. Generally, light and dark brown sugars can be used interchangeably. When you want an intense molasses and deep dark licorice flavor, Billington's organic dark brown molasses sugar is the best. In rich desserts with a slightly bitter bent, like the Gingerbread Cupcakes (page 161) and the Pumpkin Ice Cream (page 209), this sugar works particularly well.

### BARLEY MALT SYRUP

This natural liquid sweetener, produced from sprouted barley and often used in bread making, is about half as sweet as granulated sugar. Dark brown, thick, and sticky, it's great when used in combination with other sweeteners for bringing malt flavor into ice creams and chocolate sauce. Barley malt syrup is considered to be one of the healthiest sweeteners in the natural food industry, since it's produced from a whole food source and is made up of simple sugars.

## SALT

Just as it does in the savory kitchen, salt perks up and pulls forth the flavor of baked goods. Most pastries, cookies, cakes, and even ice creams contain some salt. I use kosher salt in baking because I prefer its taste to other basic salts, but you can use whatever salt you like. If you are using a finer salt, you can cut back the amount a bit to compensate. If you are sensitive to salt, you can use less than I call for. A flaky sea salt, like Maldon, makes a nice garnish for chocolate or caramel desserts.

## EGGS

You can see and taste the difference in your baked goods when you use the freshest, highest-quality eggs available. Fresh, sustainably raised, local eggs yield a creamier anglaise, a more golden cake, richer puddings, and generally better-tasting desserts than less fresh and conventionally raised eggs do.

## BUTTERS

### UNSALTED BUTTER

Since the quantity of salt in salted butter varies from brand to brand, the unsalted version is the butter of choice for most bakers and cooks. Land O'Lakes is my brand of choice. It is reasonably priced and tastes good.

### HIGH-FAT BUTTER

In recipes where butter is a key ingredient, such as shortbread cookies (page 60) and brioche (page 39), I use high-fat butter. With more fat and less water, the high-fat version has a fuller flavor than regular butter. High-fat butter can be used interchangeably with regular butter in any recipe, so feel free to make the substitution whenever you want to make something extra-special. Plugrá is a great brand, and one that is widely available in supermarkets.

## OILS

### GRAPESEED OIL

I tend to favor grapeseed oil, which has a pleasing light, neutral flavor, over vegetable or nut oils in basic baked goods like quick breads and cakes.

### OLIVE OIL

A great baking oil, olive oil lends its spectrum of fruity to peppery flavors to cakes and to sauces like Olive Oil Sabayon (page 240). Choose an oil that you like the taste of, since its flavor will come through. You may also enjoy drizzling high-quality flavored olive oils over slices of simple cakes, as I do with lemon olive oil over slices of Lemon Olive Oil Cake (page 148).

### PEANUT OIL

This is my number-one frying oil. It is mild in flavor and odor, producing crisper, less greasy fried desserts than a more pungent oil like canola. If you have an allergy to peanuts, I recommend soy oil.

## DAIRY

### MILK

I always choose hormone- and antibiotic-free milk for general baking and for drinking. When

GRANDMA RANKIN'S CASHEW BRITTLE,
HONEYCOMB BRITTLE, CACAO NIB BRITTLE, PINK
PEPPERCORN BRITTLE, AND PUMPKINSEED BRITTLE

making milk-focused desserts, such as panna cotta or ice cream, it's worth it to splurge for the higher quality local stuff, which generally offers deeper, richer flavors.

### CREAM

Don't confuse heavy cream (which is at least 38 percent fat) with whipping cream (which is only 30 percent fat) when shopping. Whipping cream cannot be substituted for heavy cream. I use hormone- and antibiotic-free cream whenever possible. I also keep an eye out for higher-fat cream (with 40 percent fat), which is especially great for adding a luxurious extra smoothness to puddings.

### BUTTERMILK

This rich-tasting milk adds a tangy taste to all sorts of baked goods. Its acidity brightens the overall flavor in a recipe.

### CRÈME FRAÎCHE

This cultured cream is similar to sour cream in tang, but richer and creamier. I like to whip it to peaks as you do with heavy cream and dollop a spoonful over sugary desserts to offset the sweetness. My all-time favorite brand is Vermont Butter & Cheese; to me their crème fraîche is unmatched in both quality and flavor.

### FRESH RICOTTA CHEESE

A soft, creamy cheese, fresh ricotta is great in cakes and beignets (page 172). Look for ricotta at your local cheese shop or buy Calabro's whole-milk ricotta at just about any super-market. Fresh ricotta needs to be drained overnight before using. Line a fine-mesh sieve with a coffee filter and set the sieve over a bowl. Put the ricotta in the filter and let the cheese drain overnight in the refrigerator. Fresh ricotta is quite perishable, so use it within a few days of purchasing.

### YOGURT

When yogurt is called for in desserts, use the whole-milk type. I favor the tangy, grassy sheep's milk variety. My brand of choice is 3-Corner Field Farm. Old Chatham Sheep-herding Company is another nice one.

## CHOCOLATE

The percentage associated with chocolates refers to the percentage of its cocoa butter and its cocoa solids. The higher the chocolate's percen-tage, the lower the percentage of sugar and the darker, more intense-tasting the chocolate will be. Percentage determines neither taste nor quality. These factors depend on many issues, including the quality, variety, sweetness, and acidity of the cacao beans, the skill with which the beans were roasted and blended, how much cocoa powder versus cocoa butter is used, and the quality and amount of the other ingredients that make up chocolate, like sugar, vanilla, and milk (in milk and white chocolates). In general, the fewer the ingredients, the better the quality of the chocolate. Avoid chocolate with chemical additives and unnatural flavorings.

### MILK CHOCOLATE

When it comes to milk chocolate, I love Scharffen Berger, which has an intensely chocolaty flavor and hints of caramel. Available only in 3-ounce bars, it can get pretty expensive. El Rey also makes a nice milk chocolate, and one that is available in more reasonably priced 2.2-pound blocks.

### DARK CHOCOLATE

Scharffen Berger's 70% chocolate has a great fruity flavor that works well in cakes, cookies, sauces, and ganache. For very special occasions, I use Amedei Toscano Black 70% for its rich tobacco flavor and smooth texture. Great in baked goods, it makes a particularly extra-luxurious ganache.

### WHITE CHOCOLATE

For a long time I avoided white chocolate because I found it to be cloyingly sweet. Once I learned how to work with it, however, I came to really enjoy its rich creaminess. White chocolate's high-pitched sweetness requires a counterpoint. Lemon, rum, and coconut milk do the trick, as you will see in my recipes that use white chocolate. My favorite white chocolate is called Selváticas Jaina, made by the Spanish chocolatier, Chocovic. It has 31 percent cacao solids and is made with yogurt, which gives it a bright flavor. El Rey makes a great white chocolate, too.

### CACAO NIBS

Cacao beans that have been roasted, hulled, and broken into bits are sold as "nibs." Slightly nutty, with a pleasing slightly bitter taste and hints of chocolate flavor, they have a wonderful crunch that's terrific in brittles and ice creams. Scharffen Berger makes great cacao nibs.

## NUTS

Nuts bring flavor, texture, and healthy fats to baked goods. Toasting nuts brings out their flavor, which is why they are most often toasted before being added to a batter or dough. All nuts are quite perishable—walnuts, pine nuts, and hazelnuts particularly so. For the freshest product, purchase nuts from a reputable source and keep them in an airtight container in the freezer.

### SICILIAN PISTACHIOS

These very special pistachios, grown in volcanic soil, have a brilliant bright green color and an exceptional pronounced flavor. In looks and taste alike, they make incomparable cakes, biscotti, candies, and ice creams.

### HAZELNUTS

Hazelnuts come blanched or with their skins. I prefer the blanched type but you can use either. Lightly toast the skin-on version and then rub them in a clean dish towel to remove the skins.

### PINE NUTS

Tiny and higher in fat than most other nuts, pine nuts add a richness to both savory and sweet dishes.

### MARCONA ALMONDS

These addictive delights from Spain are fried in olive oil and lightly salted. Use them to give a creamy nut flavor and an extra kiss of salt to any dessert that calls for almonds.

# FLAVORINGS

## COFFEE EXTRACT

I like to make my own coffee extract with Medaglia D'Oro instant espresso powder and hot water (page 79), though you can purchase it, if you prefer. A good brand is Trablit, which comes in 3-ounce bottles.

## VANILLA

As my vanilla bean supplier says, and I agree, vanilla is the salt and pepper of the baking world. Its 256 flavor compounds enhance the flavors of its fellow ingredients in anything cooked or baked. In fact, vanilla is an ingredient in all chocolate and is considered by chocolate connoisseurs to be critical in bringing out the depth and range of flavors in chocolate.

When purchasing vanilla, in bean, paste, and extract forms, quality is of the utmost importance. Inferior vanilla, such as low-quality beans or synthetic ("imitation") extracts, will leave your baked goods and custards tasting flat.

## VANILLA BEANS

Vanilla beans are cultivated in several parts of the world. My preferences are Bourbon beans, from Madagascar, and Tahitian beans.

Bourbon-Madagascar beans offer a very classic, rich, and complex (many describe it as chocolaty) vanilla flavor. They're chockful of natural vanillin, the main ingredient in pure vanilla extract, varying from 1.8 to 3 percent depending on the quality of the bean. I find this variety of bean rounds out the flavors of other ingredients in baked goods while adding its own soft, smooth flavor.

Tahitian vanilla beans are fruitier than their Bourbon counterparts, with floral, licorice, and cherry notes, and much lower in vanillin. Though they are not as widely available, it's worth the effort to track down these beans, especially when vanilla is the focus of a recipe, such as in Vanilla Bean Ice Cream (page 204). Tahitian beans are plumper than Bourbons and have fewer seeds.

Keep vanilla beans at cool room temperature, well wrapped and away from the light.

## RECYCLING VANILLA BEANS

A fresh vanilla bean pod that's been used to flavor an ice cream, custard, or dough still has a lot of flavor to offer and can be "recycled." Rinse the used bean well under cold water, washing off any stray batter or dough, and then let it dry and harden, uncovered, at room temperature, before wrapping and storing it at cool room temperature. Recycled beans will rehydrate when used for poaching or roasting fruit, or when making a fruit soup, a syrup, or a sauce. You can also use recycled beans to make a fragrant vanilla-flavored sugar to use for baking: Just add one or two beans to a canister of granulated sugar and let them sit for at least 3 days. Once the sugar is flavored, you can leave the beans in or take them out, as you like.

## VANILLA BEAN PASTE

This sweet, concentrated vanilla bean and extract mixture is a great substitute for either form of vanilla. Use half the amount of paste in place of extract, or 1 tablespoon paste for 1 bean.

### VANILLA EXTRACT

Be sure you look for a "pure" extract, which derives its flavor from vanilla beans, versus imitation, which is chemical-laden, bitter tasting, and has no actual vanilla in it.

## SPICES

Spices are best toasted just before using, to draw out their flavorful oils. Because whole spices retain their flavor longer than ground, purchase the freshest spices possible in whole form from a reputable shop and then use a spice grinder or clean coffee grinder to grind them, only as needed. Keep spices in a cool, dark place for no longer than 6 months.

### SAIGON OR VIETNAMESE CINNAMON

This very spicy cinnamon has a Red Hots–candy flavor. It comes in broken pieces, as opposed to sticks. Depending on the size, you can generally substitute two 1-inch pieces for a 3-inch stick of regular cinnamon.

### GREEN CARDAMOM PODS

Intensely aromatic, cardamom has a cool astringent flavor, similar to mint. One of my favorite spices, it is commonly used in Indian and Middle Eastern cooking. I find it works particularly well in fruit desserts and sauces, such as Maple Roasted Pineapple (page 231) and Spiced Caramel Sauce (page 246), and in Gingerbread Cupcakes (page 161). Cardamom is softer than most spices, but you can still grind it. Before using the freshly ground spice, sift it through a fine-mesh sieve to discard any larger pieces that resisted grinding.

### PINK PEPPERCORNS

Actually not a peppercorn, but a dried berry, these have a beautiful pink color and a fruity, sweet, peppery flavor. They pair well with poached or roasted summer fruit and make a great last-minute dusting over a dessert. Their mix of sweet and spicy flavors works particularly well in Pink Peppercorn Brittle (page 100).

## VITAMIN C POWDER

This intense powder packs a tangy punch. I use a small amount mixed with sugar to toss jelly candy in, for a delicious sweet-and-sour flavor. I also use it to keep sorbets from losing their brilliant color and turning brown when they are made with fruits that tend to oxidize, such as bananas, apricots, pears, and plums. Simply whisk in about $1/8$ teaspoon per cup of sorbet base. Vitamin C powder can be found at vitamin and health care stores; just be sure to purchase *regular*, not *buffered*.

# TECHNIQUES TO HELP YOU HONE
# YOUR CRAFT

Understanding basic techniques is an important factor in making great desserts. This section is helpful whether you're exploring a technique for the first time or simply refreshing your memory.

### MEASURING PANS

Using a ruler, measure baking pans between the inside edges of the pan. If your pan is a little smaller or larger than a recipe requires, you can make adjustments: use less of the batter for a smaller pan, or shorten the baking time to accommodate a larger one.

### SETTING UP AN ICE BATH

The purpose of an ice bath is to quickly cool a warm ingredient or mixture. To make an effective ice bath, use a bowl that is significantly larger than the one that includes the warm ingredient. Fill the large bowl about half way with ice, then add just enough cold water to allow the smaller bowl to submerge enough so that the ice and ice water surround its outer edges.

### WORKING WITH BUTTER

Whether you're working with cold, softened (room-temperature), or melted butter, cut the butter into small pieces before you begin. Small pieces speed up the softening and melting processes, and—whether the butter is being used cold or softened—blend more evenly and quickly into a dough than larger ones.

### CUTTING OUT COOKIE DOUGH

Dip cookie and biscuit cutters in flour between cuts. This helps keep the cuts clean and precise, giving the finished product a nice well-defined shape.

When dough is re-rolled, the glutens in the flour are further activated, which reduces the lightness and flakiness of the product once it's baked. Most dough scraps can be re-rolled once, but not more. To keep scraps to a minimum when cutting out biscuits, doughnuts, and cookies, cut the items as close together as possible.

### SHAPING PIE OR TART DOUGH TO CHILL

Shape pie or tart dough into a large (about 6 to 8 inches) uniformly thin, flattened disk, rather than a misshapen disk or ball, before chilling. When you're ready to roll out the dough, you won't have as far to roll to get a nice thin round.

### ROLLING OUT AND FITTING PIE OR TART DOUGH INTO PANS

Use a clean, well-floured surface for rolling. Allow the dough to soften at room temperature for about five minutes before rolling it out. A nice large disk of dough should only require a few rolls in each direction before fitting into the pan. I like to roll up and down, then turn the dough 180 degrees and repeat to form a uniform circle. To release the dough from the surface, slide a large metal spatula (offset is best) underneath it. To transfer the dough to a baking pan, gently roll it onto a rolling pin, then unroll it over the pan. The key here is to have the dough at the proper temperature: not too cold, which will cause it to crack, and not too warm, which will make it difficult to move without tearing. If your dough becomes too warm while you are rolling it out, simply put it back into the refrigerator to chill until it is firm enough to work with. Most pie and tart doughs are forgiving. It's fine to use scraps to patch cracks or holes; you can even patch a crust that has been blind baked before adding the filling, as long as the tart or pie will be baked again.

### BAKING WITH EGGS

In cakes, cookies, and other baked goods, use eggs at room temperature—they create a smoother batter than cold eggs do. Cold eggs, however, are easier to separate than eggs at room temperature. When separated eggs are called for, separate them first, then let them come to room temperature, if desired.

### BEATING EGG WHITES

Start with room-temperature whites, which whip to a greater volume than cold whites. Use a clean, dry stainless-steel or copper bowl. When using a standing electric mixer, loosen the whisk attachment so that it sits directly on the bottom of the bowl. You can do this by setting, but not locking, the whisk into place. This is especially helpful when beating small quantities of whites.

Begin with the mixer on low speed, allowing the whites to build volume slowly, which creates a better structure than a faster speed. When the whites appear frothy, with enough bubbles so that you cannot see the bottom of the bowl, increase the speed by one notch and add your sugar, if using. When the whites look more like shaving cream than soap bubbles, you have the beginning of a soft peak. Stop the mixer and begin to test the whites. At soft peak, whites form a point that flops when it is lifted from the whites with a whisk. Stiff-peak whites form a peak that remains standing. When the whites get close to stiff, finish beating by hand to avoid overbeating.

### USING DARK METAL OR NONSTICK BAKING PANS AND SHEETS

The recipes in this book were tested using stainless-steel pans. Dark metal or nonstick pans may brown baked goods faster. If you are using dark metal pans, reduce the oven temperature by 25 degrees. The baking time may also need to be slightly reduced.

## USING AN OVEN THERMOMETER

Purchase an inexpensive oven thermometer at any hardware store to make sure your oven setting is accurate. Set the thermometer in the center of the oven, and toward the rear, for the most accurate reading. If you find that your oven temperature is higher or lower than the thermostat setting, simply adjust the thermostat accordingly.

## TOASTING NUTS AND COCONUT FLAKES

Spread nuts and coconut flakes evenly on a pan before toasting. When stirring, be sure to pull nuts and flakes in from the outside edges of the pan, where the heat is more intense.

## FOLDING

Always add a lighter mixture to a heavier mixture (not the other way around) when folding together two elements. Use a dry rubber spatula. Cut the spatula down into the center of the two mixtures, then draw it up and around the edge of the bowl, rotating it over to bring the mixture up from the bottom and over the top. Make a deep enough movement so that the mixture at the bottom of the bowl is folded up to the top. Repeat, rotating the bowl, just until the mixtures are combined.

## SCOOPING BATTER

Ice cream scoops come in a variety of sizes and are useful for scooping batter uniformly for cookies and cupcakes. Use a tiny scoop for cookies and a larger one for cupcakes.

## FRYING

Use a large heavy-bottomed saucepan for frying, and monitor the temperature of the oil with a candy or deep-frying thermometer. Fry in batches to avoid crowding the pan; frying too many items in a pan at one time lowers the temperature of the oil and makes it harder to manage the items in the pan.

To dispose of frying oil, let the hot oil cool, and then use a small funnel to pour it back into the (empty) bottle it came from for easy and clean disposal.

## MAKING AND JUDGING CARAMEL

Making caramel can be intimidating at first, but you will quickly become more comfortable with the process.

Use a large pot to make caramel, especially if you are adding liquid, which will bubble up. Keep a small bowl of ice water nearby to dip your finger or hand into should hot caramel splatter. When adding liquid to caramel, wear an oven mitt on the hand that is whisking to prevent burns from splatter. Pour liquid into the caramel in a slow stream.

Judge the color of caramel by dropping a small spoonful onto a white plate. A yellow-gold color (think yellow labrador retriever) is the first stage, perfect for making butterscotch. The next stage is a light amber (like a golden retriever). This is usually used with caramel that is going to be cooked again, as in tarte tatin and apple butter. Following this stage is a dark amber (Irish setter color), used for caramel sauces, brittles, and candies, and then, finally, the smoking dark brown (dark chocolate labrador retriever) caramel that I use for caramel ice cream. While judging the caramel, remove the pot from the heat to slow the cooking process. You can always return it to the heat if you want to cook the caramel further.

If you think you've burned your sugar during the caramel-making process, start over before adding anything to it, like butter or cream (sugar is inexpensive; the other ingredients are not). To clean a pot of burnt caramel, carefully set the hot pan into the sink. Gently drip the water from the faucet *away* from the pan until the water is warm. Then stand back from the sink while you move the faucet over the pan to avoid splattering. Add enough water to the pot to cover the burnt sugar. Once the mixture stops bubbling, return the pot to the stove and bring the water to a boil (the burnt caramel will loosen from the pot). Then pour the mixture down the drain and clean out your pot.

## TEMPERING CHOCOLATE

When using melted chocolate to dip a cookie or to roll a truffle, it is important that the chocolate be "in temper." This means that it is emulsified (all of the fats and solids are combined), so that you end up with a glossy, hard chocolate coating. Using a chocolate that is out of temper will result in a soft, cloudy coating once the chocolate cools.

To temper chocolate, bring about 2 inches of water to a simmer in a large saucepan. Chop the chocolate into small pieces and put about two thirds of it into a clean, dry heatproof mixing bowl. Set the bowl over the simmering water and gently stir the chocolate with a heatproof rubber spatula until it is smooth and completely melted.

Remove the bowl from the saucepan (keep the water at a simmer). About 2 tablespoons at a time, add the reserved chopped chocolate to the melted chocolate, stirring to melt it. (This method of tempering is called "seeding," because the pieces of fresh chopped chocolate, or "seeds," which are in temper, bring the melted chocolate into temper.) By this point, the melted chocolate will have cooled to about 80°F. Return the bowl to the saucepan of simmering water, and in 5-second intervals, heat and then remove the bowl, stirring the entire time, until the chocolate reaches 88° to 89°F on a thermometer, or until it feels just below body temperature to the touch when a bit is dabbed on the pulse point of your wrist. Your chocolate will be in temper at this point.

To test your temper, dip the tip of a knife into the chocolate and set the knife aside at cool room temperature. Within a few minutes, the chocolate should set evenly and be shiny and glossy, with no white streaks. If your chocolate is not in temper, let the bowl of chocolate cool to 80°F (or to just before it starts to set up), then gently reheat it over the simmering water, stirring constantly, to 88°F.

Milk and white chocolate are especially sensitive to heat—more so than dark. White chocolate is the most delicate to work with because it contains milk solids. White chocolate can easily lump up if exposed to too much heat, so make sure to keep the water at a bare simmer, and stir constantly as the chocolate melts.

# MUFFINS, SCONES, QUICK BREADS & OTHER BREAKFAST TREATS

# CHOCOLATE CHIP SCONES

I started making these scones one winter when I was faced with a dearth of fresh local fruit. Now they're a must-have for me no matter what the season!

MAKES 1 DOZEN

**1¾ cups all-purpose flour, plus more for rolling**

**1 tablespoon plus ½ teaspoon baking powder**

**¼ cup plus 2 tablespoons granulated sugar**

**½ teaspoon kosher salt**

**6 tablespoons (¾ stick) chilled unsalted butter, cut into small pieces**

**½ heaping cup (3 ounces) semisweet chocolate chips**

**1 cup plus 2 tablespoons heavy cream**

**1 tablespoon Demerara sugar**

In the bowl of an electric mixer fitted with the paddle attachment, combine the flour, baking powder, granulated sugar, and salt. Add the butter. Put the bowl in the freezer for 5 minutes. Then beat the mixture on low speed until the butter is broken up into pebble-sized pieces, about 3 minutes.

Add the chocolate chips. With the mixer on low speed, add 1 cup of the cream and mix just until the dough comes together. Using your hands, knead the mixture in the bowl to bring the dough completely together.

Turn out the dough onto a lightly floured surface and roll it into a 7-inch round, about ¾ inch thick. Using a sharp knife, cut the dough into 12 wedges, like pieces of pie.

Place the pieces on a baking sheet, spacing them ½ inch apart. Cover with plastic wrap and freeze for 15 minutes or chill in the refrigerator for 1 hour. (Unbaked scones, wrapped well, can be refrigerated for up to 2 days or frozen for up to 2 weeks.) When baking frozen scones, add 5 minutes to the baking time.

While the scones are chilling, preheat the oven to 375°F.

Brush the scones with the remaining 2 tablespoons cream and sprinkle with the Demerara sugar. Bake the scones, rotating the baking sheet once, until they are golden on the edges and on the bottom and are firm to the touch, about 20 minutes. Transfer to a wire rack to cool.

The scones are best served the day they're made, but they will keep in an airtight container at room temperature for up to 3 days.

## VARYING YOUR CRAFT
### CHOCOLATE CHIP–ESPRESSO SCONES
Stir together 1 tablespoon instant espresso powder and 1 teaspoon hot water, or use 1 tablespoon homemade Coffee Extract (page 79). Add the mixture to the dough when you add the cream.

# BUILDING YOUR CRAFT
## SCONES

Scones can be easily modified to include both sweet and savory flavors of all sorts. Use the Chocolate Chip Scone recipe (opposite) as your base. By maintaining the proportion of dry ingredients (flour, sugar, baking powder, and salt) to liquid (in this case heavy cream) and fats (butter), you can let your imagination and palate guide you in creating your own flavors.

Sweet spices, like cinnamon, star anise, and cardamom, can be added to the dry ingredients. The liquid can be modified to include buttermilk, sour cream, or citrus juice. A nice citrus scone can be made using ¾ cup heavy cream, ¼ cup fresh citrus juice, plus 1 teaspoon or so of finely grated zest.

For add-ins, fresh or dried fruit can be substituted for the chocolate chips. For fruits that might seep out a lot of liquid, such as strawberries, pineapple, or juicy peaches, use 1 tablespoon less cream. When using dried fruits, I like to plump them up a bit in a warm liquid, to soften them, before mixing into the dough. If you like, you can enhance the flavor of softened dried fruits with liquor or juice before adding them to the dough, as in the recipe for Rum Raisin Scones (page 28). Toasted nuts, candied ginger, or maple sugar, and even finely chopped fresh herbs, like thyme, rosemary, or mint, are all great add-ins for sweet scones.

For savory scones, try flavor enhancers like fennel seeds, black or red chili pepper, and smoked Spanish paprika; fresh herbs, like chives, thyme, sage, and rosemary; nuts; cheeses (use cheeses that crumble well, like soft goat cheese or feta, or hard cheeses that grate well, like Parmigiano-Reggiano or cheddar); and meats, like bacon, prosciutto, and merguez sausage. You can sprinkle the tops of savory scones with crunchy bits of coarse sea salt in place of the Demerara sugar. For savory scones, you'll still want to use sugar in the dough, which, like salt, helps bring forth the flavors of the other ingredients.

### BASIC GUIDELINES

Here's how to modify the Chocolate Chip Scone base recipe. (Maintain the flour, baking powder, and butter amounts as indicated.)

- **SUGAR** For sweet scones, use ¼ cup. For savory scones, decrease the sugar to 1 teaspoon.

- **SALT** For sweet scones, use ½ teaspoon. For savory scones, use 1 teaspoon.

- **LIQUID** Can be cream, buttermilk, or a combination. When using citrus juice, ¼ cup of juice can replace ¼ cup of the cream or buttermilk.

- **ADD-INS** ½ to 1 cup of fruit, nuts, cheese, and so on can be used in place of the chocolate. You can use a single add-in or a combination. When using wet fruit, such as strawberries, or soft cheese, like goat, use only ½ cup. A complementary ingredient can be added, as long as it is dry and lightweight, such as slivered almonds or fresh herbs.

# SOUR CHERRY SCONES

The gorgeous ruby-red color and juicy-tart flavor punctuate these pretty scones.

1¾ cups unbleached all-purpose flour, plus more for rolling

1 tablespoon plus ½ teaspoon baking powder

¼ cup granulated sugar

½ teaspoon kosher salt

6 tablespoons (¾ stick) chilled unsalted butter, cut into small pieces

½ cup pitted sour cherries (about 30), fresh or unthawed frozen

1 cup plus 2 tablespoons heavy cream

1 tablespoon Demerara sugar

**TIP** More tender than their sweeter cousins, sour cherries don't cling as much to the pit as other varieties, making them quite easy to work with. Generally, you can just squeeze the pit out from the fruit with your index finger and thumb.

**NOTE** Though the season is short (late June to early July), sour cherries freeze well and the frozen version works just as well as the fresh in this recipe.

In the bowl of an electric mixer fitted with the paddle attachment, combine the flour, baking powder, granulated sugar, and salt. Add the butter. Put the bowl in the freezer for 5 minutes. Then beat the mixture on low speed until the butter is broken up into pebble-sized pieces, about 3 minutes.

Add the cherries, and mix on low speed just until they are evenly distributed, about 5 seconds. Then add 1 cup of the cream and mix just until the dough comes together. Using your hands, knead the mixture in the bowl to bring the dough completely together.

Turn out the dough onto a lightly floured surface and roll it into a 7-inch round, about ¾ inch thick. Using a sharp knife, cut the dough into 12 wedges, like pieces of pie.

Place the pieces on a baking sheet, spacing them ½ inch apart. Cover with plastic wrap and freeze for 15 minutes or chill in the refrigerator for 1 hour. (Unbaked scones, wrapped well, can be refrigerated for up to 2 days or frozen for up to 2 weeks. If using frozen cherries, it's preferable to freeze, not refrigerate, unbaked scones.) Frozen scones can be baked immediately. Add 5 minutes to the baking time.

While the scones are chilling, preheat the oven to 375°F.

Brush the scones with the remaining 2 tablespoons cream and sprinkle with the Demerara sugar. Bake the scones, rotating the baking sheet once, until they are golden on the edges and on the bottom and are firm to the touch, about 20 minutes. Transfer to a wire rack to cool.

The scones are best served the day they're made, but they will keep in an airtight container at room temperature for up to 3 days.

## VARYING YOUR CRAFT
### SOUR CHERRY–ALMOND SCONES
Add ½ cup toasted slivered almonds to the dough and sprinkle 2 tablespoons untoasted slivered almonds (along with the Demerara sugar) on top just before baking.

# RUM RAISIN SCONES

I love this grown-up twist on a simple currant scone.

MAKES 1 DOZEN

½ cup raisins

½ cup dark rum, such as Myers's

1¾ cups unbleached all-purpose flour, plus more for rolling

1 tablespoon plus ½ teaspoon baking powder

¼ cup granulated sugar

½ teaspoon kosher salt

6 tablespoons (¾ stick) chilled unsalted butter, cut into small pieces

¾ cup plus 2 tablespoons heavy cream

1 tablespoon Demerara sugar

TIP Rum raisins can be made up to 3 months ahead. The longer they sit, the more flavor they develop, so make them at least a few days ahead when you can.

NOTE Here the rum delivers much more than just flavor. It also plumps up the raisins, creating a deliciously moist crumb.

Put the raisins in a medium saucepan and cover with 1 cup water. Bring the mixture to a boil, remove from the heat, and strain. Transfer the raisins to a bowl and add the rum. Let steep at room temperature for at least 1 hour.

In the bowl of an electric mixer fitted with the paddle attachment, combine the flour, baking powder, granulated sugar, and salt. Add the butter. Put the bowl in the freezer for 5 minutes. Then beat the mixture on low speed until the butter is broken up into pebble-sized pieces, about 3 minutes.

Drain the raisins, reserving the rum. Add ¼ cup of the strained rum to ¾ cup of the heavy cream. Add the raisins to the flour mixture and beat once or twice to evenly distribute them. With the mixer on low speed, add the cream mixture; mix just until the dough comes together. Using your hands, knead the mixture in the bowl to bring the dough completely together.

Turn out the dough onto a lightly floured surface and roll it into a 7-inch round, about ¾ inch thick. Using a sharp knife, cut the dough into 12 wedges, like pieces of pie.

Place the pieces on a baking sheet, spacing them ½ inch apart. Cover with plastic wrap and freeze for 15 minutes or chill in the refrigerator for 1 hour. (Unbaked scones, wrapped well, can be refrigerated for up to 2 days or frozen for up to 2 weeks.) Frozen scones can be baked immediately. Add 5 minutes to the baking time.

While the scones are chilling, preheat the oven to 375°F.

Brush the scones with the remaining 2 tablespoons cream and sprinkle with the Demerara sugar. Bake the scones, rotating the baking sheet halfway through, until they are golden on the edges and on the bottom and are firm to the touch, about 20 minutes. Transfer to a wire rack to cool.

The scones are best served the day they're made, but they will keep in an airtight container at room temperature for up to 3 days.

# APPLE CIDER MUFFINS

If the scent of cinnamon-y baked apples wafting through your kitchen doesn't hook you (and your neighbors!), then the taste of these dense, fruity muffins will. One of my favorite fall breakfast treats, the combination of grated apples and cider creates deep flavor and moistness. Sour cream adds a little richness and balances the sugar in the fruit.

Preheat the oven to 350°F. Generously butter a standard 12-cup muffin tin or line it with paper liners.

In a medium bowl, whisk together the granulated sugar, brown sugar, and oil. Add the eggs and whisk to combine. In another bowl, sift together the flour, baking soda, salt, and cinnamon. In a third bowl, whisk together the apple cider, sour cream, and vanilla.

Add one third of the flour mixture and one third of the apple cider mixture to the sugar mixture, folding with a spatula just to combine. Add the rest of the flour and cider mixtures in two additions. Fold in the grated apple, and then divide the batter evenly among the prepared muffin cups, filling each cup three quarters of the way. Sprinkle the tops of the muffins with the Demerara sugar.

Bake, rotating the muffin tin halfway through, until the muffins spring back to the touch, 25 to 30 minutes. Transfer the pan to a wire rack and let cool for 10 minutes. Then turn out the muffins from the pan and let them cool completely on the wire rack.

These muffins are best the second day and will keep in an airtight container at room temperature for up to 3 days.

## VARYING YOUR CRAFT

### APPLE CIDER QUICK BREAD

Pour the batter into a buttered 8½ x 4½-inch loaf pan lined with parchment paper and bake, rotating the pan halfway through, until a cake tester inserted in the center of the loaf comes out clean, 45 to 55 minutes. Transfer the pan to a wire rack and let cool for 10 minutes. Then turn out the loaf from the pan and let it cool completely on the wire rack. This bread is best the second day and can be kept, wrapped in plastic wrap, at room temperature for up to 3 days.

### MAKES 1 DOZEN

Unsalted butter, for the muffin tin (optional)

1 cup granulated sugar

1 cup packed dark brown sugar

¾ cup grapeseed oil

3 large eggs

2¼ cups unbleached all-purpose flour

1½ teaspoons baking soda

1 teaspoon kosher salt

1 teaspoon ground cinnamon

1 cup apple cider

¾ cup sour cream

1½ teaspoons pure vanilla extract

2 crisp baking apples, such as Granny Smith or Mutsu, peeled, cored, coarsely grated, and drained, juices reserved and used as part of the cider measurement

1 tablespoon Demerara sugar

**TIP** I like to use grapeseed oil instead of canola, peanut, or soy oil in recipes like this that use oil as the fat. Its pleasant mild flavor and lightness is reflected in the finished muffin. Other vegetable oils can be used in a pinch.

# COFFEE CAKE MUFFINS WITH PECAN STREUSEL

I like a light, not-too-sweet coffee cake with a hint of salt, and this one fits the bill. Using the batter to make muffins is just plain fun.

**PECAN STREUSEL**

1½ cups (6 ounces) pecans, finely chopped

½ cup packed dark brown sugar

1 tablespoon ground cinnamon

¼ teaspoon kosher salt

3 tablespoons unsalted butter, melted

**MUFFINS**

8 tablespoons (1 stick) unsalted butter, very soft, plus more for the muffin tin (optional)

Finely grated zest of 2 lemons

1 cup granulated sugar

1 large egg

½ cup plus 2 tablespoons sour cream

½ teaspoon pure vanilla extract

1¾ cups all-purpose flour

1½ teaspoons baking powder

½ teaspoon kosher salt

**FOR THE STREUSEL:** Preheat the oven to 350°F.

Spread the pecans on a baking sheet and bake until toasted, about 5 minutes. Remove the nuts from the oven and let cool. In a large bowl, mix the cooled pecans with the brown sugar, cinnamon, and salt, making sure to break up and incorporate all of the brown sugar. Stir in the butter.

**FOR THE MUFFINS:** Butter a standard 12-cup muffin tin or line it with paper liners.

In the bowl of an electric mixture fitted with the paddle attachment, combine the butter, lemon zest, and sugar and beat on medium speed until light and fluffy, about 5 minutes. Scrape down the sides of the bowl.

With the mixer on medium speed, add the egg, and then the sour cream and vanilla. Scrape down the sides of the bowl. In another bowl, sift together the flour, baking powder, and salt. Add the flour mixture to the mixer bowl and beat on low speed until just combined; the batter will be soft.

Using an ice cream scoop or a large spoon, fill the prepared muffin cups with batter so they are only about one-third full. Sprinkle a generous tablespoon of streusel over the batter in each cup. Evenly divide the remaining batter among the cups, and sprinkle the muffins with the remaining streusel. The cups will be filled about three quarters of the way.

Bake, rotating the muffin tin halfway through, until the muffins spring back to the touch, about 25 minutes. Transfer the tin to a wire rack and let stand for 10 minutes. Then turn out the muffins onto the rack to cool. Serve warm or at room temperature.

The muffins will keep in an airtight container at room temperature for up to 3 days.

## VARYING YOUR CRAFT

### COFFEE CAKE

Spread a little less than half of the batter into a buttered and parchment-lined 8½ x 4½-inch loaf pan. Sprinkle half of the streusel over the cake. Top with the remaining batter. Sprinkle the remaining streusel over the top. Bake, rotating the pan halfway through, until a cake tester inserted in the center of the cake comes out clean and the cake springs back to the touch, about 50 minutes. Transfer the pan to a wire rack and let stand for 5 minutes. Then turn out the loaf onto the rack and let it cool for at least a few minutes. Serve warm or at room temperature.

The cake will keep in an airtight container at room temperature for up to 3 days.

**TIP** Allowing the butter to become very soft before using it in the batter is the key to the airy texture of these tasty muffins. For muffins first thing in the morning, I cube the butter the night before I plan to bake, and leave it out in a bowl on the kitchen counter overnight so that it's ready to go the next morning. Alternatively, it takes about 2 hours at room temperature for the butter to get soft enough, depending on the temperature in your kitchen.

# JAMMY FIG MUFFINS

These muffins are made with black Mission figs, which have a round sweetness akin to honey and a fantastic earthiness. I call them "jammy" because the fruit magically transforms into a jam while the muffins bake.

Unsalted butter, for the pan (optional)

1 cup unbleached all-purpose flour

1 teaspoon ground cinnamon

½ teaspoon baking soda

¼ teaspoon kosher salt

½ cup buttermilk

1 large egg

½ teaspoon pure vanilla extract

¾ cup packed dark brown sugar

4 tablespoons (½ stick) unsalted butter, cut into small pieces, at room temperature

5 to 6 large fresh black Mission figs, cut into ½-inch pieces (1 cup)

TIP Fresh figs have two seasons, one in spring and one in late fall into early winter. When choosing figs, look for ones that are heavy for their size and have a little softness and give. Hard figs will be dry inside, and those that are mushy are already past their prime.

NOTE Berries or ripe stone fruit work well here in place of figs.

Preheat the oven to 350°F. Generously butter a standard 12-cup muffin tin or line it with paper liners.

In a bowl, sift together the flour, cinnamon, baking soda, and salt. In a second bowl, whisk together the buttermilk, egg, and vanilla.

In the bowl of an electric mixer fitted with the paddle attachment, beat the brown sugar and the butter on medium speed until well combined, about 5 minutes. With the mixer on the lowest speed, add one third of the flour mixture and one third of the buttermilk mixture, scraping the sides of the bowl with a rubber spatula and beating until just combined. Add the rest of the flour and buttermilk mixtures in two additions. Remove the bowl from the mixer and gently fold in the figs.

Divide the batter evenly among the muffin cups, filling them three quarters of the way. Bake, rotating the muffin tin halfway through, until the muffins are firm to the touch and deep golden brown in color, 25 to 30 minutes. Transfer the pan to a wire rack and let cool for 10 minutes. Then turn out the muffins from the pan and let them cool completely on the wire rack.

The muffins will keep in an airtight container at room temperature for up to 3 days.

## VARYING YOUR CRAFT
### STREUSEL FIG MUFFINS

For a bit of crunchy texture and caramel-y flavor, fold 1 cup Marcona Almond Streusel (page 140) into the batter when you add the figs. After dividing the batter among the muffin cups, sprinkle another ⅓ cup of the streusel on top of the muffins just before baking.

Alternatively, toast ¾ cup chopped hazelnuts on a baking sheet in a 350°F oven for 5 minutes. Fold the cooled nuts into the batter, and just before baking, sprinkle the tops of the muffins with ¼ cup roughly chopped untoasted hazelnuts.

# PUMPKIN SPICE BREAD

Seeing the first pumpkins piled up at the market as early fall sets in makes me hungry for this cake-y bread. Super-moist with a warm sweet-spice, it is great toasted and spread with a thick pat of nice salty butter. The flavors deepen as the baked bread sits, so make it up to two days in advance of serving, if you like. I use canned pumpkin purée in place of baked fresh pumpkin because the canned version is consistently good in terms of moisture and flavor—and it makes this recipe quick and easy.

Position a rack in the center of the oven and preheat the oven to 350°F. Line the bottom of an 8½ x 4½-inch loaf pan with parchment, and grease the bottom and sides with butter.

In a medium bowl, whisk together the granulated sugar, brown sugar, egg, egg yolk, and oil. Add the pumpkin, sour cream, and vanilla and whisk well to combine. In another bowl, sift together the flour, baking soda, salt, nutmeg, cinnamon, cloves, and white pepper. Using a rubber spatula, fold the dry ingredients into the wet. Then whisk together gently to just combine.

Pour the batter into the prepared pan and sprinkle the top with the Demerara sugar.

Bake, rotating the pan once, until the bread is firm to the touch, well browned, and slightly cracked on top, about 55 minutes. Transfer the pan to a wire rack and let stand for 5 minutes. Then turn out the loaf onto the rack to cool. Serve warm or at room temperature.

The bread will keep in an airtight container at room temperature for up to 3 days.

**TIP** If you want to make fresh pumpkin purée, cut a pumpkin or squash (my favorites are sugar pumpkins, hubbard squash, or butternut squash) in half and remove all of the seeds and stringy pulp with a large spoon. Place the halves, cut side down, on a baking sheet; cover with foil, tightly sealing the edges; and bake at 375°F until the pumpkin is very soft to the touch and completely cooked through, 1 to 2 hours, depending on the size of the pumpkin. Cool on a wire rack until cool enough to handle. Then scrape the flesh away from the skins and purée the flesh in a food processor until smooth. Drain overnight, refrigerated, in a strainer lined with cheesecloth or with a large coffee filter.

### MAKES ONE 8½ X 4½-INCH LOAF

Unsalted butter, at room temperature, for the pan

½ cup granulated sugar

½ cup packed dark brown sugar

1 large egg

1 large egg yolk

½ cup grapeseed oil

¾ cup canned pumpkin purée

⅓ cup plus 1 tablespoon sour cream

¾ teaspoon pure vanilla extract

1 cup plus 2 tablespoons unbleached all-purpose flour

¾ teaspoon baking soda

½ teaspoon kosher salt

1 teaspoon freshly grated nutmeg

½ teaspoon ground cinnamon

Pinch of ground cloves

Pinch of freshly ground white pepper

1 tablespoon Demerara sugar

# TOASTED NUT & HONEY GRANOLA

You'll never find a fresher-tasting granola than your own. Not only is it simple to make at home, you'll also avoid any preservatives that might be hiding out in the supermarket kind.

## MAKES 5 CUPS

1 cup unsweetened coconut flakes

2¼ cups old-fashioned rolled oats

⅓ cup hazelnuts, roughly chopped

½ cup almonds, roughly chopped

⅓ cup plus 2 tablespoons grapeseed oil

2 tablespoons honey

2 tablespoons packed dark brown sugar

Finely grated zest of 1 orange

½ teaspoon kosher salt

½ cup golden raisins

½ cup dried blueberries

¼ cup dried apricots, cut into small pieces

Preheat the oven to 325°F.

Spread the coconut on a baking sheet and bake, stirring occasionally, until toasted, 5 to 7 minutes. Transfer to a bowl.

In a second bowl, combine the oats, hazelnuts, and almonds. Spread the oat mixture onto the baking sheet and bake, stirring three or four times, until toasted, 12 to 15 minutes.

While the oat mixture is toasting, in a large bowl, whisk together the oil, honey, and brown sugar. Add the orange zest and the salt, and whisk to combine.

Remove the oat mixture from the oven, immediately add it to the oil mixture, and using a spatula, fold together to combine well, making sure all of the dry ingredients are well dampened. Spread the mixture onto the baking sheet in an even layer, return it to the oven, and bake, stirring occasionally to move granola on the edges into the center, until the granola is golden and dry, about 20 minutes. If the granola is at all sticky after 20 minutes, return it to the oven and bake, checking every couple of minutes, until it is dry. Remove the granola from the oven and let it cool to room temperature on a rack.

In a bowl, combine the granola with the raisins, blueberries, apricots, and toasted coconut. Transfer the mixture to an airtight container.

The granola will keep for up to 2 weeks in an airtight container at room temperature, and for up to 1 month in the freezer.

### VARYING YOUR CRAFT
#### CHERRY PISTACHIO GRANOLA

Substitute ¾ cup chopped pistachios for the almonds and hazelnuts. Substitute 1¼ cups dried cherries for the raisins, apricots, and dried blueberries.

#### MAPLE PECAN GRANOLA

Substitute ¾ cup chopped pecans for the almonds and hazelnuts. Substitute maple syrup for the honey, and maple sugar for the brown sugar.

#### TROPICAL GRANOLA

Substitute ¾ cup chopped macadamia nuts for the almonds and hazelnuts. Substitute 2 tablespoons agave syrup for the honey, and 2 tablespoons Demerara sugar for the brown sugar. Substitute ¾ cup chopped dried pineapple and ½ cup chopped dried papaya for the raisins, apricots, and dried blueberries.

## BUILDING YOUR CRAFT
## GRANOLA

This granola recipe can be easily varied in almost countless ways. An interesting place to begin is with the honey that you choose. Experiment with different types and you'll find that your choice can really drive the flavor of the granola. My favorites include linden, which has a light lime scent and a mild flavor, and local wildflower, which is a little darker and more floral.

Any nut, from almonds and walnuts to pine nuts and pecans; any seeds, including flax, pumpkin, and sunflower; and any dried fruit can be added or left out, so use whatever you fancy. You can leave out the coconut, if you like. Vanilla and other extracts can be added as a flavoring, and maple syrup can replace the honey as a sweetener.

# APPLE FRITTERS

Simple to make, these festive fritters are great for brunch or alongside ice cream for dessert. Beer not only deepens the flavor of the fritters, its bubbles make them light and crispy. When dipping, loop the apple rings over your finger for ease and to get the fullest coverage.

MAKES 10

¾ cup plus 2 tablespoons unbleached all-purpose flour, sifted

¼ cup plus 7 tablespoons sugar

1¼ teaspoons ground cinnamon

Kosher salt

2 large eggs, separated

1½ teaspoons unsalted butter, melted

1 teaspoon pure vanilla extract

½ cup beer (lager or pilsner)

1 large firm baking apple, such as Granny Smith, Mutsu, or Crispin

Peanut oil, for frying

In a bowl, whisk together the flour, ¼ cup of the sugar, ½ teaspoon of the cinnamon, and 1 teaspoon salt.

In a large bowl, whisk together the egg yolks, butter, and vanilla. Whisk in one third of the flour mixture then one third of the beer to the egg yolk mixture, just to combine. Add the rest of the flour mixture and beer in two additions; whisk well to combine. Set the batter aside to rest for 30 minutes.

While the batter is resting, peel, core, and slice the apple into ten ⅛-inch-thick rings. Spread out the rings on a large plate. Stir together 1 tablespoon of the sugar and ¼ teaspoon of the cinnamon, and sprinkle the mixture over the apple slices. Let the slices sit for 20 minutes to soften and absorb the sugar.

Whisk the egg whites to soft peaks, and gently but thoroughly fold them into the batter.

In a wide, shallow bowl, whisk together the remaining 6 tablespoons sugar, remaining ½ teaspoon cinnamon, and a pinch of salt.

Fill a high-sided skillet or wide pot with 2 inches of oil, and heat the oil to 375°F. In batches, dip the apple rings into the batter to coat both sides, and fry, turning once, until the fritters are golden and crisp, about 3 minutes. Drain on paper towels, immediately toss in the cinnamon-sugar mixture, and serve warm.

# BROWN BUTTER
# WAFFLES

For breakfast, dress up these waffles with whatever fruit looks best at the market and a drizzle of maple syrup. But don't think of waffles as just morning fare. I often use them as a component of a playful dessert: Cut them into quarters and stack them alongside ice cream or custard—just as you would with cookies.

**6 tablespoons (¾ stick) unsalted butter, cut into small pieces**

**1 cup plus 2 tablespoons unbleached all-purpose flour**

**¼ cup plus 1 tablespoon packed dark brown sugar**

**1 teaspoon baking powder**

**¼ teaspoon baking soda**

**½ teaspoon kosher salt**

**1 cup buttermilk**

**2 large eggs, separated**

**Unsalted butter, for the waffle iron**

In a small saucepan, melt the butter over medium-high heat; continue cooking until the butter turns brown and has a nutty fragrance, about 5 minutes. Remove from the heat.

In a medium bowl, whisk together the flour, brown sugar, baking powder, baking soda, and salt. Make a well in the center and pour in the buttermilk and the egg yolks. Whisk the wet ingredients together, gently working them into the dry ingredients until just combined. Add the browned butter and whisk until fully absorbed. (At this point, the batter will keep for several hours or up to 2 days in the refrigerator.)

In the bowl of an electric mixer fitted with the whisk attachment, beat the egg whites to soft peaks. Gently fold the whites into the batter in two additions.

Lightly brush a waffle iron with butter and cook the waffles according to the manufacturer's instructions.

## COMBINING YOUR CRAFT
Cut the waffles into quarters and serve them alongside Maple Custard (page 176) and Blueberry Compote (page 238).

# BRIOCHE BAKED IN A CAN

The recipe for this brioche dough, given to me by the great French pastry chef Pierre Hermé, is unconventional and so much easier than its more traditional counterpart. The main difference is that the butter and eggs are used cold, straight from the refrigerator, which takes some of the advance planning out of the preparation (in a more traditional recipe, the butter and eggs must be at room temperature before using). Because of its lower water content, high-fat or European-style butter is a great choice for this recipe, yielding a richer, more flavorful brioche, though you can substitute regular butter with fine results. I love using soup cans in place of baking pans to bake the brioche. With all the fancy baking pans out there, none gives you the playful look you get from a simple can, and it's nice, too, to put an old can to good use (see box, page 41).

In the bowl of an electric mixer fitted with the dough hook, mix together the flour and sugar on low speed until combined.

Bring about 2 inches of water to a simmer in a medium saucepan. Whisk together the eggs and yeast in a medium heatproof bowl. Set the bowl over the saucepan of simmering water until the mixture is just warm to the touch (between 100° and 130°F), about 1 minute, whisking the entire time.

Add the warm egg mixture to the flour mixture and beat on medium speed until the dough comes together into a ball, about 4 minutes. With the machine running, slowly add the salt.

With the machine running, add the butter quickly, piece by piece. Continue to mix until the dough is shiny and makes a slapping sound on the sides of the bowl, about 6 minutes.

Lift the dough out of the bowl and transfer it between your two fists, bouncing it up and down and folding it back into a ball, until the dough begins to tighten, about 4 minutes.

Transfer the dough to a large buttered bowl, cover it well with plastic wrap or a kitchen towel, and let the dough rise at room temperature until it doubles, about 2 hours.

MAKES 6 INDIVIDUAL BRIOCHES

2½ cups high-gluten bread flour

¼ cup sugar

6 large eggs

1 (¼-ounce) packet active dry yeast

1 tablespoon kosher salt

12 ounces (3 sticks) chilled unsalted butter, preferably high-fat, cut into small pieces, plus more for the bowl and cans

RECIPE CONTINUES

RECIPE CONTINUED

Fold the dough down, return it to the same bowl, and cover it well with plastic wrap. Let it rise in the refrigerator for at least 6 hours or overnight.

Lightly grease the inside of 6 clean soup cans with butter.

Divide the brioche dough into 6 equal pieces. Roll each piece into a ball with a smooth top (like a hamburger bun). Place the dough balls, top side down, in the prepared cans. Cover the cans with plastic wrap or a kitchen towel, and let the dough rise at room temperature until it reaches the tops of the cans, about 2 hours.

Position a rack in the center of the oven and preheat the oven to 375°F.

Put the cans on a baking sheet and bake, rotating the sheet halfway through, until the brioches are dark golden brown, about 30 minutes. Remove the cans from the oven and immediately turn the brioches out, tapping the cans on the counter to loosen the bread and running a knife around the edges if necessary. Let cool on a wire rack. Serve warm or at room temperature.

You can wrap completely cooled brioche in plastic wrap and use it for pain perdu (French toast) up to 3 days later. Or freeze the well-wrapped brioche for up to 2 weeks; thaw it to room temperature before using it to make pain perdu.

## VARYING YOUR CRAFT
### TRADITIONAL BRIOCHE LOAF

After making the dough, shape it into an 8-inch square. Turn the dough over and fold it into thirds, pinching and making sure there are no air pockets; tuck in the ends. Put the dough, seam side down, into a buttered 8½ x 4½-inch loaf pan. Press down on the dough with your fists, making sure it reaches all corners of the pan. Let rise as indicated in the recipe. Bake for 50 minutes.

# PREPARING SOUP CANS FOR BAKING

The first time you use your soup cans for baking, they need to be prepared and seasoned. This is easy, and you only have to do it once.

Preheat the oven to 450°F. Remove the labels from the cans. Tap down any sharp or jagged edges around the inside rim of the cans with a small hammer. Wash and dry the cans well; then grease the insides with butter and set the cans on a baking sheet. Cook the cans for 1 hour. (This cooks off the thin lining separating the soup from the can, leaving only the metal, which will act as the pan for the bread.) Remove the cans from the oven and let them cool. Wipe out the inside of each can with a paper towel. The cans are now ready to use.

Like a cast-iron skillet, the cans get better as you use them: the more you bake in them, the more seasoned they become. As the cans become more seasoned, they will produce a more evenly golden bread that will slide more easily out of the cans. To clean the cans after use, don't run them through the dishwasher. Just wipe them out with a damp cloth and let them dry completely before storing.

# BRIOCHE CINNAMON ROLLS

Brioche dough gives these sweet, sticky rolls a much lighter texture than the average. With multiple rises, there's a fair amount of time required here; however, you can prepare the dough, roll the filling into it, and freeze it up to one week ahead. The night before baking, defrost the dough just enough to slice it, tuck the rolls into muffin cups, and let them rise in the fridge overnight. Pull the tin out of the refrigerator and let it stand for about 30 minutes before baking, and you're on your way.

MAKES 12

**Dough for Brioche Baked in a Can (page 39)**

**1¼ cups packed dark brown sugar**

**1 tablespoon ground cinnamon**

**4 tablespoons (½ stick) unsalted butter**

**½ cup heavy cream**

**½ cup confectioners' sugar**

Prepare the dough through the second rise.

To make the filling, combine the brown sugar and cinnamon in a heatproof bowl. In a small saucepan, bring the butter and ¼ cup of the cream to a boil. Immediately remove the mixture from the heat, pour it over the sugar mixture, and whisk well to combine.

Roll the dough into a rectangle, about 18 x 8 inches and about ½ inch thick. Spread the cinnamon filling evenly over the dough, leaving one inch uncovered at the top. Roll up the dough, starting at one of the long ends, into a log. Seal the top edge to the log by pressing it gently. Wrap the log tightly in plastic wrap and freeze it until it is firm enough to cut, about 1 hour, or up to 1 week.

Cut the log into 12 equal pieces and fit the pieces, cut side up, into a standard 12-cup muffin tin. Cover the tin with plastic wrap and let it sit in a warm place until the dough doubles in size, about 1 hour.

Preheat the oven to 375°F.

Uncover the cinnamon rolls and bake, rotating the muffin tin halfway through, until they are dark golden brown on top, about 30 minutes.

While the rolls are baking, make the icing: In a bowl, whisk together the remaining ¼ cup cream and the confectioners' sugar.

Remove the rolls from the oven, and immediately turn them out from the tin onto a rack. Turn them top side up, and drizzle the icing over them. Serve warm or at room temperature.

The cinnamon rolls are best served the day they are baked, but they can be kept in an airtight container at room temperature for up to 2 days and reheated to serve for 5 minutes in a 350°F oven.

## VARYING YOUR CRAFT
### APPLE-CINNAMON ROLLS
Replace the filling with 1 cup Apple Butter (page 239).

### QUINCE ROLLS
Replace the filling with 1 cup Quince Butter (page 239).

# CHOCOLATE BRIOCHE

This yeasty, bittersweet chocolate bread is a great one for dark-chocolate lovers. My favorite way to eat it is toasted and spread with a thick smear of creamy, slightly sweet mascarpone cheese. The key technique here is to beat the dough in your mixer until it releases from the sides of the bowl and forms a good tight ball around the dough hook. As it beats, the glutens build up, which gives the dough its delicate texture.

MAKES ONE
8 ½ X 4 ½-INCH LOAF

**1 (¼-ounce) packet active dry yeast**

**2 cups bread flour**

**⅓ cup plus 2 tablespoons unsweetened cocoa powder**

**1 teaspoon kosher salt**

**3 large eggs**

**8 ounces (2 sticks) chilled unsalted high-fat butter, cut into small pieces, plus more for the bowl and pan**

**½ cup sugar**

In the bowl of an electric mixer, whisk the yeast with ½ cup warm water. In a large bowl, sift together the flour, cocoa powder, and salt; add this to the yeast mixture. Using the dough hook attachment, stir the mixture on low speed until combined. Increase the speed to medium and, one at a time, add the eggs. Mix until the dough begins to pull away from the sides of the bowl, forms a ball around the dough hook, and begins to slap against the sides of the bowl, about 10 minutes.

With the machine running, add the butter quickly, piece by piece. Add the sugar. Continue to mix until the dough is shiny, about 15 minutes.

Remove the dough from the bowl, and holding it in your hands, alternate it from hand to hand, letting it hang over your fists and bouncing it up and down, about thirty times in each hand. (This action helps tighten the dough, developing the gluten, which keeps it bound together as it rises and cooks.)

Put the dough in a large buttered mixing bowl and cover it with plastic wrap or a kitchen towel. Set the dough aside in a warm place until it has risen by 50 percent, 3 hours.

Fold the dough to deflate it, and return it to the buttered mixing bowl. Cover it tightly with plastic wrap and refrigerate it for at least 6 hours or overnight.

Grease an 8½ x 4½-inch loaf pan with butter.

Shape the dough into a 8-inch square. Turn the dough over and fold it into thirds, pinching and making sure there are no air pockets; tuck in the ends.

Put the dough, seam side down, in the prepared pan and press down on the dough with your fists, making sure it reaches all corners of the pan. Cover the pan with plastic wrap and let the dough rise at room temperature until it reaches the top of the pan, about 2 hours.

Preheat the oven to 375°F.

Set the pan on a baking sheet and bake, rotating the pan once halfway through, until the brioche is dark golden on top and the bottom of the loaf has a hollow sound when unmolded and tapped, about 50 minutes. Transfer the pan to a wire rack and let stand for 5 minutes. Then turn out the loaf onto the rack to cool. Serve warm or at room temperature.

Chocolate brioche is best eaten fresh on the day it's made. It can be kept, well wrapped, at room temperature for up to 3 days or frozen for up to 3 weeks. Defrost and toast before serving.

# CHOCOLATE BABKA

This old-world cross between bread and cake is decadent deliciousness for breakfast, with afternoon coffee, or for dessert. Packed with rich dark chocolate and cinnamon swirls, the meltingly buttery pieces pull apart in strands.

MAKES TWO
8½ X 4½-INCH
LOAVES

**Dough for Brioche Baked
in a Can (page 39)**

## STREUSEL

½ cup sugar

⅓ cup unbleached all-purpose
flour, plus more for rolling the
dough

½ teaspoon ground cinnamon

¼ teaspoon kosher salt

3 tablespoons unsalted butter,
melted

## FILLING

10 ounces semisweet chocolate,
roughly chopped

⅓ cup sugar

2½ teaspoons ground
cinnamon

8 tablespoons (1 stick) unsalted
butter, at room temperature,
plus more for the pans

2 large egg yolks

Prepare the dough through the second rise.

FOR THE STREUSEL: In a small bowl, mix together the sugar, flour, cinnamon, and salt. Add the butter and stir until the mixture is damp throughout. Transfer the streusel to a baking sheet, and using your hands, crumble it into ¼-inch chunks.

FOR THE FILLING: In two batches, pulse the chocolate in a food processor until the pieces are the size of small pebbles. Transfer to a bowl. Add the sugar and cinnamon and stir to combine. Divide the mixture in half.

(The streusel and the filling can both be prepared up to 2 weeks ahead. Store the streusel in an airtight container in the freezer. The filling can be stored in an airtight container at room temperature.)

Line the bottoms of two 8½ x 4½-inch loaf pans with parchment, and grease the bottoms and sides with butter.

Divide the cold brioche dough in half. Wrap one portion in plastic wrap and return it to the refrigerator. Roll out the other half of the dough into a 12 x 14-inch rectangle, about ⅛ inch thick. Spread 4 tablespoons of the butter on top, leaving a 1-inch border all around. Sprinkle one portion of the chocolate mixture over the butter. Whisk together the yolks and 1 tablespoon cold water; brush some of the egg wash over the border.

Starting with the 14-inch side closest to you, roll the dough into a tight log. Firmly pinch the ends and the seam to seal in the filling. Twist the roll several times and then brush it with some of the egg wash. Sprinkle about 2 tablespoons of the streusel over half of the roll and then fold the dough in half, sandwiching the streusel. Fold the ends under and twist the dough to fit it into one of the prepared pans. Push the dough to the edges of the pan. Brush the top of the loaf with some of the egg wash and sprinkle with

3 more tablespoons of the streusel. Repeat with the remaining dough, filling, and streusel to form the second loaf.

Cover the loaves with plastic wrap and set them aside in a warm spot until the dough rises up to the tops of the pans, about 2 hours.

Preheat the oven to 375°F.

Bake, turning the pans halfway through, until the babkas are dark golden on top and the bottom of a loaf has a hollow sound when unmolded and tapped, about 1 hour. Transfer the pans to a wire rack and let stand for 5 minutes. Then turn out the loaves onto the rack to cool. Serve warm or at room temperature.

Babka is best on the day it's made, but it can be kept, well wrapped in plastic wrap or foil, at room temperature for up to 3 days or in the freezer for up to 1 month, thawing and then toasting it to serve.

# BRIOCHE PAIN PERDU

I was raised on good basic French toast: a couple of slices of nice bread, soaked in an egg and milk mixture, and cooked up crisp on the edges and tender inside. As a grown-up, I crave a fluffier, more flavorful version. Floating freshly baked brioche in a rich vanilla-kissed custard is the answer. Using round cans to bake the brioche provides elegant round slices, which are as nice for dessert as for breakfast. However, when time is an issue, pick up a good brioche at your favorite bakery in lieu of making your own.

**SERVES 6**

½ recipe Brioche Baked in a Can (page 39), or six 1½-inch-thick slices store-bought brioche

2 large eggs

2 large egg yolks

1 cup whole milk

1 cup heavy cream

½ cup granulated sugar

¾ teaspoon pure vanilla extract

½ teaspoon kosher salt

3 tablespoons unsalted butter

Confectioners' sugar, for dusting

Maple syrup, fresh fruit, or yogurt, for serving

If you are using the brioche baked in a can, cut it into six 1½-inch-thick slices (2 slices per loaf).

In a large bowl, whisk together the eggs and yolks.

In a medium saucepan, heat the milk, cream, granulated sugar, vanilla, and salt over medium heat, whisking occasionally, until the mixture is warm to the touch and the sugar is dissolved, about 3 minutes. Remove the mixture from the heat, and whisking constantly, pour about one quarter of it into the egg mixture. Add the remaining milk mixture and whisk to combine. Use immediately, or chill the custard for up to 2 days until ready to use.

Preheat the oven to 250°F.

Transfer the custard mixture to a large shallow baking dish (9 x 13 inches). Add the brioche slices and soak on both sides for 1 or 2 minutes, until the bread absorbs the custard like a sponge.

In a large heavy skillet, heat 1½ tablespoons of the butter over medium heat until it is hot but not smoking. Add 2 or 3 slices of brioche (or as many as will fit in one layer) and cook for 3 minutes on each side, or until puffed and golden brown. Transfer the French toast to a baking sheet and keep it warm in the oven. Repeat with the remaining butter and bread slices.

Sprinkle the French toast with confectioners' sugar, and serve with maple syrup.

### COMBINING YOUR CRAFT
Serve Pain Perdu as dessert with Rum Caramel Roasted Bananas (page 229) and Caramel Ice Cream (page 207), or with Lemon Curd (page 242) and fresh berries.

# CHOCOLATE RAISED DOUGHNUTS WITH SUGAR CRACKLE GLAZE

A simple sugar glaze helps to bring out the chocolate flavor in these slightly sweet doughnuts.

Prepare the dough through the second rise.

Lightly coat a baking sheet with nonstick cooking spray.

Turn out the dough onto a lightly floured surface and roll it out with a lightly floured rolling pin into a ½-inch-thick round. Cut out 13 rounds with a floured 3-inch cutter or inverted drinking glass, and then cut a hole in the center of each round with a 1-inch cutter. Transfer the doughnuts and the doughnut holes to the prepared baking sheet. Cover lightly with plastic wrap and let rise in a warm place until slightly puffed, about 20 minutes. Do not re-roll the scraps.

Just before frying the doughnuts and holes, prepare the glaze: whisk together the confectioners' sugar, 1 tablespoon hot water, and the vanilla in a wide, shallow bowl.

Heat 2 inches of oil in a deep, heavy 4-quart pot until it registers 350°F on a candy or deep-frying thermometer. Fry the dough-nuts, 3 at a time, turning them once with a wire skimmer or a slotted spoon, until puffed, 2 to 3 minutes per batch. Transfer them to paper towels to drain. While they are still warm, dip the doughnuts into the glaze, turning to coat them well. Place the doughnuts on a rack set over a baking sheet to catch the drips. Let stand for 1 to 2 minutes to set the glaze before serving.

Fry the doughnut holes until puffed, turning once, about 45 seconds; then drain and dip in the glaze.

Serve the doughnuts warm or at room temperature on the day they are fried.

**MAKES A BAKER'S DOZEN**

Dough for Chocolate Brioche (page 44)

Nonstick cooking spray

Unbleached all-purpose flour, for rolling

¾ cup confectioners' sugar

¼ teaspoon pure vanilla extract

Peanut oil, for frying

# GLAZED BUTTERMILK CAKE DOUGHNUTS

These are my simplest doughnuts. Nothing fancy, but so good.

MAKES A BAKER'S
DOZEN

¾ cup buttermilk

1 large egg

3 large egg yolks

⅓ cup grapeseed oil

3¾ cups cake flour, plus extra
for dusting

1 cup granulated sugar

2 teaspoons baking powder

½ teaspoon baking soda

1½ teaspoons ground cinnamon

¼ teaspoon freshly grated
nutmeg

1 teaspoon kosher salt

Finely grated zest of 1 lemon

Nonstick cooking spray

2 cups confectioners' sugar

Peanut oil, for frying

In a medium bowl, whisk together the buttermilk, egg, egg yolks, and grapeseed oil. Sift 2 cups of the flour into another bowl and set it aside.

In the bowl of an electric mixer fitted with the paddle attachment, combine the remaining 1¾ cups flour, the granulated sugar, baking powder, baking soda, cinnamon, nutmeg, salt, and lemon zest. Mix on low speed just to combine. Add the buttermilk mixture and continue mixing just until the dough comes together. Remove the bowl from the mixer, and using a spatula, gently fold in the reserved flour. The dough will be very sticky.

Transfer the dough to a 12 x 14-inch sheet of waxed paper. Place a second sheet of waxed paper on top, and roll out the dough between the paper to an 8 x 10-inch oval, about ¾ inch thick. Set the dough, still between the sheets of waxed paper, on a baking sheet and freeze until it is firm enough to cut, about 30 minutes.

Remove the dough from the freezer and remove the top sheet of waxed paper. Dust the dough with flour and replace the waxed paper. Flip the dough over; remove and discard the bottom sheet of waxed paper. Now the dough is loosened from the waxed paper and is easy to cut.

Lightly coat a baking sheet with nonstick cooking spray.

Using a floured 3-inch round cutter or inverted drinking glass, cut out doughnuts. Cut out the centers with a floured 1-inch cutter. Transfer the doughnuts to the prepared baking sheet. Re-roll the scraps and repeat to make a total of 13 doughnuts and 13 holes. Cover with plastic wrap and chill in the refrigerator for at least 30 minutes or up to 1 day (if making the dough ahead, bring it to room temperature before frying).

Just before frying the doughnuts and holes, prepare the glaze: In a wide, shallow bowl, whisk together the confectioners' sugar and ¼ cup hot water.

In a large high-sided skillet or a wide pot, heat 2 inches of oil to 350°F. Working in batches of 3, fry the doughnuts, carefully turning them with a wire skimmer or slotted spoon halfway through, until golden brown, about 1½ minutes per side. Transfer the doughnuts to paper towels to drain, and then immediately dip one side of each doughnut into the glaze. Transfer them, glaze side up, to a rack set over a baking sheet, and let sit until the glaze sets, about 3 minutes.

Fry the doughnut holes for 1 minute per batch. Drain, dip in the glaze, and transfer to the wire rack.

Serve the doughnuts warm or at room temperature on the day they are fried.

## BUILDING YOUR CRAFT
# DOUGHNUTS

Making doughnuts at home might seem daunting, but it's actually quite easy, and of course, there are few things better than a fresh-from-the-fryer doughnut.

Doughnuts fall into two basic categories: cake and yeast. Cake doughnuts are leavened with baking powder and baking soda. They have a tender crumb, like a cake. The yeast sort get their loft from yeast, and like bread, they require a rise. They are lighter and have little air pockets and a touch of yeasty flavor. If you're a first-time doughnut maker or are short on time, start with the cake doughnuts (page 50 and 53).

Except for an inexpensive candy (or deep-frying) thermometer, you don't need any fancy equipment. The key to making a great doughnut at home is to set up your tools before you begin. Once you begin to fry the doughnuts, you'll be working quickly, so it's best to have everything within arm's reach. While your dough is chilling or rising, clean your tools and clear your work surface. Set up a mini assembly line: on a work surface near the stove, position a slotted spoon or skimmer for turning and transferring doughnuts, a timer, a paper towel–lined plate for draining, your bowl of glaze or sugar topping so the warm doughnuts can be dunked right in, and a baking sheet with a rack fitted over it, for cooling and to let a glaze topping drip off. Fry and sugar or glaze doughnuts in batches of three.

# CHOCOLATE CAKE DOUGHNUTS WITH CHOCOLATE CRACKLE GLAZE

The glaze for these doughnuts is very thick when first mixed together, and then it melts onto the doughnuts as they're dipped. When it cools off, it crackles.

Bring 1 inch of water to a simmer in a medium saucepan. Put the chocolate and the butter in a heatproof bowl and set it over (but not touching) the simmering water. Turn off the heat; stir occasionally until they have melted completely.

In a large bowl, whisk together 1 cup of the flour, the granulated sugar, cocoa powder, baking powder, baking soda, and salt. In a second bowl, whisk together the buttermilk, egg, and egg yolk.

Make a well in the center of the dry ingredients, pour in the buttermilk mixture, and using a spatula, fold two or three times. Add the chocolate mixture and fold together until the dough is smooth and shiny. Sift the remaining ¾ cup flour over the mixture, and fold to combine well.

Transfer the dough to a 12 x 14-inch sheet of waxed paper. Place a second sheet of waxed paper on top, and roll out the dough between the paper into a 10 x 12-inch oval that is about ¾ inch thick. Set the dough, still between the sheets of waxed paper, on a baking sheet and freeze until it is firm enough to cut, about 30 minutes.

Remove the dough from the freezer and remove the top sheet of waxed paper. Dust the dough with flour and replace the waxed paper. Flip the dough over; remove and discard the bottom sheet of waxed paper. Now the dough is loosened from the waxed paper and is easy to cut.

Lightly coat a baking sheet with nonstick cooking spray.

RECIPE CONTINUES

MAKES 10

## DOUGHNUTS

3 ounces best-quality bittersweet chocolate (70%), finely chopped

3 tablespoons unsalted butter

1¾ cups cake flour, plus more for dusting

½ cup granulated sugar

1 tablespoon unsweetened cocoa powder

2 teaspoons baking powder

½ teaspoon baking soda

½ teaspoon kosher salt

⅓ cup plus 1 tablespoon buttermilk

1 large egg

1 large egg yolk

Nonstick cooking spray

## GLAZE

1 cup confectioners' sugar

2 tablespoons unsweetened cocoa powder

½ teaspoon pure vanilla extract

¼ teaspoon kosher salt

Peanut oil, for frying

Using a floured 3-inch round cutter or inverted drinking glass, cut out doughnuts. Cut out the centers with a floured 1-inch cutter. Transfer the doughnuts to the prepared baking sheet. Re-roll the scraps and repeat to make a total of 10 doughnuts and 10 holes.

Cover with plastic wrap and chill in the refrigerator for at least 30 minutes or up to 1 day (if preparing the dough ahead, bring it to room temperature before frying).

Just before frying the doughnuts and holes, prepare the glaze: Whisk together the confectioners' sugar, cocoa powder, vanilla, and salt in a wide, shallow bowl. Add 2 tablespoons hot water and whisk until the glaze is smooth. (The glaze will be very thick. The warm doughnuts will melt the glaze as you dip them. Still, if the glaze begins to thicken too much as you are using it, adjust the consistency by adding a few more drops of hot water.)

In a large high-sided skillet or a wide pot, heat 2 inches of oil to 350°F. Working in batches of 3, fry the doughnuts, carefully turning them with a wire skimmer or slotted spoon halfway through, until cooked through, about 45 seconds per side. Test the first doughnut by breaking it open about 30 seconds after removing it from the oil, and if it is over- or underdone, adjust the time accordingly. Transfer the doughnuts to paper towels to drain, and then immediately dip one side of each doughnut into the glaze. Transfer them to a rack, glaze side up, and let sit until the glaze sets, about 3 minutes.

Fry the doughnut holes for 35 seconds per batch. Drain and dip in the glaze in the same way.

Serve the doughnuts warm or at room temperature on the day they are fried.

# RAISED CINNAMON-SUGAR DOUGHNUTS

Made with brioche dough, these doughnuts are less sweet and more yeasty than a traditional doughnut. I like to serve them with a seasonal fruit compote.

Prepare the dough through the second rise.

Lightly grease a baking sheet with nonstick cooking spray.

Turn out the brioche dough onto a clean lightly floured work surface and roll it out with a lightly floured rolling pin to a ¾-inch-thick round. Cut out 13 rounds with a floured 3-inch cutter or inverted drinking glass, and then cut a hole in the center of each round with a floured 1-inch cutter. Transfer the doughnuts and holes to the prepared baking sheet. Cover with plastic wrap or a clean kitchen towel and let rise in a warm place until slightly puffed, about 20 minutes. Do not re-roll the scraps.

Just before frying the doughnuts and holes, stir together the sugar, cinnamon, and salt in a wide, shallow bowl.

Heat 2 inches of oil in a deep heavy 4-quart pot until it registers 350°F on a deep-frying thermometer. Fry the doughnuts, 3 at a time, turning them occasionally with a wire mesh skimmer or a slotted spoon, until they are puffed and dark golden brown, about 1 minute per side. Transfer them to paper towels to drain. Fry the holes until they are puffed and dark golden brown, 30 to 45 seconds per side, and transfer them to paper towels. Toss the doughnuts and holes in the sugar mixture to coat.

Serve warm or at room temperature. The doughnuts are best on the day they are fried.

**MAKES A BAKER'S DOZEN**

**Dough for Brioche Baked in a Can (page 39)**

**Nonstick cooking spray**

**Unbleached all-purpose flour, for rolling**

**¾ cup sugar**

**1 teaspoon ground cinnamon**

**⅛ teaspoon kosher salt**

**Peanut or soy oil, for frying**

SIMPLE SUGAR COOKIES

# COOKIES, BROWNIES & CANDIES

# SIMPLE SUGAR COOKIES

This is my favorite recipe for festive cut-out cookies. Roll the dough out nice and thin and you'll get a buttery cookie with a good crunch. Enjoy these as is or bring out the icing, dragées, candy pearls, glittery or matte sprinkles, sparkly sugar, cinnamon candies, and gold or silver dust, and go to town. From Valentine's Day to Easter, Halloween, and Christmas, these cookies are fun to decorate all year long. I divide the dough into two parts here, making one part chocolate and leaving the other part plain, but you can leave all of the dough plain or make all of it chocolate, if you like.

In the bowl of an electric mixer fitted with the paddle attachment, beat the butter, sugar, and vanilla on medium speed until well combined, about 3 minutes. Add the egg and beat until well combined. Reduce the speed to low. In three additions, add the flour and salt, beating after each addition until combined.

Divide the dough in half and return one portion to the mixer bowl. With the mixer on low speed, add the chocolate and mix just until combined.

Wrap the doughs separately in plastic wrap and chill for about 1 hour (or up to 2 days), so that they are easier to roll out. (This dough can be frozen, well wrapped, for up to 1 month.)

Preheat the oven to 350°F.

On a lightly floured work surface, roll the light dough out into a 10-inch round, about ¼ inch thick. Cut the dough into desired shapes with cookie cutters, rerolling the scraps once.

Transfer the cookies to a parchment-lined baking sheet and bake for 20 minutes, rotating the sheet once halfway through. Transfer the cookies to a wire rack to cool.

Repeat with the chocolate dough.

If you are icing the cookies, whisk together the confectioners' sugar, milk, and vanilla. Add food coloring, if using. Brush the icing on top of the cooled cookies, and sprinkle with dragées or other embellishments, if using.

The cookies can be kept in an airtight container at room temperature for up to 1 week.

MAKES 2 DOZEN

### DOUGH

12 tablespoons (1½ sticks) unsalted butter, at room temperature

½ cup granulated sugar

1 teaspoon pure vanilla extract

1 large egg

2 cups unbleached all-purpose flour, plus more for rolling

1 teaspoon kosher salt

1 ounce unsweetened chocolate, melted

### ICING (OPTIONAL)

1 cup confectioners' sugar

3 tablespoons milk

½ teaspoon pure vanilla extract

Food coloring (optional)

### DECORATIONS (OPTIONAL)

Dragées, sprinkles, and/or other embellishments, such as finely ground Pink Peppercorn Brittle (page 100)

# PECAN SHORTBREAD COOKIES

Using both vanilla bean and vanilla extract gives these buttery, nut-filled cookies a rich, round character. As the vanilla bean tumbles around in your mixer, its flavorful oils mix into the dough. High-fat butter lends an extra richness, but you can use regular butter with fine results, if you like.

MAKES 2½ DOZEN

¾ cup pecans, roughly chopped

10 tablespoons (1¼ sticks) unsalted butter, preferably high-fat, at room temperature

½ cup confectioners' sugar

½ vanilla bean, split lengthwise, seeds scraped out, bean and seeds reserved

½ teaspoon pure vanilla extract

½ teaspoon kosher salt

1½ cups unbleached all-purpose flour, plus more for rolling

1 large egg yolk, lightly beaten

3 tablespoons Demerara sugar

Preheat the oven to 350°F.

Spread the pecans out on a baking sheet and bake until fragrant and toasted, about 5 minutes. Let them cool completely on the baking sheet placed on a wire rack.

In the bowl of an electric mixer fitted with the paddle attachment, beat the butter, confectioners' sugar, vanilla bean and seeds, vanilla extract, and salt on medium speed until no visible chunks of butter remain, about 3 minutes.

With the mixer on low speed, add the flour in three additions, mixing each well before adding the next. Stir in the pecans.

Turn out the dough onto a lightly floured work surface. Remove the vanilla bean and recycle it for another use (see page 16). Roll the dough into a log about 1½ inches in diameter. Wrap it in parchment paper, making sure to cover the ends completely, and refrigerate until firm, at least 1 hour or overnight. (The dough can be frozen, well wrapped, for up to 1 month.)

Preheat the oven to 350°F.

Let the dough stand at room temperature until it is soft enough to slice, about 5 minutes.

Brush the dough with the egg yolk, roll it in the Demerara sugar to coat it evenly, and then slice it into ½-inch-thick rounds. Place the rounds about 1 inch apart on a parchment-lined baking sheet. Bake, rotating the sheet halfway through, until the cookies are lightly golden and fragrant, 25 to 30 minutes. Transfer them to a wire rack to cool completely.

The cookies can be kept in an airtight container at room temperature for up to 1 week.

# CORNMEAL SHORTBREAD COOKIES

Cornmeal not only infuses these light, vanilla-flecked shortbreads with flavor, it also gives them a fantastic sandy texture.

MAKES 2 DOZEN

¾ cup plus 2 tablespoons unbleached all-purpose flour, plus more for rolling

½ cup coarse yellow cornmeal or fine yellow polenta

½ teaspoon kosher salt

9½ tablespoons unsalted butter, preferably high-fat, cut into small pieces, at room temperature

½ cup confectioners' sugar

¼ vanilla bean, split lengthwise, seeds scraped out, bean and seeds reserved; or 1 teaspoon pure vanilla extract

2 tablespoons Demerara sugar

In a mixing bowl, whisk together the flour, cornmeal, and salt.

In the bowl of an electric mixer fitted with the paddle attachment, beat the butter, confectioners' sugar, and vanilla bean and seeds on low speed until just well combined, about 1 minute. With the mixer running, add the flour mixture in two additions, mixing until just combined. Remove the vanilla bean from the dough and recycle it for another use (see page 16).

Flatten the dough into a disk and wrap it in plastic wrap. Chill it in the refrigerator for 30 minutes or up to 2 days. (The dough can be frozen, well wrapped, for up to 1 month.)

Preheat the oven to 350°F.

On a lightly floured surface, roll the dough out to ¼-inch thickness. With a 4-inch round cutter or inverted bowl, cut out rounds of dough. Take each round and cut it into 6 wedges, like a pizza.

Arrange the wedges on a parchment-covered baking sheet, spacing them ½ inch apart, and sprinkle with the Demerara sugar. Bake, turning the sheet halfway through, until the cookies are golden, 30 to 35 minutes. Transfer them to a wire rack to cool completely.

Cornmeal Shortbread Cookies will keep in an airtight container at room temperature for up to a week.

# GINGERSNAPS

Don't let these innocent-looking little cookies fool you—they pack a punch of spicy ginger and have a fabulous crunch.

Preheat the oven to 350°F.

In a bowl, whisk together the flour, baking soda, cinnamon, and salt.

In the bowl of an electric mixer fitted with the paddle attachment, beat together the granulated sugar and butter on medium speed until light and fluffy, 2 to 3 minutes. Beat in the eggs, molasses, and ginger to combine. With the mixer on low speed, gradually add the flour mixture, beating just until incorporated.

Line two baking sheets with parchment.

Shape the dough into twenty-four ¾-inch balls. Put the Demerara sugar in a shallow bowl and roll the balls in it to coat them completely. Space the balls evenly on two baking sheets. Bake, rotating the sheets once halfway through, until dark golden brown, about 15 minutes. Transfer the baking sheets to wire racks to cool.

The gingersnaps can be kept in an airtight container at room temperature for up to 5 days.

## VARYING YOUR CRAFT
These gingersnaps make a great crust for pies and tarts (see page 108 for instructions).

## COMBINING YOUR CRAFT
Serve gingersnaps with Butterscotch Pudding (page 196) and a spoonful of crème fraîche.

MAKES 3 DOZEN

**2 cups unbleached all-purpose flour**

**1½ teaspoons baking soda**

**1 teaspoon ground cinnamon**

**½ teaspoon kosher salt**

**1 cup granulated sugar**

**12 tablespoons (1½ sticks) unsalted butter, cut into pieces, at room temperature**

**2 large eggs**

**¼ cup blackstrap molasses**

**1 tablespoon finely grated fresh ginger**

**½ cup Demerara sugar**

# CRISP HONEY GRAHAMS

One bite of these homemade grahams and you'll never go back to the store-bought version. You can make these your own by varying the type of honey you use. A darker honey like buckwheat will give you an earthier, more molasses-y tasting cookie than a lighter honey, like linden.

In a bowl, sift together the all-purpose flour, whole-wheat flour, salt, baking soda, and cinnamon.

In the bowl of an electric mixer fitted with the paddle attachment, combine the butter, dark brown sugar, granulated sugar, and honey. Mix on medium speed until well combined, about 1 minute. In two additions, add the dry ingredients, letting the first fully incorporate before you add the second.

Flatten the dough into a rectangular shape, wrap it tightly in plastic wrap, and refrigerate until chilled, about 30 minutes or up to 2 days. (The dough can be frozen, well wrapped, for up to 1 month.)

Preheat the oven to 350°F. Line two baking sheets with parchment.

Unwrap the chilled dough, and on a lightly floured surface, roll it out into a rectangle about ⅛ inch thick. Using a ruler and a pastry cutter or a sharp knife, cut the dough into 1½ x 3-inch rectangles; use a spatula to transfer the rectangles to the prepared baking sheets as you go. Reroll the scraps of dough once, and cut out more cookies. Using a fork, pierce each rectangle with two rows of four to six marks.

Bake the graham crackers, rotating the baking sheets halfway through, until they are golden brown, 15 to 20 minutes. Cool on a wire rack.

The graham crackers will keep in an airtight container at room temperature for up to 1 week.

RECIPE CONTINUES

**MAKES 3 DOZEN**

2 cups unbleached all-purpose flour, plus more for rolling

½ cup whole-wheat flour

¾ teaspoon kosher salt

½ teaspoon baking soda

½ teaspoon ground cinnamon

8 ounces (2 sticks) unsalted butter, cut into small pieces, at room temperature

¼ cup packed dark brown sugar

¼ cup granulated sugar

¼ cup honey

TIP Using a ruler and a fluted pastry wheel is a nice, easy way to create a cute cookie with a deckled edge.

RECIPE CONTINUED

## VARYING YOUR CRAFT

These grahams make a great crust for pies and tarts (see page 108 for instructions).

## COMBINING YOUR CRAFT

For a twist on the classic cherry cheesecake, dollop Cream Cheese Panna Cotta (page 180) with a spoonful of Sour Cherry Compote (page 235) and serve a stack of graham crackers alongside.

# S'MORES

For each s'more, you'll need 2 graham crackers, one 2-inch square Coconut Marshmallow (page 98), and 1 tablespoon milk chocolate ganache (see instructions below).

3 ounces milk chocolate, chopped
1½ tablespoons unsalted butter, cut into small pieces
¼ cup heavy cream
¼ teaspoon kosher salt

Bring about 2 inches of water to a simmer in a small saucepan. Combine the chocolate, butter, cream, and salt in a mixing bowl and place it over the simmering water. Whisk the mixture gently to combine as it melts. Let the ganache cool to room temperature.

Preheat the oven to broil and position an oven rack 8 inches from the heat source.

Spread 1 tablespoon of the ganache on 1 graham cracker and top with the marshmallow. Repeat for each s'more you would like to make. Place them on a baking sheet and broil for 3 minutes, rotating the sheet after 2 minutes, until the marshmallow is golden brown and soft. Remove from the oven and sandwich with another graham cracker. Serve immediately.

# CANDIED LEMON SLICES

It's so nice to have these pretty stained-glass-like candies on hand. Enjoy them on their own, drop them into fresh lemonade, or use them to garnish cupcakes, steamed puddings, and sorbets. They're easy to make and they keep for months in the fridge.

Trim the ends of each lemon so that they are even and flat. Slice the lemons as thin as possible while keeping the slices intact (the pulp should be firmly attached to the skin all the way around). Using a paring knife, carefully remove any seeds from the slices.

In a medium saucepan, combine the sugar and 1 cup water. Stir to make sure that the sugar is wet throughout (dry pockets of sugar will caramelize and burn rather than dissolve into the water) and then bring the mixture to a boil.

Add the lemon slices and gently press with a wooden spoon to submerge them. Reduce the heat so the mixture barely simmers, and cover the surface with a round piece of parchment. Cook without stirring or touching until the lemon slices become translucent, about 30 minutes.

Remove the pan from the heat and transfer the slices, with the syrup, to a bowl. Set the bowl in an ice bath, or chill it in the refrigerator, until completely cooled. Transfer the lemons and syrup to a covered container and store in the refrigerator.

MAKES ABOUT 45

3 medium lemons, preferably organic, washed and dried

2 cups sugar

TIP Use fresh, fairly firm lemons with smooth, even skins. A mandoline makes very thin, even slices, though a sharp knife will work, too.

# BLACKBERRY JELLIES

**Jellies make a great gift.** Tuck them into little candy papers and pack them into pretty boxes.

Lightly coat the bottom and sides of an 8-inch square baking pan with nonstick cooking spray. Line the bottom with parchment paper, and spray the parchment. Have a fine-mesh sieve handy.

In a blender, purée the blackberries and ½ cup water. Strain through the sieve into a 2-cup measuring cup. You should have 1¼ cups of purée. Add water if needed to reach 1¼ cups.

In a medium heatproof bowl, using a dry whisk, whisk together 3 tablespoons plus 1 teaspoon of the sugar and the pectin. (Using dry tools will prevent lumps of pectin from forming.)

In a medium saucepan, bring to a boil 1¾ cups plus 2 tablespoons of the sugar with the blackberry purée, cider, and corn syrup. Remove from the heat, pour one third of the mixture over the pectin mixture, and whisk to combine. Using a rubber spatula, scrape the pectin mixture into the saucepan. Over medium heat, return the mixture to a boil and cook for 3 minutes.

Spoon a few drops of the liquid onto a plate. If it sets up enough so that you can peel it off the plate, it is ready; strain the liquid through a sieve into the prepared baking pan. If not, continue cooking, testing every 2 minutes, until it does. Set the baking pan of jelly on a flat surface and do not disturb until the jelly cools completely, about 30 minutes.

In a small bowl, whisk together the remaining 1 cup sugar and the vitamin C powder. Sprinkle a thin layer over the jelly (to prevent sticking) and top with parchment. Invert a baking sheet over the baking pan, and flip over to release the jelly onto the baking sheet. Peel off the parchment, and sprinkle the jelly with some of the sugar mixture. Using a 1-inch round cutter, cut out the jellies, tossing each one in the sugar mixture and transferring it to a large plate or baking sheet as you go.

The jellies will keep well, layered between sheets of parchment paper in an airtight container, for 2 weeks. Toss them again in the sugar and vitamin C mixture just before serving.

MAKES ABOUT 60

Nonstick cooking spray

2½ cups fresh blackberries

About 3¼ cups sugar

2 tablespoons plus 2 teaspoons powdered pectin (see Sources)

½ cup plus 2 tablespoons apple cider

¼ cup light corn syrup

1 teaspoon vitamin C powder (see Sources)

# BUILDING YOUR CRAFT
## JELLIES

Making jellies at home is fun, and you wind up with a delicious natural fruit candy with a smooth, tender texture, rather than one that has that cloyingly sweet, stick-to-your-teeth quality found in commercial brands. While the hunting down of powdered pectin (the recipe does not work with liquid) and vitamin C powder can be a little labor-intensive, once you have everything on hand, the jellies are quick to put together. Using vitamin C powder adds a tang that you can vary as you please by adding less or more than I call for, or none at all.

I like a round shape, which you can create with a simple round cutter, as it recalls that of traditional gumdrops. To get the most jellies possible out of a batch with the least amount of scraps left over, cut your jellies as close as possible to one another, or if you prefer to avoid scraps altogether, simply cut the jelly into squares with a knife.

Varying the flavor of jellies is easy. The base should always include apple cider (an important source of pectin), sugar, pectin, and corn syrup. The fruit purée can vary.

Using the Blackberry Jellies as a base recipe, you can simply substitute 1¼ cups of just about any strained fruit purée for the blackberry purée to make your own flavors, adding spices if you like. The only fruit that does not work well for jellies is pineapple, which contains enzymes that prevent the jelly from setting. As a rule of thumb, use the best-quality, most intensely flavored fruit you can get your hands on. Try raspberry, strawberry, peach, pear, passion fruit, even rhubarb (which will require a juicer).

# SPICED APPLE CIDER JELLIES

Cinnamon, cloves, star anise, and black peppercorns enhance the warm flavor of the cider in these jellies.

Lightly coat the bottom and sides of an 8-inch square baking pan with nonstick cooking spray. Line the bottom with parchment paper, and spray the parchment. Have a fine-mesh sieve handy.

In a medium heatproof bowl, using a dry whisk, whisk together the pectin and 3 tablespoons of the sugar. (Using dry tools prevents lumps of pectin from forming.)

In a medium saucepan, bring to a boil the cider, 1¾ cups of the sugar, the cinnamon, cloves, star anise, peppercorns, and corn syrup. Remove from the heat, pour one third of the cider mixture over the pectin mixture, and whisk to combine. Using a rubber spatula, scrape the pectin mixture into the saucepan. Over medium heat, return the mixture to a boil and cook for 3 minutes.

Spoon a few drops of the liquid onto a plate. If it sets up enough so that you can peel it off the plate, it is ready; strain the liquid through the sieve into the prepared baking pan. If not, continue cooking, testing every 2 minutes, until it does. Set the baking pan of jelly on a flat surface and do not disturb until the jelly cools completely, about 30 minutes.

In a small bowl, whisk together the remaining 1 cup sugar and the vitamin C powder. Sprinkle a thin layer of this mixture over the jelly (to prevent sticking) and place a piece of parchment on top. Invert a baking sheet over the baking pan, and holding the two together, flip them over to invert the jelly onto the baking sheet. Carefully peel off the parchment from the top of the jelly, and sprinkle the jelly with some of the sugar mixture. Using a 1-inch round cutter, cut out the jellies, tossing each one in the sugar mixture and transferring it to a large plate or baking sheet as you go.

The jellies will keep well, layered between sheets of parchment paper in an airtight container, for 2 weeks. Toss them again in the sugar and vitamin C mixture just before serving.

## MAKES ABOUT 60

Nonstick cooking spray

1 tablespoon plus 2 teaspoons powdered pectin (see Sources)

2¾ cups plus 3 tablespoons sugar

1¾ cups apple cider

2 cinnamon sticks

2 whole cloves

2 whole star anise

5 black peppercorns

⅓ cup light corn syrup

1 teaspoon vitamin C powder (see Sources)

# HAZELNUT LINZER COOKIES

Hazelnuts replace the traditional almonds in this version of the linzer cookie, which, to me, gives the cookies a nice wintry feeling. Apple Butter and Quince Butter (page 239) are my favorite fillings, but you can also use the more classic raspberry jam or any other flavor you like. Sometimes I use three or four jams with one batch of cookies for fun and easy variation.

MAKES 1½ DOZEN

1½ cups hazelnuts, finely ground

12 tablespoons (1½ sticks) unsalted butter, at room temperature

1 cup confectioners' sugar, plus more for sprinkling

Finely grated zest of 1 lemon

Finely grated zest of 2 oranges

3 large egg yolks

1¼ cups unbleached all-purpose flour, plus more for rolling

2 teaspoons ground cinnamon

1 teaspoon baking powder

½ teaspoon freshly grated nutmeg

½ teaspoon kosher salt

¼ cup fruit preserves

**TIP** As long as you have two cookie cutters of the same or compatible shape, one smaller than the other to make the cutout, you can shape these cookies anyway you like—hearts, stars, butterflies, and more.

Preheat the oven to 350°F.

Spread the ground hazelnuts on a baking sheet and bake for 5 minutes, until lightly toasted. Remove from the oven and set the baking sheet on a rack to cool. Turn the oven off if you won't be baking the cookies right away.

In the bowl of an electric mixer fitted with the paddle attachment, beat together the butter, confectioners' sugar, and lemon and orange zests on medium speed until well mixed, about 4 minutes. Beat in the egg yolks, scraping down the sides of the bowl as needed.

In another bowl, sift together the flour, cinnamon, baking powder, nutmeg, and salt. With the mixer on low speed, add the dry ingredients to the butter mixture and beat until combined. Add the hazelnuts and beat until combined. Turn out the dough onto a sheet of plastic wrap and shape it into a flattened disk. Wrap it in the plastic and chill until firm, 30 minutes or up to 2 days. (The dough can be frozen, well wrapped, for up to 1 month.)

On a lightly floured surface, roll out the dough to ⅛-inch thickness. Using a 2-inch round cutter, cut out 36 cookies. Transfer the cookies to parchment-covered baking sheets, spacing them at least ½ inch apart. Using a ½-inch round cutter, cut out and remove the centers of half of the cookies; these cookies will be the tops. Chill the tops and bottoms in the refrigerator until firm, 10 to 15 minutes.

While the cookies are chilling, preheat the oven to 350°F if necessary.

Bake, rotating the sheets halfway through, until the cookies are golden brown, 15 to 20 minutes. Transfer the cookies, still on the parchment, to a wire rack and let cool completely.

When they are cool, sprinkle the cut-out top cookies with confectioners' sugar. Spoon about ½ teaspoon preserves on each whole bottom cookie; then set the cut-out cookies over the whole ones to sandwich them together.

Unfilled, the cookies can be kept in an airtight container at room temperature for up to 1 week. Once filled, they are best eaten on the same day.

# OATMEAL RAISIN BISCOTTI

A bowl of oatmeal in a cookie! These are, in fact, as great for breakfast as they are for tea or dessert. I love them studded with golden raisins and pecans, but the additions can be as varied as your taste for serving oatmeal. Maple sugar, available in specialty shops or by mail order, brings all of the flavors together. If you don't have maple sugar, substitute ¾ cup packed dark brown sugar.

**MAKES ABOUT 3 DOZEN**

¾ cup pecans, roughly chopped

1 cup old-fashioned rolled oats

1¾ cups unbleached all-purpose flour, plus more for rolling

¾ cup maple sugar

1 teaspoon baking powder

½ teaspoon baking soda

½ teaspoon ground cinnamon

½ teaspoon kosher salt

2 large eggs

¼ cup dark molasses, such as Grandma's

2 tablespoons vegetable oil

¾ teaspoon pure vanilla extract

¾ cup golden raisins

Preheat the oven to 350°F. Line a baking sheet with parchment paper.

Spread the pecans in a single layer on a second baking sheet. Toast them in the oven until they are lightly golden and fragrant, about 5 minutes. Remove from the heat and set the sheet on a wire rack to cool. Keep the oven on.

In a food processor or blender, grind ½ cup of the oats to make a fine flour. In the bowl of an electric mixer fitted with the paddle attachment, whisk together the oat flour, remaining ½ cup oats, all-purpose flour, maple sugar, baking powder, baking soda, cinnamon, and salt.

In a separate bowl, whisk together the eggs, molasses, and oil. With the mixer on low speed, slowly add the egg mixture to the dry ingredients, scraping down the sides of the bowl as necessary, until combined. Mix in the cooled nuts, vanilla, and raisins, just to combine.

Turn out the dough onto a lightly floured surface and divide it in half. Shape each portion into a 16 x 2-inch log and transfer them to the prepared baking sheet, placing them about 3 inches apart. Bake, rotating the sheet once, until the logs are golden and firm to the touch, about 30 minutes. Transfer the logs, still on the parchment paper, to a wire rack and let cool slightly, about 5 minutes.

Reduce the oven temperature to 250°F.

One at a time, transfer the warm logs to a cutting board and use a serrated knife to cut them on the diagonal into ⅓-inch-thick slices. Arrange the slices, cut side up, on the baking sheet. Bake until the biscotti are dry and firm to the touch, about 1 hour. Remove the baking sheet from the oven and let the sheet of biscotti cool completely on the rack.

The biscotti can be kept in an airtight container at room temperature for up to 1 month.

## VARYING YOUR CRAFT

### OATMEAL APRICOT BISCOTTI
Use ¾ cup roughly chopped almonds in place of the pecans, and ¾ cup chopped dried apricots in place of the raisins.

### OATMEAL BLUEBERRY BISCOTTI
Use ¾ cup roughly chopped unsalted pistachios in place of the pecans, and ¾ cup dried blueberries in place of the raisins.

### OATMEAL CHERRY BISCOTTI
Use ¾ cup roughly chopped walnuts in place of the pecans, and ¾ cup chopped dried cherries in place of the raisins.

# CHERRY ANISE BISCOTTI

These little cookies are packed with multiple flavors that all work well together. Anise is a warm spice that pairs perfectly with the tang of dried cherries. Cornmeal lends a golden color, pleasant gritty texture, and natural sweetness, and toasted almonds add a delicate richness that balances the slight pucker of the fruit.

**MAKES ABOUT 3 DOZEN**

1 cup blanched whole almonds, roughly chopped

1 cup granulated sugar

8 tablespoons (1 stick) unsalted butter, cut into small pieces, at room temperature

2 teaspoons anise seeds

2 large eggs

1½ cups unbleached all-purpose flour, plus more for rolling

½ cup yellow coarsely ground cornmeal or fine polenta

1½ teaspoons baking powder

½ teaspoon kosher salt

¾ cup dried cherries

Preheat the oven to 350°F. Line a baking sheet with parchment paper.

Spread the almonds in a single layer on a second baking sheet. Toast them in the oven until they are lightly golden and fragrant, stirring occasionally, about 5 minutes. Remove from the heat and cool the sheet on a wire rack. Keep the oven on.

In the bowl of an electric mixer fitted with the paddle attachment, combine the sugar, butter, and anise seeds. Beat on medium-low speed until the ingredients are well combined and no butter pieces are visible, about 4 minutes.

Add the eggs, one at a time, beating to incorporate after each addition.

In another bowl, whisk together the flour, cornmeal, baking powder, and salt. In three additions, add the dry ingredients to the mixer bowl and beat on medium-low speed, scraping down the sides of the bowl as needed, until combined. Add the toasted almonds and dried cherries, and beat just to combine.

Turn out the dough onto a lightly floured work surface and divide it in half. Shape each portion into a 16 x 2-inch log and transfer them to the prepared baking sheet, spacing them about 3 inches apart.

Bake, rotating the baking sheet halfway through, until the logs are golden brown and firm to the touch, about 25 minutes. Transfer the logs, still on the parchment paper, to a wire rack and let cool slightly, about 5 minutes.

Reduce the oven temperature to 250°F.

Transfer the warm logs to a cutting board. Using a serrated knife, cut the logs on the diagonal into ⅓-inch-thick slices. Arrange the slices, cut side up, on the baking sheet. Bake until the biscotti are dry and firm to the touch, about 1 hour. Remove the pan from the oven and let the sheet of biscotti cool completely on the rack.

The biscotti can be kept in an airtight container at room temperature for up to 3 weeks.

# CHOCOLATE WALNUT BISCOTTI

These light, crispy cookies are deeply chocolaty but not too sweet. I use coffee extract here (which you can make yourself, using instant espresso powder and water; opposite). The coffee extract acts similarly to vanilla extract, adding a fantastic depth and roundness to the chocolate flavor without adding a discernible coffee flavor. Without the extract, the flavor of these cookies falls flat.

**MAKES ABOUT 3 DOZEN**

**1 cup walnut pieces, roughly chopped**

**1 cup unbleached all-purpose flour, plus more for rolling**

**⅓ cup unsweetened cocoa powder**

**½ cup packed dark brown sugar**

**¼ cup granulated sugar**

**2 tablespoons unsalted butter, cut into small pieces, at room temperature**

**¼ teaspoon baking soda**

**¼ teaspoon kosher salt**

**2 large eggs**

**1 large egg yolk**

**2 teaspoons Coffee Extract (recipe follows)**

**¾ teaspoon pure vanilla extract**

**½ cup semisweet chocolate chips**

**TIP This dough is very sticky, so use ample flour on your work surface and hands when rolling it out.**

Preheat the oven to 350°F. Line a baking sheet with parchment paper.

Spread the walnuts in a single layer on a second baking sheet. Toast them in the oven, stirring occasionally, until they are lightly golden and fragrant, about 5 minutes. Remove from the heat and cool the sheet on a wire rack. Keep the oven on.

In the bowl of an electric mixer fitted with the paddle attachment, combine the flour, cocoa powder, brown sugar, granulated sugar, butter, baking soda, and salt. Beat on low speed until the ingredients are well combined and no butter pieces are visible, about 4 minutes.

In a medium bowl, whisk together the eggs, egg yolk, coffee extract, and vanilla. Add the mixture to the flour mixture and beat on low speed to combine. Add the cooled nuts and the chocolate chips, and beat just to combine.

Turn out the dough onto a generously floured work surface and divide it in half. Shape each portion into a 16 x 2-inch log, and transfer them to the prepared baking sheet, spacing them about 3 inches apart.

Bake, rotating the sheet halfway through, until the logs are firm to the touch, about 20 minutes. Transfer the logs, still on the parchment paper, to a wire rack and let cool slightly, about 5 minutes.

Reduce the oven temperature to 250°F.

Transfer the warm logs to a cutting board. Using a serrated knife, cut the logs on the diagonal into ⅓-inch-thick slices. Arrange the slices, cut side up, on the baking sheet. Bake until the biscotti are dry and firm to the touch, about 1 hour. Remove the baking sheet from the oven and let the sheet of biscotti cool completely on the rack.

The biscotti can be kept in an airtight container at room temperature for up to 3 weeks.

## COFFEE EXTRACT

¼ cup hot water

One 2-ounce jar instant espresso powder, preferably Medaglia D'Oro

Slowly stir the hot water directly into the jar of espresso powder. Cover the jar with the lid, close the lid tightly, and shake well to combine. Use immediately or keep in a dark cupboard at room temperature for up to 6 months.

### VARYING YOUR CRAFT

**CHOCOLATE-DIPPED CHOCOLATE WALNUT BISCOTTI**

Bake the biscotti, omitting the chocolate chips. Melt and temper 12 ounces semisweet chocolate (see page 21). Dip one side, or one end, of each cookie into the chocolate. Scrape off any excess chocolate on the edge of the bowl. Place the biscotti, dipped side down, on a parchment-covered baking sheet. Let the chocolate set at room temperature, about 5 minutes. The biscotti can be kept in an airtight container for up to 3 weeks.

# PEANUT BUTTER SANDWICH COOKIES WITH MILK CHOCOLATE FILLING

These playful, crunchy cookie sandwiches with their gooey filling are great for kids of all ages. Using a commercial peanut butter is the key to evoking that childhood taste (my favorite is Skippy creamy; try crunchy for variation and see which you like best). Be sure to let the cookies cool completely before filling them, or bake them a day in advance and fill them the next day. Unfilled peanut butter cookies are also great to use for ice cream sandwiches, and are delicious alongside Chocolate Pudding (page 192).

Preheat the oven to 350°F. Line two baking sheets with parchment paper.

In a large bowl, sift together the flour, baking powder, baking soda, and salt.

In the bowl of an electric mixer fitted with the paddle attachment, beat the butter, brown sugar, and confectioners' sugar on medium-high speed until light and fluffy, about 2 minutes. Add the peanut butter and beat to combine, scraping down the sides of the bowl as needed. With the mixer on low speed, slowly add the oil, vanilla, and egg and beat until just combined, about 20 seconds. Add the flour mixture, beating just to combine.

Lightly flour the palms of your hands, and roll the dough into balls about ½ inch in diameter. Place them about 1 inch apart on the prepared baking sheets. Bake, rotating the sheets halfway through, until the cookies are golden brown on the edges, about 12 minutes. Transfer the baking sheets to wire racks and let cool completely. (The cookies can be stored, unfilled, in an airtight container at room temperature for up to 1 week.)

RECIPE CONTINUES

**MAKES ABOUT 2 DOZEN**

**COOKIES**

1¾ cups unbleached all-purpose flour, plus more for rolling

1 teaspoon baking powder

½ teaspoon baking soda

½ teaspoon kosher salt

6 tablespoons (¾ stick) unsalted butter, at room temperature

½ cup plus 1 tablespoon lightly packed dark brown sugar

¾ cup plus 1 tablespoon confectioners' sugar

½ cup creamy peanut butter

½ cup vegetable oil

1½ teaspoons pure vanilla extract

1 large egg

## FILLING

**6 ounces milk chocolate,
roughly chopped**

**½ cup creamy peanut butter**

**¼ cup confectioners' sugar**

**¼ teaspoon kosher salt**

**¾ cup heavy cream**

RECIPE CONTINUED

To make the filling, combine the chocolate, peanut butter, confectioners' sugar, and salt in a medium bowl. In a small saucepan, bring the cream to a boil. Remove the cream from the heat and pour it over the chocolate mixture. Stir with a spatula until the chocolate is completely melted. Set the bowl in an ice bath, or chill it in the refrigerator, until the filling has cooled to room temperature and is thick enough to spread. Then use it immediately or transfer it to an airtight container and refrigerate it for up to 1 week (let it come to room temperature before using).

Using an offset spatula, spread 1 teaspoon of the filling over the flat sides of half of the cookies. Sandwich with the remaining cookies, flat sides together.

Once filled, the cookies are best eaten the same day, but they can be kept in an airtight container in the refrigerator for up to 3 days.

## VARYING YOUR CRAFT
### PEANUT BUTTER ICE CREAM SANDWICHES

Fill these cookies with Vanilla Bean Ice Cream (page 204) in place of the chocolate filling, allowing the ice cream to soften slightly before making the sandwiches. You will need at least 2 cups of ice cream and 16 cookies to make 8 sandwiches. Place a small scoop of ice cream between 2 cookies and gently press together. Once the sandwiches are made, let them firm up in the freezer for at least 30 minutes. Then either serve them or wrap them individually in plastic wrap, place in freezer bags, and store in the freezer until ready to serve. Let frozen sandwiches stand at room temperature for 5 minutes before serving.

# CARROT CAKE SANDWICH COOKIES WITH CREAM CHEESE FILLING

Using ground oats and all-purpose flour, instead of just flour alone, is the secret to the rich flavor of these whoopie pie–like cookies.

Preheat the oven to 350°F. Line two baking sheets with parchment paper.

Grind the oats in a food processor to make a fine flour. In a medium bowl, whisk together the oat flour, all-purpose flour, cinnamon, nutmeg, baking soda, and salt.

In the bowl of an electric mixer fitted with the paddle attachment, beat the butter, brown sugar, granulated sugar, and vanilla extract on medium speed until well combined. Add the egg and beat to combine, scraping down the sides of the bowl with a rubber spatula. With the mixer on the lowest speed, add the dry ingredients in two additions, scraping down the sides of the bowl after each one. Add the carrots and raisins, mixing just to combine. The dough will be very sticky.

Drop 1-tablespoon mounds of the dough onto the prepared baking sheets, spacing them ½ inch apart. Bake, rotating the sheets once halfway through, until the cookies are golden brown and spring back when gently touched in the center, about 12 minutes. Cool the cookies completely, on the baking sheets set on a wire rack, before filling.

To make the filling, in the bowl of an electric mixer fitted with the paddle attachment, beat the cream cheese, butter, lemon zest, sugar, and salt on medium speed until well combined, scraping down the sides of the bowl as needed. (The filling can be kept in a covered container in the refrigerator for up to 1 week. Let it come to room temperature before using.)

Using a small spoon or spatula, spread 1 teaspoon of the filling over the flat side of half of the cookies. Sandwich with the remaining cookies, flat sides together.

The cookies can be kept in an airtight container for up to 2 days.

MAKES 1½ DOZEN

## COOKIES

¾ cup old-fashioned rolled oats

1 cup unbleached all-purpose flour

¾ teaspoon ground cinnamon

¼ teaspoon freshly grated nutmeg

½ teaspoon baking soda

½ teaspoon kosher salt

8 tablespoons (1 stick) unsalted butter, at room temperature

½ cup packed dark brown sugar

¼ cup granulated sugar

½ teaspoon pure vanilla extract

1 large egg

¾ cup roughly grated carrots (about 1½ medium carrots)

¼ cup raisins

## FILLING

3 ounces cream cheese, at room temperature

4 tablespoons (½ stick) unsalted butter, at room temperature

Finely grated zest of 1 lemon

1 tablespoon granulated sugar

Pinch of kosher salt

# BACK-TO-SCHOOL RASPBERRY GRANOLA BARS

These nutty fruit cookies are perfect for a lunch sack, last-minute bake sale, or early autumn picnic. They are quick to put together with pantry staples and everyone seems to love them.

MAKES 16 BARS

**12 tablespoons (1½ sticks) unsalted butter, plus more for the pan**

**1 cup pecans, roughly chopped**

**1½ cups unbleached all-purpose flour**

**1¼ cups old-fashioned rolled oats**

**⅓ cup granulated sugar**

**⅓ cup packed dark brown sugar**

**1 teaspoon kosher salt**

**½ teaspoon baking soda**

**1 cup raspberry preserves**

Preheat the oven to 350°F. Butter an 8-inch square baking pan and line the bottom with parchment.

In a small saucepan, melt the butter. Remove from the heat and let cool to room temperature.

Spread the pecans on a baking sheet. Bake until lightly golden and fragrant, about 5 minutes. Cool the sheet completely on a wire rack.

In a large bowl, whisk together the flour, oats, granulated sugar, brown sugar, salt, baking soda, and pecans. Pour in the melted butter, and using a wooden spoon, mix together until well combined. Transfer about two thirds of the dough to the prepared baking pan. Press the dough evenly into the pan, forming a firmly packed layer.

Using an offset or rubber spatula, spread the preserves over the dough. Evenly sprinkle the remaining dough over the preserves. Bake, rotating the pan halfway through, until the top is golden brown and fragrant, about 40 minutes. Transfer the pan to a wire rack and let it cool completely. Then cut into 2-inch squares.

The bars can be kept in an airtight container at room temperature for up to 1 week.

## VARYING YOUR CRAFT
### FIG BARS
Substitute Fig and Spiced Wine Preserves (page 228) for the raspberry preserves.

# LITTLE LEMON BARS

I like to keep these bars small because they pack such a tart citrus punch. They're elegant, yet homey and easy to make.

## CRUST

**12 tablespoons (1½ sticks) chilled unsalted butter, cut into small pieces, plus more for the pan**

**¼ cup plus 2 tablespoons confectioners' sugar**

**½ teaspoon kosher salt**

**1½ cups unbleached all-purpose flour, plus more for rolling**

## FILLING

**4 large eggs**

**2 cups granulated sugar**

**Finely grated zest of 2 lemons**

**⅓ cup fresh lemon juice (about 3 lemons), strained**

**½ cup unbleached all-purpose flour, plus more for rolling**

**¾ teaspoon baking powder**

**¼ teaspoon kosher salt**

FOR THE CRUST: In the bowl of an electric mixer fitted with the paddle attachment, beat together the butter, confectioners' sugar, and salt on low speed until there are no longer any visible chunks of butter, about 3 minutes. Add half of the flour, and mix just until combined; repeat with the remaining flour. Form the dough into a 5 x 5-inch square, wrap it in plastic wrap, and refrigerate until firm, about 1 hour (or overnight).

Preheat the oven to 350°F. Line the bottom of an 8-inch-square pan with parchment and grease it with butter.

On a lightly floured surface, roll the chilled dough into a 10-inch square, about ⅛ inch thick. Transfer it to the prepared baking pan by rolling the dough around the rolling pin and then unrolling it over the pan. Fit the dough into the corners and sides of the pan (the dough should come up about 1 inch on all sides of the pan). Chill for 10 minutes in the freezer (or, well wrapped, for up to 1 month).

Remove the crust from the freezer and bake, rotating the pan once halfway through, until golden, about 30 minutes.

While the crust is baking, prepare the filling: In a large bowl, whisk together the eggs, sugar, lemon zest, and lemon juice. In another bowl, sift together the flour, baking powder, and salt. Whisk the flour mixture into the egg mixture just to combine.

Remove the crust from the oven and pour the filling into it. Return the pan to the oven and bake, rotating the pan once halfway through, until the filling is golden brown and firm to the touch, about 40 minutes. Transfer the pan to a wire rack and let it cool completely. Then cut into thirty-two 1 x 2-inch bars.

Store in an airtight container at room temperature for up to 3 days.

# ULTIMATE CHOCOLATE BROWNIES

If you like a moist, chewy-type brownie, this is the recipe for you. Instead of using cocoa powder, as is done in many brownie recipes, I use unsweetened chocolate, which gives them richness and a smooth mouth feel. For a shiny, crackly top, keep the batter thin and warm. Mix the warm chocolate with the rest of the ingredients quickly and pop the pan right into the hot oven.

Preheat the oven to 375°F. Butter an 8-inch square baking pan and line the bottom with parchment.

Bring about 2 inches of water to a simmer in a medium saucepan. Put the butter and the unsweetened chocolate in a heatproof bowl and set it over (but not touching) the simmering water. Stir the mixture frequently with a rubber spatula until it is completely melted and combined. Remove the pan from the heat but keep the bowl over the water to keep the mixture warm.

In a large bowl, whisk together the eggs, sugar, and vanilla. In another bowl, sift together the flour and salt. Pour the warm chocolate mixture over the egg mixture and whisk together. With a rubber spatula, quickly fold in the flour mixture. Fold in the chocolate chips and immediately pour the mixture into the prepared baking pan, spreading it evenly.

Bake for 10 minutes. Then rotate the pan and bake until the brownies are shiny and cracked on top, 10 minutes more. Transfer the pan to a wire rack and let it cool completely. Then cut into 1½-inch squares.

Keep the brownies at room temperature in an airtight container for up to 3 days or frozen, well wrapped, for up to 1 month.

**MAKES 25 SQUARES**

**12 tablespoons (1½ sticks) unsalted butter, plus more for the pan**

**3 ounces unsweetened chocolate, roughly chopped**

**3 large eggs, at room temperature**

**1½ cups sugar**

**¾ teaspoon pure vanilla extract**

**1 cup unbleached all-purpose flour**

**1 teaspoon kosher salt**

**1 heaping cup semisweet chocolate chips**

**TIP** These are a great make-ahead because they freeze so well. After they've cooled, cut them, then wrap the brownies either individually or together tightly in plastic wrap and freeze them for up to 1 month. When you are ready to serve them, unwrap them and heat them in a 300°F oven for about 5 minutes. They'll taste as good as freshly baked.

# NUT & CHERRY NOUGAT

This version of Italian nougat mixes cherries and almonds with the classic pistachios. Traditionally, Italian nougat is rolled between sheets of edible wafer paper. I prefer to leave the paper off, making the candy easier to cut into even pieces for serving or to chop into misshapen pieces and fold into or sprinkle over ice cream. This is a fairly labor-intensive recipe, but it's worth the effort. The candy keeps well and makes a beautiful and very special gift.

Preheat the oven to 350°F.

In a mixing bowl, whisk together the confectioners' sugar and cornstarch. Pour the cornstarch mixture into a fine-mesh sieve and liberally sprinkle some over a 12 x 17-inch baking sheet. Set aside the sieve with the remaining cornstarch mixture.

Spread the pistachios and almonds on a baking sheet lined with parchment paper, and toast in the oven for 5 minutes. Turn off the oven and leave the nuts inside to keep warm. Put the honey in a small heat-resistant bowl and place that in the turned-off oven as well.

Put ½ cup plus 2 tablespoons of the corn syrup and ½ cup of the granulated sugar into a small saucepan and stir to make sure all of the sugar is damp. Attach a candy thermometer to this pan.

Put the remaining ½ cup plus 2 tablespoons corn syrup and ¾ cup of the granulated sugar into another small saucepan and stir to make sure all of the sugar is damp. Put both pans over high heat.

Put the egg whites in the bowl of an electric mixer fitted with the whisk attachment. Set the whisk attachment so that the whisk drops down to touch the bottom of the bowl (see page 19). With the mixer on medium speed, slowly add the remaining 1 tablespoon plus 1 teaspoon of the sugar to the egg whites. Leave the mixer running while the sugar in the saucepans continues to heat.

MAKES ABOUT
50 SQUARES

¾ cup confectioners' sugar

⅓ cup cornstarch

1 cup unsalted pistachios, roughly chopped

1½ cups sliced blanched almonds

2 tablespoons honey

1¼ cups light corn syrup

1¼ cups plus 1 tablespoon plus 1 teaspoon granulated sugar

¼ cup egg whites (from about 2 large eggs)

½ teaspoon kosher salt

½ cup dried cherries

Nonstick cooking spray

**TIP** I tend to make this candy in the wintertime when the air is nice and dry. The less humidity there is, the longer the nougat will stay dry. If you are stacking the finished pieces together in a box or container, use parchment or wax paper between the layers to prevent sticking.

Success depends on having everything set up (timers, rolling pin, everything). Read through the recipe before you begin.

**TIP** This is a very small amount of sugar to cook, so use the smallest saucepans you have. If the sugar is too shallow to be measured by your candy thermometer, use the cooking times as a guide, and when you think it is hot enough, tilt the saucepan so you can hold the thermometer in the syrup to check the temperature. If the sugar gets a little too hot, simply pull the saucepan off the heat and wait for it to cool to the correct temperature before adding it to the egg whites. This works only if the sugar has not yet begun to turn to caramel. If it caramelizes, you have cooked it for too long and will have to start over.

When the sugar in the saucepan fitted with the thermometer comes to 250°F (about 4 minutes), remove the pan from the heat. Transfer the thermometer to the second pan of sugar (continue to cook that pan of sugar). In a slow and steady stream, pour the first pan of sugar syrup down the side of the mixer bowl and into the whipping egg whites.

When the second pan of sugar reaches 293°F (about 2 more minutes), pour that sugar syrup down the side of the mixer bowl in a slow and steady stream. Increase the speed to high and whip until the egg white mixture turns white and thick, about 5 minutes. Then add the warm honey and the salt.

Turn the mixer off and switch to the paddle attachment. With the mixer on low speed, add the warm nuts and the cherries. Beat just until the nuts and cherries are evenly dispersed; then remove the bowl from the mixer. Scrape the nougat onto the prepared baking sheet. Sift enough of the cornstarch mixture over the top of the nougat to cover it liberally. With a rolling pin, roll the nougat until it is ¾ inch thick and covers most of the baking sheet.

Set the baking sheet on a wire rack to cool until the nougat is at room temperature, about 30 minutes. Transfer the nougat to a cutting board. Using a knife lightly coated with nonstick cooking spray or butter, cut the nougat into 1½-inch squares.

The nougat will keep well in an airtight container at room temperature for 3 weeks.

# BITTERSWEET
# CHOCOLATE MERINGUE

A hint of salt heightens all the complex and delicious flavor notes of a good-quality chocolate in this dark, crispy candy.

Preheat the oven to 350°F. Lightly coat a 12 x 17-inch baking sheet with nonstick cooking spray or line it with a silicone liner.

Bring about 2 inches of water to a simmer in a large saucepan. Put the chocolate in a heatproof bowl and place it over (but not touching) the simmering water. Stir frequently until it has melted. Remove the saucepan from the heat without removing the bowl, so that the chocolate remains warm.

In the bowl of an electric mixer fitted with the whisk attachment, beat the egg whites on medium-low speed until they become opaque and frothy and begin to increase in volume, about 3 minutes. Slowly add the sugar and continue beating for 5 minutes. Increase the speed to high and beat until the mixture becomes thicker and shiny, about 10 minutes. Add the vanilla and salt, followed by the warm chocolate, and beat just to combine.

Remove the bowl from the mixer and gently fold to fully incorporate the chocolate.

Using a rubber spatula, spread the meringue evenly onto the prepared baking sheet. It will be about ¼ inch thick. Bake the meringue, rotating the sheet halfway through, until it is fragrant, crackled, and shiny, about 20 minutes. (You can test for doneness by breaking off a piece of meringue and setting it on the counter until it cools to room temperature, about 10 seconds. It should be dry and crunchy all the way through.) Set the meringue on the baking sheet on a wire rack until it is completely cool; then break it into pieces.

The meringue can be kept in an airtight container at room temperature for up to 2 weeks. If it loses its crunch, dry it in a 300°F oven for 5 to 10 minutes.

SERVES 8

Nonstick cooking spray (optional)

6 ounces bittersweet chocolate (70%), roughly chopped

½ cup egg whites (from about 4 large eggs), at room temperature

1 cup sugar

1 teaspoon pure vanilla extract

1 teaspoon kosher salt

# TOASTED COCONUT MERINGUE

The warm, toasty flavor of freshly baked coconut is so intense in this feather-light candy that, even days after being made, it tastes and smells fresh out of the oven. Serve the shards of coconut meringue as is, use them to top fruit sorbets, or layer them into ice cream sundaes.

SERVES 8

Nonstick cooking spray (optional)

½ cup egg whites (from about 4 large eggs), at room temperature

½ cup granulated sugar

⅓ cup confectioners' sugar

½ teaspoon pure vanilla extract

½ teaspoon kosher salt

1 cup unsweetened shredded coconut

Preheat the oven to 300°F. Lightly coat a 12 x 17-inch baking sheet with nonstick cooking spray or line it with a silicone liner.

In the bowl of an electric mixer fitted with the whisk attachment, beat the egg whites on medium-low speed until they become opaque and frothy and begin to increase in volume, about 3 minutes. Slowly add the granulated sugar and then the confectioners' sugar, and continue beating for 5 minutes. Increase the speed to high and beat until the mixture becomes thicker and shiny, about 10 minutes. Add the vanilla and salt, and beat just to combine. Remove the bowl from the mixer and gently fold in the coconut.

Using a rubber spatula, spread the meringue evenly onto the prepared baking sheet. It will be about ¼ inch thick. Bake the meringue, rotating the sheet halfway through, until it is fragrant and lightly golden, about 30 minutes. (You can test for doneness by breaking off a piece of meringue and setting it on the counter until it cools to room temperature, about 10 seconds. It should be dry and crunchy all the way through.) Cool the meringue on the baking sheet on a wire rack until it is completely cool. Then break it into pieces.

The meringue can be kept in an airtight container at room temperature for up to 2 weeks. If it loses its crunch, dry it in a 300°F oven for 5 to 10 minutes.

# BUILDING YOUR CRAFT
# MERINGUE

Meringue is easy and quick to make, and if you have a lot of egg whites left over from making ice cream or custard, this is a great way to use them up. I like to make sheets of the candy, which I then break into shards of all shapes and sizes. Great for eating on their own, the crispy pieces can be sprinkled over ice creams, sorbets, or sundaes, or packed into cellophane bags and tied with pretty ribbons for gifts. If you like, you can spoon the meringue into puffs of any size; just be sure to adjust the baking time accordingly.

A few basic rules, and then you're on your way to playing around with meringue flavors: Always start with warm or room-temperature egg whites, which build more volume and have a stronger composition than those that are whipped when cold. Allow the whites to reach their full volume before incorporating any add-ins. With meringue you don't have to worry about overwhipping because the large amount of sugar alters the structure of the whites, protecting them from overwhipping, which can be a problem in other desserts. But you can easily underwhip your whites, which will create a dense, flat meringue.

Use the Toasted Coconut Meringue (page 92) as a base for a plain meringue, folding in your own add-ins, which can include spices, nuts, bits of chocolate, and more. Use the Bittersweet Chocolate Meringue (page 91) as a base to create your own as well, using any of the add-ins mentioned above, or coffee or other extracts, crispy bits of ground cacao nibs, and more.

# WHITE CHOCOLATE TRUFFLES

A little lemon zest really brightens this classic ganache.

Preheat the oven to 350°F.

In a food processor, finely chop the pistachios. Spread them onto a baking sheet and toast until they are fragrant, 5 minutes. Remove from the oven and cool the sheet on a rack. When cool, grind the pistachios to a fine flour in the food processor. Transfer them to a shallow bowl.

Pour about 2 inches of water into a medium saucepan and bring it to a simmer. Put the white chocolate, lemon zest, and salt into a heatproof bowl and place it over the simmering water. Stir until the white chocolate has melted. Remove the bowl from the heat and gently whisk in the heavy cream until completely smooth.

Let the ganache cool to room temperature, about 2 hours. Then cover the surface with a piece of plastic wrap and refrigerate it until it has set, about 1 hour.

Using a melon baller or a ½-teaspoon measure, and a cup of warm water to clean the scoop as needed between balls, scoop the ganache into 28 one-inch balls. Roll each ball between your hands until it is round, and then roll it in the toasted ground pistachios to coat.

The truffles can be kept in an airtight container at room temperature for up to 3 days, or in the refrigerator for up to 2 weeks. Store them with extra toasted pistachios sprinkled over the top, which keeps the truffles coated and prevents them from rubbing against one another.

## VARYING YOUR CRAFT
### WHITE CHOCOLATE COCONUT TRUFFLES
Substitute canned coconut milk for the heavy cream. Toast ½ cup unsweetened shredded coconut in a 250°F oven for 5 minutes, and substitute the coconut for the toasted ground pistachios. Substitute 1 tablespoon spiced dark rum, such as Myers's, for the lemon zest.

MAKES 28

¾ cup unsalted pistachios

8 ounces white chocolate, finely chopped

Finely grated zest of 1 lemon

¼ teaspoon kosher salt

⅓ cup heavy cream

# MILK CHOCOLATE TRUFFLES

Ground cacao nibs lend a nice bitterness and crunch to these creamy rich truffles. Fans of dark chocolate can simply swap bittersweet chocolate (70%) for the milk chocolate.

MAKES 40

**8 ounces milk chocolate, finely chopped**

**3 tablespoons unsalted butter, cut into small pieces**

**¼ teaspoon kosher salt**

**¾ cup heavy cream**

**¼ cup unsweetened cocoa powder**

**½ cup cacao nibs, ground**

Combine the chocolate, butter, and salt in a mixing bowl.

In a small saucepan, bring the cream to a boil. Remove the pan from the heat and pour about half of the hot cream over the chocolate mixture. Stir gently with a whisk. When most of the chocolate has melted, pour in the remaining cream. Slowly whisk together until the mixture forms a smooth and glossy ganache.

Let the ganache cool to room temperature, about 2 hours. Then cover the surface with a piece of plastic wrap and chill it in the refrigerator until set, about 1 hour.

Whisk together the cocoa powder and ground cacao nibs in a large shallow bowl. Using a melon baller or a ½-teaspoon measure, and a cup of warm water to clean the scoop as needed between balls, scoop the ganache into forty 1-inch balls. Roll each ball between your hands until it is round, and then roll in the cocoa powder mixture.

The truffles can be kept in an airtight container at room temperature for up to 3 days, or in the refrigerator for up to 2 weeks. Store them with the extra cocoa powder mixture sprinkled over the top, which keeps the truffles coated and prevents them from rubbing against one another.

## VARYING YOUR CRAFT
### CINNAMON MILK CHOCOLATE TRUFFLES

In a small saucepan, combine the cream with 5 cinnamon sticks and bring to a boil. Remove the pan from the heat and pour the mixture into a heatproof bowl. Cool to room temperature, cover, and let it steep overnight in the refrigerator. Then strain through a fine-mesh sieve. Substitute this cinnamon-infused cream for the cream in the recipe.

## BUILDING YOUR CRAFT
# TRUFFLES

It's a funny thing about truffles: they are easier to prepare than most cookies, and yet they are one of the most luxurious little gifts you can give. Learn to be creative with truffles and you'll never lack for a last-minute something special when you need one.

I've included my recipes for milk and white chocolate truffles here, which you can vary to your heart's content. Truffles are nothing more than a simple ganache (heated heavy cream and chocolate whisked together). They can be flavored by infusing the cream with tea, herbs, spices, coffee, or nuts, and can be finished with cocoa powder or tempered chocolate.

Dried fruit should be plumped up with boiling water, strained, and, if you like, then steeped in alcohol for at least 1 hour. Chopped pitted prunes and Armagnac is one of my favorite combinations. Stir ⅓ cup strained fruit into one recipe of ganache.

Alcohol or liqueurs—everything from brandy to grappa, rum, and flavored liquors—can be used to flavor truffles, with or without dried fruit. Use 2 to 4 tablespoons of alcohol and increase the amount of chocolate from 8 to 9 ounces. (Alcohol creates a softer base, so the extra ounce of chocolate will help firm up the truffles.)

All sorts of teas can be steeped in the cream that you use to make truffles. Green jasmine and chamomile work well with white chocolate, and many, including mint and Earl Grey, work well with milk chocolate. To infuse truffles with tea, bring the cream to a boil, add 2 tablespoons of loose tea, remove from the heat, and let the mixture steep for 10 minutes. Strain and discard the tea leaves before proceeding with the recipe.

To infuse truffles with coffee flavor, infuse the cream the day before you make the truffles. Bring 2 tablespoons of very fresh coffee beans to a boil with the cream. Let the cream mixture cool to room temperature; then chill it in the refrigerator overnight. Strain and discard the coffee beans before proceeding with the recipe. The same thing can be done with 2 tablespoons of finely ground toasted nuts, if you want to infuse the ganache with a nut flavor. Adding nuts this way is preferable to stirring them into the ganache base, where they quickly lose their crunch.

And then there are all the little extras—like toasted ground nuts and cacao nibs, and crushed toffee, brittle, or peppermint candies—that you can use to coat the truffles once they are rolled. These lend both flavor and texture. Rolled truffles can be dusted with unsweetened cocoa powder or confectioners' sugar or dipped in tempered chocolate (see page 21).

# COCONUT MARSHMALLOWS

You will realize how much you love marshmallows when you taste one that's homemade.

MAKES ABOUT
4 DOZEN

Nonstick cooking spray

¾ cup confectioners' sugar

⅓ cup cornstarch

2 tablespoons plus 2 teaspoons (about 2½ envelopes) powdered gelatin

¾ cup plus 2 tablespoons light corn syrup

3 tablespoons honey

1¾ cups granulated sugar

1 tablespoon pure vanilla extract

¾ teaspoon salt

3 cups unsweetened shredded coconut

**TIP** For thicker marshmallows, use an 8-inch-square pan instead of a baking sheet.

Lightly coat a 12 x 17-inch baking sheet with nonstick cooking spray, and then line it with plastic wrap. (The spray will hold the plastic in place.) Using a metal spatula, smooth out any wrinkles in the plastic; then lightly coat the plastic with nonstick spray. Lightly coat the metal spatula with nonstick spray.

Whisk together the confectioners' sugar and cornstarch in a medium mixing bowl. Set aside.

In the bowl of an electric mixer, whisk together the gelatin and 1 cup of cold water. Set the whisk attachment so that the whisk drops down to touch the bottom of the bowl (see page 19).

In a small saucepan, combine the corn syrup, honey, and granulated sugar. Add ⅓ cup of water and carefully stir together so that all of the sugar is damp but is not on the sides of the pan.

Attach a candy thermometer to the side of the pan, and set the pan over high heat. Cook until the sugar reaches firm ball stage (245°F), 6 to 8 minutes. Remove the pan from the heat and let the sugar cool to 225°F, about 12 minutes.

With the mixer on low speed, slowly pour a stream of the sugar syrup down the inside edge of the mixer bowl. When all of the sugar syrup has been added, increase the speed to medium-high. The mixture will begin as a liquid and continue to build volume and thicken as it cools. After 5 minutes, add the vanilla and salt. Continue mixing until the marshmallow becomes very thick and the bowl feels cool, about 15 minutes more.

Remove the bowl from the mixer, and using a rubber spatula, fold in the coconut. Scrape the marshmallow mixture onto the prepared baking sheet. Smooth the mixture with the prepared metal spatula, making sure it reaches all edges of the pan and is a uniform thickness. Let the marshmallow stand at room temperature until set up, 2 to 3 hours.

Sift about half of the confectioners' sugar mixture in a light layer on a clean work surface. Invert the marshmallows from the baking sheet on top. Remove the plastic wrap and sift some confectioners' sugar mixture over the top. Using a chef's knife coated with nonstick spray and a ruler, cut the marshmallows into 2-inch squares. Toss in the remaining confectioners' sugar mixture.

The marshmallows will keep in an airtight container at room temperature for up to 1 week.

### VARYING YOUR CRAFT

**LEMON MARSHMALLOWS**
Substitute the finely grated zest of 3 lemons for the coconut.

**SPICED MARSHMALLOWS**
Substitute 1 teaspoon ground cinnamon, ¼ teaspoon ground cardamom, and ½ teaspoon ground star anise for the coconut.

**MOCHA MARSHMALLOWS**
Substitute ¼ cup unsweetened cocoa powder and 1 tablespoon coffee extract (page 79) for the coconut.

# GRANDMA RANKIN'S CASHEW BRITTLE

My Grandma Rankin started making what became her famous cashew brittle as a young adult, using a recipe passed down by her mother. Years later, she decided to give the salty-sweet candy as Christmas gifts. Before long she was sending my grandfather to the nut factory to buy nuts in bulk. For years she made 150 pounds of the candy every holiday season!

**MAKES 1¾ POUNDS**

Nonstick cooking spray

2 cups sugar

8 tablespoons (1 stick) unsalted butter

⅓ cup light corn syrup

½ teaspoon baking soda

1½ tablespoons kosher salt

1½ cups (12 ounces) salted roasted cashews

Lightly coat a rimmed baking sheet with nonstick cooking spray; set it aside.

Combine the sugar, butter, corn syrup, and ½ cup water in a large saucepan. Stir together so that all of the sugar is wet. Cook the mixture over high heat without stirring until it turns a dark amber color, about 10 minutes. Remove from the heat. Carefully whisk in the baking soda, followed by the salt; the caramel will rise and bubble. Using a wooden or metal spoon, fold in the cashews. Pour the brittle onto the prepared baking sheet, and using the back of the spoon, spread it out into a layer about ½ inch thick. Let it cool completely. Break the brittle into bite-size pieces, using a mallet or the back of a heavy knife.

The brittle can be stored in an airtight container at room temperature for up to 2 weeks.

## VARYING YOUR CRAFT

### CACAO NIB BRITTLE
Replace the cashews with 1½ cups (6 ounces) cacao nibs.

### PINK PEPPERCORN BRITTLE
Replace the cashews with 1 cup (4 ounces) pink peppercorns.

### PUMPKIN SEED BRITTLE
Replace the cashews with 1½ cups (6 ounces) toasted pumpkin seeds.

### HONEYCOMB BRITTLE
Double the amount of baking soda. This makes the caramel bubble up, making the finished brittle look like a honeycomb. The end result is a very light, airy, crunchy candy.

# SPICY CARAMEL
# POPCORN

This crunchy treat makes a fun and unexpected dessert or a great movie snack. I also love packing it into cellophane bags and tying the bags with ribbon for gifts or Halloween treats.

Lightly coat two large heatproof rubber spatulas and a large mixing bowl with nonstick cooking spray.

In a large saucepan or pot with a lid, heat the vegetable oil over medium-high heat. Add the popcorn kernels, cover, and keep the saucepan moving until all of the kernels have popped, about 4 minutes. Transfer the popped popcorn to the prepared bowl, removing any unpopped kernels.

In a small bowl, whisk together the baking soda and cayenne pepper.

In a medium saucepan, combine the sugar, butter, salt, and ½ cup water. Cook over high heat, without stirring, until the mixture becomes a light golden-yellow caramel, about 10 minutes. Remove from the heat and carefully whisk in the baking soda mixture (the mixture will bubble up).

Immediately pour the caramel mixture over the popcorn. Working quickly and carefully, use the prepared spatulas to toss the caramel and popcorn together, as if you were tossing a salad, until the popcorn is well coated.

Pour the popcorn onto a large baking pan and quickly flatten and separate it into small pieces while it is still warm. Cool to room temperature, about 15 minutes. Once it is cool, store it in a well-sealed airtight container.

Caramel popcorn will keep in an airtight container for up to 2 weeks.

MAKES ABOUT
4 QUARTS

Nonstick cooking spray
3 tablespoons vegetable oil
½ cup popcorn kernels
1½ teaspoons baking soda
¾ teaspoon cayenne pepper
3 cups sugar
3 tablespoons unsalted butter
1½ tablespoons kosher salt

GRAHAM CRACKER CRUST

# TARTS, PIES, COBBLERS & CRISPS

# BASIC PIE DOUGH

A combination of butter and vegetable shortening produces a tender, flaky dough. For best results, measure out and chill the flour, sugar, butter, and shortening in the freezer for 15 minutes before you begin.

MAKES ENOUGH FOR
ONE 8- TO 10-INCH
SINGLE-CRUST PIE

1½ cups unbleached all-purpose flour

1½ teaspoons sugar

¾ teaspoon kosher salt

8 tablespoons (1 stick) chilled unsalted butter, cut into small pieces

¼ cup solid vegetable shortening

¼ cup ice water, plus more if needed

In the bowl of a food processor, combine the flour, sugar, and salt; pulse to combine. Add the butter and shortening, and pulse until the mixture resembles coarse crumbs, with some larger pieces remaining.

With the machine running, add the ice water through the feed tube in a slow, steady stream, processing just until the dough begins to bind and holds together when squeezed in the palm of your hand, 5 to 10 seconds. If the dough is too dry, add a bit more water, 1 tablespoon at a time.

Turn out the dough onto a clean work surface and shape it into a flattened disk. Wrap it in plastic wrap and refrigerate it for at least 1 hour, or overnight. (The dough can be frozen for up to 1 month; thaw it overnight in the refrigerator before using.)

# CORNMEAL TART DOUGH

Cornmeal lends great texture to this dough, and buttermilk gives it a touch of tartness.

In the bowl of an electric mixer fitted with the paddle attachment, beat the butter and sugar on medium speed until well combined. Add the buttermilk and vanilla extract, scrape down the sides of the bowl with a rubber spatula, and beat on medium speed until combined.

In a bowl, whisk together the cornmeal, flour, and salt. In two additions, add the cornmeal mixture to the butter mixture, beating just to combine.

Remove the bowl from the mixer, and if there are dry ingredients remaining in the bottom of the bowl, use your hands to knead them into the dough. Divide the dough in half, shape each portion into a flattened disk, and wrap each disk in plastic wrap. Refrigerate for at least 1 hour, or overnight. (The dough can be frozen for up to 1 month; thaw it overnight in the refrigerator before using.)

**MAKES ENOUGH FOR TWO 8- TO 10-INCH SINGLE-CRUST TARTS**

10 tablespoons (1¼ sticks) unsalted butter, at room temperature

¾ cup sugar

¼ cup buttermilk

¾ teaspoon pure vanilla extract

½ cup yellow cornmeal or fine polenta

1½ cups unbleached all-purpose flour

1 teaspoon kosher salt

# ALMOND SABLÉ DOUGH

I love the buttery taste and crumbly texture of this dough.

In a bowl, whisk together the all-purpose flour, almond flour, and salt.

In the bowl of an electric mixer fitted with the paddle attachment, combine the butter and confectioners' sugar. Mix on medium-low speed until well combined, about 4 minutes.

Mix in the egg and then the yolk, allowing each to be incorporated before adding the next. In two additions, add the flour mixture, scraping down the sides of the bowl after each addition.

Turn out the dough onto a clean lightly floured work surface. Divide it in half, shape into flattened disks, and wrap each one in plastic wrap. Refrigerate for at least 1 hour, or overnight. (The dough can be frozen for up to 1 month; thaw it overnight in the refrigerator before using.)

**MAKES ENOUGH FOR TWO 8- TO 10-INCH TARTS**

2¼ cups unbleached all-purpose flour, plus more for dusting

¾ cup almond flour (see page 10)

½ teaspoon kosher salt

14 tablespoons (1¾ sticks) chilled unsalted butter, cut into small pieces

½ cup plus 1 tablespoon confectioners' sugar

1 large egg

1 large egg yolk

# GRAHAM CRACKER CRUST

The sweet molasses-y flavor of this crust is a perfect match for slightly tart fruits, like blackberries, cherries, and apricots.

MAKES ONE 9-INCH
PIE CRUST

1¾ cups graham cracker crumbs (from ½ batch Crisp Honey Grahams, page 65)

¼ cup packed dark brown sugar

1 tablespoon unbleached all-purpose flour

½ teaspoon kosher salt

4 tablespoons (½ stick) unsalted butter, melted

Preheat the oven to 350°F.

In a large bowl, whisk together the graham cracker crumbs, brown sugar, flour, and salt. Add the butter and stir until the mixture is well combined. If the crumbs are not holding together when you press them against the sides of the bowl, add up to 1 tablespoon cold water and stir to combine.

Press the crumbs into a 9-inch pie plate, evenly covering the bottom and sides. Chill in the freezer for 10 minutes.

Place the pie plate on a baking sheet and bake, rotating the pie plate halfway through, until the crust is fragrant and set, about 14 minutes. Transfer the pie plate to a wire rack and let the crust cool completely.

# GINGERSNAP CRUST

Quick and easy to put together, this crust bakes in just 10 minutes.

MAKES ONE 9-INCH
PIE CRUST

1¾ cups gingersnap crumbs (from about ½ batch Gingersnaps, page 63)

¼ cup packed dark brown sugar

1 tablespoon unbleached all-purpose flour

½ teaspoon kosher salt

4 tablespoons (½ stick) unsalted butter, melted

TIP Stored in a well-sealed bag, gingersnap crumbs will keep in the freezer for up to a month.

Preheat the oven to 350°F.

In a large bowl, whisk together the gingersnap crumbs, brown sugar, flour, and salt. Add the butter and stir until the mixture is well combined. If the crumbs are not holding together when you press them against the sides of the bowl, add up to 1 tablespoon cold water and stir to combine.

Press the crumbs into a 9-inch pie plate, evenly covering the bottom and sides. Chill in the freezer for 10 minutes. Place the pie plate on a baking sheet and bake until the crust is fragrant and set, about 10 minutes. Transfer the pie plate to a wire rack and let the crust cool completely.

# CHOCOLATE SABLÉ DOUGH

Use this bittersweet dough to complement a chocolate filling or to lend contrast to a nut-, fruit-, or even cheese-based one.

In a bowl, sift together the flour, cocoa powder, and salt.

In the bowl of an electric mixer fitted with the paddle attachment, beat the butter and sugar on low speed until there are no visible pieces of butter, about 3 minutes. Add the egg and mix just until incorporated. Add the flour mixture in three additions, mixing each in completely before adding the next.

Turn out the dough onto a clean lightly floured work surface. Divide it in half, shape into flattened disks, and wrap each one in plastic wrap. Refrigerate for at least 1 hour, or overnight. (The dough can be frozen for up to 1 month; thaw it overnight in the refrigerator before using.)

# CREAM CHEESE DOUGH

I love this crust for fruit pies, especially apple. It also works well for savory dishes, like quiche.

In a mixer fitted with the paddle attachment, beat the butter, cream cheese, and sugar on medium speed until the mixture is smooth and there are no visible chunks of butter or cream cheese, about 5 minutes. Add the flour and salt and mix until just combined.

Turn out the dough onto a clean lightly floured work surface. Divide it in half, shape into flattened disks, and wrap each one in plastic wrap. Refrigerate for at least 1 hour, or overnight. (The dough can be frozen for up to 1 month; thaw it overnight in the refrigerator before using.)

# KEY LIME MERINGUE PIE

A topping of sweet cloudlike meringue complements the puckery lime curd in this refreshing and very pretty pie.

On a lightly floured surface, roll out the dough to an 11-inch round. Roll the dough onto a rolling pin, center it over a 9-inch pie plate, and fit it into the plate, pressing the dough into the edges. Trim the dough, leaving a 1-inch overhang. Fold the overhang under, and crimp the edges to form the top edge of the crust. Freeze the pie crust for 10 minutes.

Meanwhile, preheat the oven to 375°F.

Line the chilled pie shell with a round of parchment paper or foil, leaving a 1-inch overhang. Fill it with pie weights or dried beans. Bake until the edges of the crust are just beginning to turn golden, 20 to 25 minutes. Remove the parchment and pie weights. Return the crust to the oven and continue baking until it is golden all over, about 10 minutes more. Transfer the pie plate to a wire rack and let it cool completely. Turn off the oven.

Bring about 2 inches of water to a simmer in a large saucepan.

In a large heatproof bowl, whisk together the Key lime zest, Key lime juice, lemon juice, sugar, eggs, egg yolks, and salt. Set the bowl over the saucepan, and whisking constantly (be sure to whisk into the corners of the bowl), cook the curd until it is thick enough that a trail can be pulled across its surface with the whisk without it immediately filling in, 12 to 15 minutes.

Remove the bowl from the heat and whisk in the butter, one piece at a time, whisking until the mixture is well combined and smooth. Strain the curd through a fine-mesh sieve into another bowl. Cover the surface of the curd with plastic wrap, and chill it in the refrigerator for 30 minutes.

RECIPE CONTINUES

MAKES ONE 9-INCH PIE

## DOUGH

**Basic Pie Dough (page 106)**

**Unbleached all-purpose flour, for dusting**

## KEY LIME CURD

**Finely grated zest of 4 Key limes**

**⅓ cup fresh Key lime juice (from about 9 Key limes)**

**3 tablespoons fresh lemon juice**

**½ cup granulated sugar**

**3 large eggs**

**3 large egg yolks**

**¼ teaspoon kosher salt**

**8 tablespoons (1 stick) chilled unsalted butter, cut into small pieces**

**1 cup heavy cream**

## MERINGUE

**⅔ cup egg whites (from about 4 large eggs)**

**⅔ cup granulated sugar**

**¼ cup confectioners' sugar**

**1 teaspoon pure vanilla extract**

**¼ teaspoon kosher salt**

RECIPE CONTINUED

In a medium mixing bowl, whip the cream to soft peaks. Gently fold the whipped cream into the cooled lime curd. Pour the lightened curd into the cooled pie crust, spreading the curd evenly with a spatula to cover the bottom.

Preheat the oven to 375°F.

MAKE THE MERINGUE: In the bowl of an electric mixer fitted with the whisk attachment, beat the egg whites on low speed until bubbles begin to form. Increase the speed to medium-low and continue to beat until the whites become opaque and begin to increase in volume, about 5 minutes. Slowly add the granulated sugar and confectioners' sugar. Add the vanilla and salt. Increase the speed to medium and beat until the meringue becomes very thick, about 10 minutes.

Spread the meringue over the curd, pushing it right to the edges of the crust so that the curd is completely covered. Using a metal spatula or offset spatula, create swirls and peaks in the meringue.

Position a rack about 8 inches from the top of the oven.

Put the pie on a baking sheet, and place it on the oven rack. Bake, rotating the baking sheet once halfway through, until the meringue is golden brown, darker on the "peaks" but still white in the "valleys," 10 to 12 minutes. Transfer the pie to a wire rack and let it cool completely. Then chill it for 1 hour before serving.

The pie is best eaten the day it is baked, but it can be kept chilled, loosely covered in plastic wrap, for up to 2 days.

# RICOTTA CHEESE TART

This light, lemon-kissed tart suits any season. Nice on its own, it also pairs well with all sorts of sauces and sides. In the spring, serve it with fresh berries. During the summer, try compotes and sorbets. And when cooler weather sets in, Spiced Red Wine Roasted Figs (page 228) make a great match.

Preheat the oven to 350°F.

On a lightly floured surface, roll out the dough to an 11-inch round. Fit it into a 9½-inch fluted tart pan with a removable bottom. Press the dough into the edges of the pan, and use a paring knife to trim off the excess dough along the top edge. Save the scraps of dough to patch any holes. Prick the bottom of the tart all over with a fork, and chill it for 10 minutes in the freezer.

Line the chilled tart shell with a piece of parchment paper or aluminum foil, leaving a 1-inch overhang. Fill it with pie weights or dried beans. Bake until the edges of the crust are just beginning to turn golden brown, 15 to 20 minutes. Remove the parchment and pie weights. Rotate the crust, return it to the oven, and continue baking until it is golden all over, 15 to 20 minutes more. Transfer the tart shell to a wire rack and let it cool completely. Keep the oven on.

Place the cooled tart pan on a baking sheet. In a large bowl, whisk together the drained ricotta, sugar, egg, egg yolks, cream, crème fraîche, vanilla, salt, and lemon zest to make a smooth batter. Pour the batter into the baked tart shell. Bake, rotating the pan halfway through, until the tart is set, puffed around the edges, and slightly loose in the center, 25 to 30 minutes. Transfer it to a wire rack and let it cool completely.

Remove the outer ring of the tart pan and serve at room temperature.

MAKES ONE 9½-INCH TART

Unbleached all-purpose flour, for dusting

½ recipe Almond Sablé Dough (page 107)

1 pound fresh whole-milk ricotta cheese, drained overnight (see Tip)

¼ cup plus 2 tablespoons sugar

1 large egg

3 large egg yolks

¼ cup heavy cream

¼ cup crème fraîche

1 teaspoon pure vanilla extract

¼ teaspoon kosher salt

Finely grated zest of 3 lemons

**TIP** To drain fresh ricotta, line a large strainer with a double layer of cheesecloth or a coffee filter and set it over a deep bowl. Spoon the ricotta into the strainer, cover with plastic wrap, and refrigerate overnight. Discard the drained liquid.

# RUSTIC BLUEBERRY CORNMEAL TART

When I lived in Maine, I could hardly wait until the tiny, deep blue, exceptionally sweet and slightly tangy wild blueberries began to show up on their low-bush branches in late July. If you can get your hands on a few pints of these, by all means use them for this tart. If not, seek out the freshest, sweetest cultivated blueberries you can find.

The dough is rolled out on parchment paper and no tart pan is needed, making this tart a great one for new bakers and for those who prefer unfussy desserts; the edges of the dough are simply folded over the fruit. I love the way the gritty texture of the cornmeal crust plays off the tender, jammy blueberries. Try it warm with vanilla ice cream, fresh whipped cream, or crème fraîche.

## MAKES ONE 9-INCH TART

½ recipe Cornmeal Tart Dough (page 107)

3 cups blueberries, or 1 (15-ounce) bag frozen blueberries (see Tip)

⅓ cup granulated sugar

1 tablespoon unbleached all-purpose flour, plus more for rolling

1 tablespoon fresh lemon juice

2 tablespoons Demerara sugar

**TIP** If you are using frozen berries, mix them with the sugar, flour, and lemon juice, and then let the berries come to room temperature; this allows the sugar and flour to mix with the juices from the berries. Also add an extra teaspoon of flour, since frozen berries tend to release more liquid than fresh.

On a piece of parchment paper lightly dusted with flour, roll out the dough to an 11-inch round. Transfer the dough, on the parchment, to a baking sheet. Chill until slightly firm, about 5 minutes.

Toss the blueberries with the granulated sugar, flour, and lemon juice. Mound them up in the center of the dough, leaving a 4-inch border all around. Fold the exposed edges of the dough over the berries. Sprinkle the tart with the Demerara sugar. Refrigerate until firm, about 20 minutes.

Meanwhile, preheat the oven to 375°F.

Bake the tart, rotating the baking sheet halfway through, until the berries are bubbling and the crust is golden brown, about 40 minutes. Transfer the baking sheet to a wire rack and let the tart cool. Serve warm or at room temperature.

# CHERRY CUSTARD TART

Over the years, I've experimented with several versions of clafouti, the French baked custard, never quite satisfied with the results. Then I played around with the base of the filling, adding sour cream and swapping flour for almond flour, and poured it into an almond crust. The result: a sumptuous, sweet-tangy custard filling, chockful of bright juicy cherries, with nutty pieces of buttery, tender shortbread-like crust in every bite.

On a lightly floured surface, roll out the dough to an 11-inch round. Fit the dough into a 9½-inch fluted tart pan with a removable bottom. Press the dough into the edges of the pan, and use a paring knife to trim off the excess dough along the top edge. With a fork, prick the bottom of the dough all over. Chill in the freezer for 10 minutes.

Meanwhile, preheat the oven to 350°F. Spread the almonds on a baking sheet and toast for 5 minutes; set aside.

Line the chilled tart shell with a round of parchment paper or foil, leaving a 1-inch overhang. Fill it with pie weights or dried beans. Bake until the edges of the crust are just beginning to turn golden, 15 to 20 minutes. Remove the parchment and pie weights. Rotate the pan, return the crust to the oven, and continue baking until it is golden all over, 15 to 20 minutes more. Transfer the tart shell to a wire rack and let it cool completely. Keep the oven on.

In a bowl, whisk together the sour cream, egg, egg yolks, granulated sugar, vanilla, and salt. Fold in the almond flour.

Set the tart pan on a baking sheet.

Spoon the cherries into the cooled tart shell, arranging the fruit in a snug single layer. Pour the custard mixture over the cherries, and then sprinkle the top with the almonds and Demerara sugar. Bake, rotating the pan halfway through, until the almonds are toasted and the edges of the filling are set (the center will be a bit loose), about 30 minutes. Transfer the pan to a wire rack and let it cool completely. Remove the outer ring of the pan before serving.

The tart is best eaten the day it is baked but can be kept at room temperature, loosely covered in plastic wrap, for up to 2 days.

MAKES ONE 9½-INCH TART

Unbleached all-purpose flour, for rolling

½ recipe Almond Sablé Dough (page 107)

¼ cup sliced blanched almonds

1 cup sour cream

1 large egg

2 large egg yolks

¼ cup granulated sugar

½ teaspoon pure vanilla extract

½ teaspoon kosher salt

¼ cup almond flour (see page 10)

3 cups fresh or frozen sour cherries, pitted

2 tablespoons Demerara sugar

# PINE NUT TART WITH ROSEMARY CREAM

Often thought of as savory ingredients, pine nuts and rosemary make an exciting, unexpected pairing in sweets. This play on a classic Tuscan dessert makes a nice ending to a fall or wintertime meal, be it simple or fancy. The fragrant, lightly sweetened whipped cream and the caramel tones of the filling seem to magically warm up a chilly day. You can candy a sprig of rosemary for a pretty garnish, if you like, or leave it fresh.

Preheat the oven to 350°F.

Spread the pine nuts out on a baking sheet and toast in the oven for 5 minutes, until fragrant. Transfer the sheet to a wire rack and let the nuts cool completely. Keep the oven on.

On a lightly floured surface, roll out the dough to an 11-inch round. Fit the dough into a 9½-inch fluted tart pan with a removable bottom. Press the dough into the edges of the pan, and use a paring knife to trim off the excess dough along the top edge. Prick the bottom all over with a fork and freeze until the dough is firm, about 10 minutes.

Line the chilled tart shell with a round of parchment paper or aluminum foil, leaving a 1-inch overhang. Fill it with pie weights or dried beans. Bake until the edges of the crust are just beginning to turn golden, 15 to 20 minutes. Remove the parchment and pie weights. Return the crust to the oven and continue baking until it is dry all over, about 5 minutes more. Transfer the tart shell to a wire rack and let it cool completely.

In a small saucepan, melt the butter over high heat until it is golden brown with a nutty fragrance, about 4 minutes. Remove it from the heat and set it aside.

In a large bowl, whisk together the brown sugar, corn syrup, salt, and vanilla. Add the eggs and whisk well to combine. Then add the browned butter. Fold in the pine nuts just to combine. Pour the filling into the tart shell and place the pan on a baking sheet.

RECIPE CONTINUES

MAKES ONE 9½-INCH TART

1¼ cups pine nuts

Unbleached all-purpose flour, for rolling

½ recipe Almond Sablé Dough (page 107)

4 tablespoons (½ stick) unsalted butter

1 cup packed dark brown sugar

1 cup light corn syrup

1 teaspoon kosher salt

1 teaspoon pure vanilla extract

3 large eggs

1½ cups heavy cream

3 sprigs rosemary

4 tablespoons granulated sugar, for garnish (optional)

2 teaspoons confectioners' sugar

RECIPE CONTINUED

Bake, rotating the baking sheet once halfway through, until the filling is set around the edges but still slightly loose in the center, about 45 minutes. (If the crust is getting too dark, cover the tart loosely with foil for the last 10 minutes.) Transfer the tart to a wire rack to cool.

Meanwhile, make the rosemary cream: In a small saucepan, bring ¾ cup of the cream just to a boil. Remove the pan from the heat and stir in 2 of the rosemary sprigs. Cover and let steep for 10 minutes.

While the cream is steeping, make the candied rosemary sprig for garnish, if you like: In a bowl, whisk together 2 tablespoons of the granulated sugar and 2 tablespoons of hot water. Put the remaining 2 tablespoons of sugar in a shallow bowl. Dip the remaining rosemary sprig in the sugar syrup to coat. Tap off any excess liquid on a paper towel, and then gently toss the wet sprig in the bowl of sugar. Set it on a paper towel to dry, about 5 minutes.

Set up an ice bath. Strain the steeped cream into a metal bowl, set the bowl into the ice bath, and chill the cream until cold, about 5 minutes. Whisk in the remaining ¾ cup cream and the confectioners' sugar. Continue to whisk until the cream forms soft peaks. Remove the outer ring and serve the tart with the cream, garnished with the fresh or candied rosemary sprig.

# ALMOND RHUBARB TART

Rhubarb is often paired with strawberries, which soften and balance its tang. I like to let the fruit stand on its own, using a sweetened almond cream in this recipe to complement the fruit's flavor.

On a lightly floured surface, roll out the dough to an 11-inch round. Fit the dough into a 9½-inch fluted tart pan with a removable bottom. Press the dough into the edges of the pan, and use a paring knife to trim off the excess dough along the top edge. Prick the bottom all over with a fork and freeze until firm, about 10 minutes.

Meanwhile, preheat the oven to 350°F.

MAKE THE ALMOND CREAM: In a small bowl, whisk together the cake flour and salt. In the bowl of an electric mixer fitted with the paddle attachment, combine the butter, almond paste, granulated sugar, and vanilla. Mix on medium speed until fully combined and light in color, about 2 minutes. Add the egg and mix until incorporated. Add the flour mixture and mix just to combine.

Spread the almond cream over the entire bottom of the chilled tart shell, using all of the cream. Place the sliced rhubarb into the tart and spread it out evenly. Sprinkle with the Demerara sugar and almonds. Place the tart on a baking sheet and bake, rotating the pan halfway through, until the crust is golden and the almonds are toasted, 25 to 30 minutes. Transfer the pan to a wire rack to cool. Remove the outer ring and serve warm or at room temperature.

The tart is best eaten the day it is baked but can be kept at room temperature, loosely covered in plastic wrap, for up to 2 days.

MAKES ONE 9½-INCH TART

Unbleached all-purpose flour, for rolling

½ recipe Almond Sablé Dough (page 107)

2 tablespoons cake flour

¼ teaspoon kosher salt

3½ tablespoons unsalted butter, at room temperature

3 tablespoons almond paste

3 tablespoons granulated sugar

⅛ teaspoon pure vanilla extract

1 large egg

4 medium rhubarb stalks, trimmed to 12 inches in length and cut into ¼-inch-thick pieces (4 cups)

2 tablespoons Demerara sugar

½ cup sliced blanched almonds

# BANANA TARTE TATIN

As this classic French upside-down tart bakes, the buttery caramel coaxes the natural sugars from the fruit, then bubbles up into the pastry, melding the two together.

MAKES ONE 8-INCH TART

**Half of a 14- to 17-ounce package frozen all-butter puff pastry sheets, thawed**

**½ cup sugar**

**3 tablespoons unsalted butter, cut into small pieces**

**4 ripe bananas**

**TIP** To keep the pastry crisp, do not invert the tart until just before serving.

Lay the puff pastry onto a sheet of parchment paper. Cut a 10-inch round of dough from the pastry, and using the tines of a fork, prick the entire surface of the round. Transfer the pastry round (on the parchment) to a baking sheet, and refrigerate until the dough is firm, about 20 minutes.

Preheat the oven to 375°F.

In an 8-inch ovenproof skillet, preferably cast iron, combine the sugar and 2 tablespoons water. Cook over high heat (do not stir) until the sugar turns to a deep golden caramel, about 7 minutes. Remove from the heat and whisk in the butter.

Cut the bananas on the diagonal into 2-inch-thick pieces. Arrange the pieces, cut side down and snugly together, in a single layer over the caramel. Cover with the puff pastry round.

Line a baking sheet with aluminum foil. Place the skillet on top of the baking sheet and bake, rotating the sheet halfway through, until the puff pastry is deep golden brown, about 50 minutes. Transfer the skillet to a wire rack and let the tart cool completely so that the fruit absorbs the caramel.

To serve, rewarm in a 350°F oven for 10 minutes, and invert the tart onto a serving plate. The tart is best eaten the day it is baked.

## VARYING YOUR CRAFT

### PEACH TARTE TATIN
Decrease the butter to 2 tablespoons (because peaches are juicier than bananas). Use 3 medium peaches, pitted and cut into quarters, in place of the bananas. Fan the peach wedges over the entire surface of the caramel.

### APPLE TARTE TATIN
Use 3 large crisp baking apples, such as Mutsu, Cortland, or Granny Smith, peeled, halved lengthwise, cored, and thinly sliced.

Closely pack the slices on their edges over the caramel, forming the shape of apple halves with the rounded edges up.

### MAKING INDIVIDUAL TATINS

You can use six 4-ounce reusable foil cups to make small tatins. Preheat the oven to 375°F. Line a baking sheet with foil. Make the caramel as directed and divide it among the foil cups. Pack the fruit into the cups on top of the caramel. Top each cup of fruit with a 3½-inch round of puff pastry. Put the foil cups on the prepared baking sheet and bake, turning the sheet halfway through, until the pastry is deep golden brown, 30 to 35 minutes.

Transfer tatins to a wire rack and let them cool completely.

To serve, rewarm in a 350°F oven for 5 minutes and invert them onto individual serving plates.

# BROWN BUTTER
## PECAN PIE

The simple technique of browning butter brings an additional layer of deep nutty flavor to this Thanksgiving staple. I like to serve this with a simple dollop of unsweetened whipped cream or vanilla ice cream.

**Unbleached all-purpose flour, for rolling**

**Basic Pie Dough (page 106)**

**1½ cups pecans, roughly chopped**

**5 tablespoons unsalted butter, cut into small pieces**

**1 cup packed dark brown sugar**

**1 cup light corn syrup**

**1 teaspoon kosher salt**

**1 teaspoon pure vanilla extract**

**3 large eggs**

**TIP** When browning butter, use a light-colored saucepan; a dark-coated one will make it difficult to see the butter and judge when it's done.

On a lightly floured surface, roll out the dough to an 11-inch round. Roll the dough onto a rolling pin, center it over a 9-inch pie plate, and fit it into the plate, pressing the dough into the edges. Trim the dough right to the top edge, with no overhang. Shape the scraps into a disk, wrap it in plastic wrap, and refrigerate it for 10 minutes. (This will be used to create a top edge to the crust after it is blind-baked—a technique that keeps the edge from becoming overly browned while allowing the bottom crust to stay crisp.) Freeze the pie crust for 10 minutes.

Meanwhile, preheat the oven to 375°F.

Spread the pecans on a baking sheet and bake until fragrant and lightly toasted, about 3 minutes. Transfer the sheet to a wire rack and let the nuts cool completely.

Line the chilled pie shell with a round of parchment paper or aluminum foil, leaving a 1-inch overhang. Fill it with pie weights or dried beans. Bake until the edges of the crust are just beginning to turn golden, 20 to 25 minutes. Remove the parchment and pie weights. Return the crust to the oven and continue baking until it is golden all over, about 10 minutes more. Transfer the pie plate to a wire rack and let the crust cool completely. Keep the oven on.

While the pie shell is cooling, roll the disk of dough scraps on a lightly floured surface to about ¼-inch thickness. Using a ½-inch cookie cutter of any shape (for example, a leaf is nice for the fall), cut out 40 pieces of dough. When the pie shell is cool, gently fan and press the cutouts around the edge of the crust to form a lip of crust. Freeze the crust for 10 minutes, or until the filling is ready.

In a small saucepan, melt the butter over high heat until it is golden brown and fragrant, about 4 minutes. Remove the pan from the heat and set it aside.

In a large bowl, whisk together the brown sugar, corn syrup, salt, and vanilla. Add the eggs and whisk until well combined. Add the browned butter, whisking well to combine. Using a rubber spatula, fold in the pecans.

Pour the filling into the chilled pie shell. Place the pie plate on a baking sheet and bake, rotating the baking sheet once halfway through and tenting the pie with foil if the crust becomes too brown, until the filling is set around the edges and slightly loose in the center, about 1 hour. Transfer the pie to a wire rack and let it cool. Serve warm or at room temperature.

The pie is best eaten the day it is baked but can be kept at room temperature, loosely covered in plastic wrap, for up to 2 days.

# BLACKBERRY PIE WITH GRAHAM CRACKER CRUST

Using fresh berries on top of a jammy filling brings a little complexity to both the flavor and texture of this otherwise very simple fruit pie. The dark molasses flavor of the graham cracker crust is the perfect complement to the sweet-tart taste of the berries.

In a medium bowl, combine 3 cups of the blackberries with the sugar and cornstarch. Mash the mixture with a fork to create juice. Let the berries sit at room temperature to macerate for about 15 minutes.

Transfer the berries and their juices to a saucepan, and cook over medium heat, stirring frequently, until thickened, about 10 minutes. Remove from the heat and let cool for about 10 minutes.

Taste the blackberry mixture. If it is too tart, add extra sugar to taste. Spoon the mixture into the graham cracker crust and spread it out evenly. Spread the remaining 1½ cups berries over the top.

In a bowl, whip the cream to soft peaks, if using.

Serve the pie at room temperature, topped with whipped cream if desired.

The pie is best eaten the day it is prepared but can be kept at room temperature, loosely covered with plastic wrap, for up to 2 days.

## COMBINING YOUR CRAFT
Serve the pie with Vanilla Bean Ice Cream (page 204).

MAKES ONE 9-INCH PIE

4½ cups fresh blackberries

½ cup sugar, or more if needed

3 tablespoons cornstarch

Graham Cracker Crust (page 108)

1 cup heavy cream, for whipping (optional)

# CONCORD GRAPE PIE

With their deep purple-black color, intense floral aroma, and sweet and slightly tangy flavor, Concord grapes make for a stunning and delicious pie. Some supermarkets stock the grapes during their autumn season, but you'll most often find them at farm stands and farmer's markets.

**Unbleached all-purpose flour, for rolling**

**2 recipes Basic Pie Dough (page 106)**

**3 pounds Concord grapes, stemmed and washed**

**1 cup sugar**

**¼ cup cornstarch**

On a lightly floured surface, roll out 1 disk of the dough to an 11-inch round. Roll the dough onto a rolling pin, center it over a 9-inch pie plate, and fit the dough into the plate, pressing the dough into the edges. Trim the dough right to the top edge, with no overhang. Combine the scraps with the second disk of dough, which will be the top crust, and return it to the refrigerator. Freeze the pie shell until firm, about 10 minutes.

Meanwhile, preheat the oven to 375°F.

Line the chilled pie shell with a round of parchment paper or aluminum foil, leaving a 1-inch overhang. Fill it with pie weights or dried beans. Bake until the edges of the crust are just beginning to turn golden, 20 to 25 minutes. Remove the parchment and the pie weights. Return the crust to the oven and continue baking until it is dark golden all over, 10 minutes more. Transfer the pie shell to a wire rack and let it cool completely. Keep the oven on.

Roll the second disk of dough between two pieces of waxed paper to a 12-inch round. Transfer the dough, still between the waxed paper, onto a baking sheet and refrigerate it.

Take about two thirds of the grapes and pop them out of their skins by pressing them between your thumb and index finger. Save half of the skins; discard the other half. In a medium saucepan, combine the flesh of the grapes with the sugar and cook over medium heat until the grapes break down enough for the pulp to separate from the seeds, about 5 minutes. Put this grape mixture through a food mill, or push it through a large-holed strainer, into a bowl to separate the pulp from the seeds. Discard the seeds. Return the strained pulp to the saucepan, and stir in the cornstarch and the reserved skins. Over medium heat, cook until the mixture thickens, about 5 minutes.

Halve the remaining grapes with a paring knife. Using the tip of the knife, remove the seeds and discard them. Fold the seeded grape halves into the cooked pulp.

Pour the grape mixture into the cooled pie shell. Cover the filling with the top crust, and trim it so that there is a 1-inch overhang the entire way around. Fold the dough under itself and seal the top crust to the bottom by crimping the edge around the entire pie. With a paring knife, cut four horizontal slits, each about 6 inches long, across the top of the pie.

Place the pie plate on a baking sheet. Bake until the crust is golden brown and the filling is bubbly and thick, 50 minutes to 1 hour. Transfer the pie to a wire rack to cool. Serve at room temperature or chilled.

The pie is best eaten the day it is baked but can be kept at room temperature or in the refrigerator, loosely covered in plastic wrap, for up to 2 days.

## VARYING YOUR CRAFT
### CONCORD GRAPE STREUSEL PIE
Make this a single-crust pie: When fitting the dough into the pie pan, leave a 1-inch overhang. Fold the overhang under and crimp the edges to form the top edge of the crust. Continue, following the recipe above. Instead of the top crust, top the grapes with 1½ cups Marcona Almond Streusel (page 140). Reduce the baking time to 40 to 50 minutes.

# BUTTERSCOTCH CREAM PIE WITH GINGERSNAP CRUST

There's something refreshingly old-fashioned about icebox pies, where the crust is baked, the filling is poured in, and the refrigerator does the rest of the work. This combination of creamy, slightly salty butterscotch cream filling and crumbly spice-laden crust is one of my favorites. Serve it spread or dolloped with fresh unsweetened whipped cream or with crème fraîche.

¾ cup sugar

5 large egg yolks

¼ cup cornstarch

½ vanilla bean, split lengthwise, seeds scraped out, bean and seeds reserved

1 cup heavy cream

2 cups whole milk

½ teaspoon kosher salt

2 tablespoons unsalted butter, cut into small pieces

Gingersnap Crust (page 108)

1½ cups heavy cream, for whipping

½ cup chopped Honeycomb Brittle (page 100; optional)

In a bowl, whisk together ¼ cup of the sugar, the egg yolks, and the cornstarch until pale in color.

Combine the remaining ½ cup sugar, ¼ cup water, and the vanilla bean and seeds in a medium saucepan. Stir until the sugar is well dampened throughout. Then heat the mixture over high heat until the sugar becomes a yellow-golden caramel, about 8 minutes. Remove from the heat. Slowly whisk in the cream, being careful to avoid splatters, and then stir in the milk.

Return the caramel mixture to the stove, bring it to a boil, and then remove it from the heat. Pour one third of the caramel mixture over the egg mixture in a thin stream, whisking to combine. Then pour all of the egg mixture into the caramel mixture in the pan, and whisk until combined. Bring to a boil over medium-low heat and cook, whisking constantly, until the custard thickens, about 8 minutes. Remove the pan from the heat and whisk in the salt and the butter.

Strain the custard through a fine-mesh sieve into a bowl, and then pour it into the prepared pie crust. Transfer the pie plate to a wire rack and let the filling cool completely. Then chill the pie until cold, about 1 hour. Whisk the cream to soft peaks and spread it over the top of the pie.

Sprinkle the Honeycomb Brittle all over the top of the pie, if using, right before serving. The pie is best eaten the day it is baked but can be kept, loosely covered in plastic wrap, in the refrigerator for up to 2 days.

# FIG & WALNUT BRIOCHE TART

For this tart you make a simple frangipane, or nut-flavored cream, made with walnuts in place of the more traditional almonds. When local strawberries are in season, I like to add them, using half strawberry and half fig.

Preheat the oven to 350°F.

Spread the chopped walnuts on a baking sheet and bake until golden and fragrant, about 5 minutes. Transfer the baking sheet to a wire rack and let the nuts cool completely. Turn the oven off.

In a bowl, whisk together the flour, salt, and baking powder.

In the bowl of an electric mixer fitted with the paddle attachment, beat the granulated sugar, brown sugar, and butter on medium speed until light and fluffy, about 4 minutes. Add the eggs, one at a time, waiting until the first is fully incorporated before adding the next. Add the flour mixture, beating just to combine, and then mix in the walnuts. (The frangipane can be made several days in advance and kept in an airtight container in the refrigerator until ready to use. Bring to room temperature before using.)

On a piece of parchment paper, roll out the brioche dough to a 12 x 16-inch rectangle, about ¼ inch thick. Transfer the dough (on the parchment) to a baking sheet. Spread the walnut frangipane over the surface of the dough, leaving a ½-inch border all around. Lay the figs, cut side up, in a single snug layer over the frangipane. Loosely cover with plastic wrap and let sit at room temperature until the dough looks soft and has risen slightly, about 1 hour.

Preheat the oven to 375°F.

Sprinkle the tart with the Demerara sugar and bake, rotating the baking sheet halfway through, until the edges of the tart are golden and the frangipane is set, about 35 minutes. Transfer to a wire rack to cool. Serve warm or at room temperature.

The tart is best eaten the day it is baked, but it can be kept for up to 2 days at room temperature, well wrapped.

**MAKES ONE 12 X 16-INCH TART**

¾ cup walnuts, roughly chopped

½ cup unbleached all-purpose flour

¾ teaspoon kosher salt

¼ teaspoon baking powder

⅓ cup granulated sugar

¼ cup packed dark brown sugar

8 tablespoons (1 stick) unsalted butter, cut into small pieces, at room temperature

2 large eggs

½ recipe dough for Brioche Baked in a Can (page 39), prepared through the second rise

2 pints ripe black Mission figs, trimmed and cut into quarters

2 tablespoons Demerara sugar

# CHOCOLATE CUSTARD TART

This tart combines a rich chocolate cookie-like crust with a glossy, creamy, deep dark chocolate filling for the ultimate double hit of chocolate. A little spoonful of crème fraîche or simple unsweetened whipped cream looks pretty on top of a slice and cuts the richness.

MAKES ONE 9½-INCH TART

Unbleached all-purpose flour, for rolling

½ recipe Chocolate Sablé Dough (page 109)

5 ounces bittersweet chocolate (70%), roughly chopped

4 ounces semisweet chocolate (62%), roughly chopped

1¼ cups heavy cream

⅔ cup whole milk

¼ cup sugar

2 large eggs

½ teaspoon kosher salt

**TIP** The secret to the silky, creamy texture of this custard is to whisk as slowly and gently as possible when combining the ingredients so no air bubbles are created.

On a lightly floured surface, roll out the dough to an 11-inch round. Roll the dough onto a rolling pin, center it over a 9½-inch tart pan with a removable bottom, and fit it into the pan, pressing the dough into the edges. With a paring knife, trim the excess dough right to the top edge of the pan. Prick the bottom all over with a fork, and freeze until firm, about 10 minutes.

Meanwhile, preheat the oven to 350°F.

Line the chilled tart shell with aluminum foil or parchment paper, leaving a 1-inch overhang, and fill it with pie weights or dried beans. Set the tart pan on a baking sheet, and bake for 15 minutes. Remove the foil and pie weights, rotate the pan, and continue baking until the crust is fragrant and feels dry to the touch, 15 to 20 minutes more. Place the baking sheet on a wire rack and let the crust cool completely.

Reduce the oven temperature to 275°F.

Combine the bittersweet and semisweet chocolates in a mixing bowl. Pour the cream, milk, and sugar into a small saucepan and bring to a boil, stirring to dissolve the sugar. Pour about one third of the hot cream mixture over the chocolate and very gently whisk together until the chocolate is melted. Add the remaining cream mixture and gently whisk to combine.

Whisk the eggs in a bowl until well combined. Pour about one third of the chocolate mixture over the eggs and gently whisk just to combine. Return the egg mixture to the chocolate mixture, add the salt, and very gently whisk until smooth.

Fill the cooled crust with the chocolate custard. Carefully transfer the tart, on the baking sheet, to the oven and bake, rotating the

sheet halfway through, until the edges of the custard are set and the center is slightly loose, about 30 minutes. Transfer the tart to a wire rack and let it cool completely. Remove the outer ring of the tart pan, and serve at room temperature.

The tart is best eaten the day it is baked but can be kept at room temperature, loosely covered in plastic wrap, for up to 2 days.

# FRESH STRAWBERRY TART WITH LEMON CREAM

Everything about this tart says "summer." The lemon cream is light and tangy; the strawberries, bright and sweet. It's refreshing in both looks and taste. I like to use the small strawberries that I find at the farmer's market.

On a lightly floured surface, roll out the dough to an 11-inch round. Fit the dough into a 9½-inch fluted tart pan with removable bottom. Press the dough into the edges of the pan, and use a paring knife to trim the excess dough along the top edge. Prick the bottom all over with a fork, and freeze until firm, about 10 minutes.

Meanwhile, preheat the oven to 350°F.

Line the chilled tart shell with a round of parchment paper or aluminum foil, leaving a 1-inch overhang. Fill it with pie weights or dried beans. Bake until the edges of the crust are just beginning to turn golden, 15 to 20 minutes. Remove the parchment and pie weights. Return the crust to the oven and continue baking until it is golden all over, 15 to 20 minutes more. Transfer the tart pan to a wire rack and let the tart shell cool completely.

In a medium mixing bowl, whip the heavy cream until it becomes thick enough to hold a peak. Fold about half of it into the lemon curd, and then fold in the rest of the whipped cream. Pour the lightened lemon curd into the tart shell and spread it out evenly.

Arrange the strawberries close together in concentric circles over the lemon curd, placing any halved strawberries cut side down. Lightly cover the tart with plastic wrap, and chill it in the refrigerator until cold, about 1 hour, or up to 4 hours. Remove the outer ring of the tart pan before serving.

The tart is best eaten the day it is prepared.

MAKES ONE 9½-INCH TART

Unbleached all-purpose flour, for rolling

½ recipe Cream Cheese Dough (page 109)

1 cup heavy cream

Lemon Curd (page 242)

2 pints fresh strawberries, hulled, large strawberries halved

# APPLE TURNOVERS

Few treats are more comforting, or more perfect for a chilly winter's day, than warm caramel-apple cubes encased in buttery, flaky puff pastry.

Half of a 14- to 17-ounce package all-butter frozen puff pastry sheets, thawed

4 large firm baking apples, such as Mutsu or Granny Smith

¼ cup granulated sugar

2 cups apple butter, homemade (page 239) or store-bought

1 large egg

2 tablespoons Demerara sugar

Vanilla bean ice cream, homemade (page 204) or store-bought

Line a baking sheet with parchment paper. Lay out the puff pastry sheet, and roll it out to 11 x 14 inches. Using a ruler and a pizza cutter, cut out six 4½-inch squares; discard scraps. Prick each square all over with a fork. Arrange the squares a couple of inches apart on the prepared baking sheet, and refrigerate until cold, about 30 minutes.

Meanwhile, peel, core, and cut the apples into 1-inch cubes.

In a large skillet, stir together the granulated sugar and ¼ cup water. Cook over medium heat until the mixture turns to a golden brown caramel, about 7 minutes. Add the apple cubes and cook until golden and tender, 5 to 7 minutes. Strain the mixture, discarding the liquid. In a bowl, combine the apple cubes and the apple butter; fold them together.

In a small bowl, whisk the egg with 1 tablespoon water. Using a pastry brush, brush the edges of each puff pastry square with the egg mixture. Spoon 1 heaping tablespoon of the apple mixture onto the center of each square (reserve the leftover filling). Fold the pastry over the apples, making a triangle shape. Using the tines of a fork, seal the edges of the pastry together. Brush the tops of the turnovers with egg mixture. Refrigerate the turnovers, on the baking sheet, for 30 minutes, or up to 3 hours.

Preheat the oven to 375°F.

Sprinkle the turnovers with the Demerara sugar, and bake, rotating the baking sheet halfway through, until they are a deep golden brown on the top and bottom, about 30 minutes. Serve warm, with the extra apple filling and the ice cream alongside.

## VARYING YOUR CRAFT

### APRICOT OR SOUR CHERRY TURNOVERS
Use 2½ cups of either Apricot Compote (page 237) or Sour Cherry Compote (page 235), well drained, in place of the apple filling.

# APPLE QUINCE BROWN BETTY

Colonial Americans, the originators of this baked fruit dessert, probably used whatever bread was left in the larder to make the sugary crumb that they packed between layers of spiced fruit filling. I mix buttery brioche with brown sugar and cinnamon and use the bread as a topping, rather than making layers.

Combine 2 cups water and the granulated sugar in a large saucepan and bring to a boil. Add the quince and return to a boil. Then reduce the heat to a simmer and cook until the quince is tender and easily pierced with a knife, about 10 minutes. Remove the pan from the heat and let the quince cool completely in the liquid. (The quince can be poached and kept refrigerated, in the poaching liquid in an airtight container, for up to 1 week.)

Drain the quince and put it into a large bowl. Stir in the apples and ⅓ cup of the brown sugar, and let the mixture sit at room temperature until the sugar begins to draw the juices out of the fruit, about 30 minutes.

Meanwhile, preheat the oven to 375°F.

Cut the brioche into 1-inch cubes. You should have 3 cups. In a large mixing bowl, whisk together the remaining ½ cup brown sugar, the cinnamon, and the salt. Add the butter and whisk to combine. Add the brioche and fold together with a spatula, allowing the bread to absorb the buttery sugar.

Scrape the fruit and the juices into an 8-inch square baking dish. Pour the bread mixture over the top of the fruit, and spread it out evenly to cover. Cover the baking dish tightly with aluminum foil.

Bake for 30 minutes. Then remove the foil, rotate the baking dish, and continue baking until the brown betty is golden brown and the fruit is thick and bubbly, about another 30 minutes. Serve warm, or transfer to a wire rack to cool. (Heat it in a 350°F oven for 10 minutes just before serving.)

The brown betty is best eaten the day it is baked.

SERVES 6

1½ cups granulated sugar

4 medium quince, peeled, quartered, cored, and diced

4 medium apples, peeled, quartered, cored, and diced

½ cup plus ⅓ cup packed dark brown sugar

One 8½ x 4½-inch loaf brioche, homemade (page 40) or store-bought

2 teaspoons ground cinnamon

½ teaspoon kosher salt

10 tablespoons (1¼ sticks) unsalted butter, melted

# PEACH & PLUM COBBLER

Though they're most often considered summertime sweets, I love to play around with fall and wintertime fruit combinations and make cobblers all year long.

SERVES 6

**FRUIT**

**4 ripe peaches, pitted and cut into eighths (3 cups)**

**8 ripe plums, pitted and cut into sixths (3 cups)**

**⅓ cup plus 2 tablespoons granulated sugar**

**1 tablespoon unbleached all-purpose flour**

**BISCUITS**

**1¾ cups unbleached all-purpose flour, plus more for shaping**

**1 tablespoon plus ½ teaspoon baking powder**

**¼ cup granulated sugar**

**½ teaspoon kosher salt**

**6 tablespoons (¾ stick) chilled unsalted butter, cut into small pieces**

**1 cup plus 2 tablespoons heavy cream**

**2 tablespoons Demerara sugar**

**Confectioners' sugar, for serving**

In a bowl, stir together the peaches, plums, granulated sugar, and flour. Let the mixture sit for 30 minutes.

To make the biscuits, in the bowl of an electric mixer fitted with the paddle attachment, beat the flour, baking powder, granulated sugar, salt, and butter on medium-low speed until the mixture resembles a coarse meal, about 4 minutes. Reduce the speed to low, add 1 cup of the cream, and mix just until combined.

Turn out the dough onto a clean lightly floured work surface. Roll out the dough to ¾-inch thickness. Using a 2-inch cutter or inverted drinking glass dipped in flour, cut out 6 rounds.

Preheat the oven to 375°F. Line a baking sheet with aluminum foil.

Scrape the fruit and its juices into a 6-cup casserole or an 8-inch square baking dish, and top with the biscuits. Brush the tops of the biscuits with the remaining 2 tablespoons cream, and sprinkle with the Demerara sugar.

Place the baking dish on the prepared baking sheet. Bake, rotating the sheet halfway through, until the juices are bubbling and thickened and the biscuits are cooked and dark golden brown, about 1 hour. Transfer the baking dish to a wire rack to cool. Serve warm or at room temperature, sprinkled with confectioners' sugar.

The cobbler is best eaten the day it is baked.

RECIPE CONTINUES

## VARYING YOUR CRAFT

With these seasonal variations you can make wonderful cobblers all year long. Simply substitute the fruit and sugar listed in each variation for the peaches, plums, and sugar in the recipe above.

### WINTER
# APPLE & GOLDEN RUM RAISIN COBBLER

1 cup golden raisins

¾ cup dark rum, such as Myers's

5 baking apples, such as Granny Smith or Mutsu, peeled, cored, and diced

⅓ cup sugar

Put the raisins in a saucepan, cover with cold water, and bring to a boil; remove from the heat. Strain the raisins and transfer them to a small bowl. Cover with the rum and let them sit for at least 2 hours at room temperature, or up to 1 month in a covered container in the refrigerator. Strain the raisins before combining them with the apples for the cobbler. (These raisins make a great topping for ice cream, custard, or pound cake, if you want to make extra.)

### SPRING
# RHUBARB ROSE COBBLER

6 medium rhubarb stalks, trimmed to 12 inches in length and cut into ¼-inch-thick pieces (6 cups)

1 teaspoon rose water

¼ cup rose-petal jam (see Sources)

⅓ cup sugar

### SUMMER
# MIXED BERRY COBBLER

2 cups hulled fresh strawberries

2 cups fresh blueberries

1 cup fresh blackberries

1 cup fresh raspberries

⅓ cup sugar

# BUILDING YOUR CRAFT
## FRUIT CRISPS
## & COBBLERS

My secret to whipping up a great dessert at a moment's notice is keeping batches of streusel and biscuits in the freezer for fruit crisps and cobblers, which make a great end to a meal all year long. With the streusel or biscuits made and ready to use, all you have to do is chop some nice ripe fruit, heat up the oven, assemble, and bake. You can vary the streusel, using any type of nut or nut combination you like.

Once you begin to make crisps and cobblers, you will see how easy and fun it is to make up your own combinations, or even to use single fruits. Fruit can vary in sweetness from one harvest to the next—for example, one pint of strawberries can be sweeter than another—so it's always good to taste your fruit before you begin baking. If you have very sweet fruits, you can cut back the sugar a bit, or if your fruits are tart, you can add a little more. When combining fruits, you can use equal amounts of two or more varieties, or let one take the lead by using unequal amounts. If you have one that's more dominant in flavor than the other, and you want a more equal balance of flavor throughout, use less of the assertive fruit. The key to the most delectable crisps and cobblers is using the best fruit you can find. My approach is to use what looks best at the farmer's market, as fruit exudes its deepest flavor when it is ripe and freshly picked. This approach applies to pies as well.

Ice cream (homemade or store-bought) is always a nice accompaniment. You can also top a crisp or cobbler with crème fraîche or Greek yogurt, or serve it simply, without a topping.

# PEAR & CONCORD GRAPE CRISP WITH MARCONA ALMOND STREUSEL

My basic rule of thumb for crisps is to use two fruits that are quite different in taste, yet complement and enhance one another. This way, once everything is baked together, you can still discern the unique flavors of each fruit. Here, the sweet, earthy qualities of pear slightly mellow the assertive tangy tones of Concord grapes.

## FRUIT

**5 ripe Bartlett or Anjou pears, peeled, halved, cored, and diced (5 cups)**

**1 cup seedless or seeded Concord grapes (see Tip opposite)**

**⅓ cup sugar**

**1 tablespoon unbleached all-purpose flour**

## STREUSEL

**1½ cups all-purpose flour**

**½ cup granulated sugar**

**⅓ cup packed dark brown sugar**

**1 cup (4 ounces) Marcona almonds, roughly chopped**

**½ teaspoon ground cinnamon**

**½ teaspoon salt**

**12 tablespoons (1½ sticks) unsalted butter, melted**

**TIP** This makes 3½ cups streusel. It will keep, well sealed in an airtight container, in the refrigerator for up to 3 days or in the freezer for up to 1 month. Frozen streusel can be used without thawing.

Position a rack in the center of the oven and heat the oven to 350°F. Line a baking sheet with aluminum foil.

FOR THE FRUIT: In a large bowl, mix together the pears, grapes, sugar, and flour. Let the mixture stand at room temperature until juices begin to draw out from the fruit, about 30 minutes.

FOR THE STREUSEL: Combine the flour, granulated sugar, brown sugar, almonds, cinnamon, and salt in the bowl of an electric mixer fitted with the paddle attachment. Mix just to combine. Add the butter and mix just until the streusel comes together. Spread onto a baking sheet and chill in the refrigerator until firm, about 15 minutes.

Crumble the streusel with your fingers, and store it in an airtight container in the refrigerator or freezer until ready to use (see Tip).

Pour the fruit and juices into a 6-cup casserole or an 8-inch square baking dish. Top with the streusel. Place the baking dish on the prepared baking sheet and bake, rotating the sheet halfway through, until the fruit is tender, the juices are bubbling and thickened, and the topping is browned, about 40 minutes. Transfer the baking dish to a wire rack and let the crisp cool for at least 10 minutes before serving. Serve warm or at room temperature.

The crisp is best eaten the day it is baked.

## VARYING YOUR CRAFT

With these seasonal variations you can make delicious crisps all year round. Simply substitute the fruit and sugar listed in each variation for the pears, grapes, and sugar in the recipe opposite.

WINTER

# PEAR & FRESH GINGER CRISP

**6 ripe Bartlett or Anjou pears, peeled, halved, cored, and diced**

**1 tablespoon finely grated fresh ginger**

**⅓ cup sugar**

SPRING

# STRAWBERRY RHUBARB CRISP

**4 cups diced rhubarb**

**2 cups hulled and halved fresh strawberries**

**⅓ cup plus 2 tablespoons sugar**

SUMMER

# NECTARINE & BLACKBERRY CRISP

**8 to 9 nectarines, halved, pitted, and diced (4 cups)**

**2 cups fresh blackberries**

**⅓ cup sugar**

FALL

# APPLE & FIG CRISP

**4 baking apples, such as Granny Smith or Mutsu, peeled, quartered, cored, and diced (about 4 cups)**

**2 cups ripe black Mission figs, stemmed and quartered**

**⅓ cup sugar**

**TIP** To seed Concord grapes, cut them in half with a sharp paring knife, pull out the seeds with the tip of the knife, and discard the seeds.

YELLOW CAKE WITH MILK
CHOCOLATE BUTTERCREAM

# CAKES & CUPCAKES

# ALMOND POUND CAKE

Almond paste lends extra moistness and a deep marzipan flavor to this buttery pound cake. When you want to add a little something for serving, just about any fruit works well. Maple Roasted Pineapple (page 231) makes a nice wintertime combination; fresh peaches and whipped cream are great in the summer.

MAKES ONE
8½ X 4½-INCH LOAF

**1 cup cake flour**

**1½ teaspoons baking powder**

**½ teaspoon kosher salt**

**⅓ cup plus 1 tablespoon almond paste (see Sources)**

**¾ cup granulated sugar**

**8 ounces (2 sticks) unsalted butter, cut into small pieces, very soft, plus more for the pan**

**½ teaspoon pure vanilla extract**

**3 large eggs**

**1 tablespoon Demerara sugar**

Preheat the oven to 350°F. Line the bottom of an 8½ x 4½-inch loaf pan with parchment paper; butter the pan and the paper.

In a bowl, sift together the flour, baking powder, and salt.

In the bowl of an electric mixer fitted with the paddle attachment, combine the almond paste and granulated sugar. Beat on medium speed until well combined, about 5 minutes. Add the butter and vanilla extract, and beat until light and fluffy, about 5 minutes. Increase the speed to medium-high and add the eggs, one at a time, waiting until each is incorporated before adding the next.

Remove the bowl from the mixer and add the flour mixture. Fold the batter gently with a spatula, to fully incorporate the dry ingredients. Scrape the batter into the prepared pan and sprinkle it with the Demerara sugar. Bake for 40 minutes (do not open the oven door during this time). Then rotate the pan and continue baking until the cake is golden and firm to the touch, 5 to 10 minutes more.

Unmold the cake from the loaf pan and let it cool completely on a wire rack. Serve at room temperature or toasted.

The cake is best eaten the day it is baked but can be kept at room temperature, wrapped in plastic wrap, for up to 3 days.

## COMBINING YOUR CRAFT
Spoon some Apricot Compote (page 237) on each slice of cake, and top the compote with a dollop of Lillet Sabayon (page 240).

# BUILDING YOUR CRAFT
## POUND CAKE

If you've ever baked a pound cake that sank in the center or wound up with a dense rather than a light, airy crumb, you know this cake is not as easy to make as it might seem. That said, once you understand a few basic principles, you will bake this delicious classic with great success every time.

Start by making sure that your butter is very soft. While you do not want it to be melted or seeping, the butter should be soft enough so that a gentle press with your finger creates an easy and immediate indentation. I leave mine out for at least several hours, saving myself some time by letting the butter sit overnight at room temperature when I plan to start baking in the morning. Cutting the butter into small pieces before softening helps speed up the process. A very soft butter works into the batter quickly and easily, allowing more air into the structure of the cake, and in turn increasing volume as well as creating a better environment for the emulsification of the eggs.

As you make the batter, adding the eggs one by one, you really want to let each egg fully incorporate before adding the next. This action also allows air to work into the batter, while at the same time helping to keep the batter well emulsified, which helps build structure. This combination of light airiness and stable structure creates a level cake (no sinking!) with a moist, delicate crumb. When you go to add the flour, you want to be as gentle as possible. Fold with a light hand and no more than is necessary to fully incorporate the dry ingredients. Be gentle again as you pour the batter into the pan and move the pan into the oven. At each step of the way, you want to help maintain the stability you've created.

After you put the pan in the oven, do not open the oven door until after the first 40 minutes of baking. This allows the cake to set. Again, you're protecting the structure of the cake. If you think your oven might run hotter or cooler than the temperature indicated, purchase an inexpensive oven thermometer at any hardware store to check. This will give you added confidence and help ensure great results.

# CARAMELIZED-APPLE SKILLET CAKE

Just a touch of cornmeal adds a light sweet flavor and a golden hue to this incredibly moist cake. Baked upside-down, it's at once easy and impressive.

Preheat the oven to 350°F.

In an 8-inch ovenproof skillet, preferably cast iron, combine ¼ cup of the sugar with 2 tablespoons water, stirring to make sure all of the sugar is damp. Cook over high heat, stirring occasionally, until the sugar turns a golden brown caramel, about 2 minutes. Remove the pan from the heat and whisk in 2 tablespoons of the butter.

Peel, core, and using a mandoline or a sharp knife, cut the apples crosswise into ⅛-inch-thick rings. Tightly shingle all of the apple rings over the caramel, starting around the outside of the skillet and working toward the center, overlapping the slices.

In the bowl of an electric mixer fitted with the paddle attachment, combine the remaining ¾ cup sugar, the remaining 6 tablespoons butter, and the vanilla. Beat on medium speed until light and fluffy, about 3 minutes. Mix in the egg yolks, one at a time.

In another bowl, whisk together the flour, cornmeal, baking powder, and salt. In three additions, add the flour mixture, alternating with the milk, to the butter mixture. Using a rubber spatula, scrape the batter into a large bowl.

Clean and dry the bowl of the electric mixer well. Add the egg whites and, using the whisk attachment on medium speed, beat to soft peaks, about 4 minutes. In three additions, fold the whites into the batter.

Spread the batter evenly over the apples in the skillet. Bake, rotating the skillet halfway through, until the cake is golden brown and firm to the touch, 45 to 50 minutes. Place the skillet on a wire rack and let it cool just until the cake is warm, about 30 minutes. Then run a knife around the edge of the cake and invert it onto a plate. Serve warm or at room temperature.

The cake is best eaten the day it is baked but can be kept at room temperature, wrapped in plastic wrap, for up to 2 days.

MAKES ONE 8-INCH CAKE

1 cup sugar

8 tablespoons (1 stick) unsalted butter, very soft

2 tart baking apples, such as Mutsu or Granny Smith

¾ teaspoon pure vanilla extract

2 large eggs, separated

¾ cup plus 3 tablespoons unbleached all-purpose flour

3 tablespoons coarse yellow cornmeal or fine polenta

1½ teaspoons baking powder

¼ teaspoon kosher salt

⅓ cup whole milk

# LEMON
# OLIVE OIL CAKE

Though I use a little butter in this cake, most of the fat comes from olive oil, which creates an extremely moist yet light crumb and offers a special flavor you don't get from using butter alone. I like a drizzle of high-quality lemon-flavored oil over the top to add an extra hint of citrus. The flavor of the oils really comes through, so use brands that you like.

**MAKES ONE
8½ X 4½-INCH LOAF**

Unsalted butter, softened, for the pan

¾ cup plus 2 tablespoons unbleached all-purpose flour

¾ teaspoon baking powder

½ teaspoon kosher salt

2 large eggs

½ cup granulated sugar

Finely grated zest of 1 lemon

⅓ cup extra-virgin olive oil

1½ tablespoons whole milk

1½ teaspoons fresh lemon juice, strained

3½ tablespoons unsalted butter, melted

1 tablespoon Demerara sugar

Good-quality lemon olive oil, for drizzling (optional)

Preheat the oven to 350°F. Line the bottom of an 8½ x 4½-inch loaf pan with parchment paper; butter the pan and the paper.

In a bowl, sift together the flour, baking powder, and salt.

Fill a medium saucepan with 2 inches of water and bring it to a simmer. In the bowl of an electric mixer, combine the eggs, granulated sugar, and lemon zest. Set the bowl over the saucepan of simmering water and whisk until the mixture is warm to the touch, about 2 minutes. Transfer the bowl to an electric mixer fitted with the whisk attachment. Beat on medium speed until the mixture thickens, is pale yellow, and forms ribbons when the whisk is lifted, 5 to 6 minutes.

Meanwhile, in another bowl, whisk together the extra-virgin olive oil, milk, and lemon juice. When the egg mixture has thickened, slowly drizzle in the oil mixture with the machine running. Reduce the speed to low, add the flour mixture, and mix just to combine. Drizzle in the butter and mix just to combine.

Pour the batter into the prepared pan and sprinkle the top with the Demerara sugar. Bake, rotating the pan once after 40 minutes, until the top of the cake is golden, the center bounces back when touched, and a cake tester inserted in the center comes out clean, about 50 minutes. Unmold the cake from the loaf pan and let it cool completely on a wire rack. Serve at room temperature or toasted, with slices drizzled with lemon olive oil, if desired.

The cake is best eaten the day it is baked but can be kept at room temperature, wrapped in plastic wrap, for up to 3 days.

# YELLOW CAKE WITH MILK CHOCOLATE BUTTERCREAM

This is my go-to birthday cake. I love its ultra-moist crumb and rich, creamy filling. Serve generous slices with tall glasses of ice-cold milk.

FOR THE CAKE: Butter the bottoms and sides of three 8-inch cake pans and line the bottoms of the pans with rounds of parchment paper. Butter the tops of the paper liners, and then dust the pans with the all-purpose flour, tapping off any excess.

Preheat the oven to 350°F.

In the bowl of an electric mixer fitted with the paddle attachment, mix the butter, 1½ cups of the sugar, and vanilla extract on medium speed, scraping down the sides of the bowl several times, until pale and fluffy, 5 minutes. Add the egg yolks, one at a time, letting each become incorporated into the batter before adding the next.

In a separate bowl, sift together the cake flour, salt, baking powder, and baking soda. Reduce the mixer speed to low and alternate adding the flour mixture and the sour cream to the butter mixture, adding one third of each at a time and letting them fully mix in before adding the next. When all of the flour mixture and sour cream have been added, turn the mixer to medium-high speed and mix for about 2 minutes to fully incorporate the ingredients and help build the structure.

Scrape the batter into a large mixing bowl. Clean the bowl to the mixer well and, using the whisk attachment, whip the egg whites on low speed until frothy, about 5 minutes. Add the remaining ¼ cup sugar and increase speed to medium high. Whip whites to soft peaks, then fold them into the batter in 3 additions.

Divide the batter between the three prepared cake pans and spread it out evenly with a spatula. Place pans on two baking sheets. Bake the cakes, rotating the pans and switching the

MAKES ONE 10-INCH LAYER CAKE

### CAKE

**2 tablespoons unbleached all-purpose flour**

**12 tablespoons (1½ sticks) unsalted butter, very soft, plus extra for the pans**

**1¾ cups sugar**

**1½ teaspoons pure vanilla extract**

**7 large egg yolks**

**3 cups cake flour**

**1 teaspoon kosher salt**

**¾ teaspoon baking powder**

**¾ teaspoon baking soda**

**1 cup plus 2 tablespoons sour cream**

**7 large egg whites**

### BUTTERCREAM

**4½ ounces milk chocolate, roughly chopped**

**12 ounces (3 sticks) unsalted butter, at room temperature**

**¾ cup egg whites (about 5 large egg whites)**

**¾ cup sugar**

**¾ teaspoon pure vanilla extract**

**¾ teaspoon kosher salt**

RECIPE CONTINUES

RECIPE CONTINUED

TIP It's best to frost this cake with the buttercream at room temperature. The buttercream can be made ahead and kept in an airtight container in the refrigerator for up to 1 week, or in the freezer for up to 1 month. Simply bring it to room temperature before using. To restore its original creamy silkiness, return it to the bowl of an electric mixer fitted with the whisk attachment and beat until smooth.

cakes between the upper and lower racks of the oven halfway through, until they are lightly golden on top, gently bounce back when touched, and a cake tester inserted in the center of the cake comes out clean, 30 to 35 minutes.

Transfer the cake pans to a wire rack and let the cakes cool for 30 minutes. Then remove them from the pans and let them cool completely, at least 3 hours, before frosting.

FOR THE BUTTERCREAM: Pour about 2 inches of water into a saucepan and bring it to a simmer. Place the chocolate in a heat-proof bowl and set it over, but not touching, the simmering water. When the chocolate has melted, remove the bowl from the heat and whisk in 4 tablespoons of the butter; set aside.

Combine the egg whites and the sugar in the bowl of an electric mixer, and set it over the same pot of simmering water. Whisking constantly so that the eggs don't cook, heat the mixture until the sugar is completely dissolved, about 2 minutes. Transfer the bowl to the mixer fitted with the whisk attachment, and starting on low speed, beat the whites. When they become frothy and translucent, after about 3 minutes, increase the speed to medium. Beat until the whites become shiny and thick, about 2 minutes. Add the remaining 10 ounces (2½ sticks) butter, 1 tablespoon at a time, without waiting for each to be absorbed. The buttercream will appear thin and broken. Add the chocolate mixture, vanilla, and salt, and beat to combine, until it becomes shiny, smooth, and silky.

Using a serrated knife, trim the tops of the cake layers to make them level. Place one layer on a cake plate and spread the top with ¾ cup of the buttercream. Repeat with the second layer. Place the third layer on top. Using an offset spatula, spread the remaining buttercream over the entire cake, swirling to decorate.

The cake is best eaten the day it is assembled but can be kept at room temperature, loosely covered in plastic wrap, for up to 2 days.

## VARYING YOUR CRAFT
### YELLOW CUPCAKES WITH MILK CHOCOLATE BUTTERCREAM FROSTING

Use this batter to make 18 standard-size cupcakes, filling the muffin cups about three-quarters full with batter. Bake at 350°F, rotating the muffin tins once halfway through, until the tops are lightly golden and a cake tester inserted in the center of a cupcake comes out clean, about 20 minutes. Once the cupcakes are completely cool, frost with the Milk Chocolate Buttercream, prepared as described opposite. Decorate the tops of the cupcakes with dragées or sprinkles, if you like.

# BURNT ORANGE
# CHEESECAKE

I love the way the bittersweet tang of the orange sauce bleeds into the creamy richness of this cake.

## BURNT ORANGE SAUCE

**4 mandarin or other small juicy oranges**

**1 cup sugar**

## GRAHAM CRACKER CRUST

**Unsalted butter, for the pan, at room temperature**

**1¾ cups graham cracker crumbs (from ½ batch Crisp Honey Grahams, page 65)**

**¼ cup packed dark brown sugar**

**1 tablespoon unbleached all-purpose four**

**½ teaspoon kosher salt**

**4 tablespoons (½ stick) unsalted butter, melted**

## CHEESECAKE

**1 pound plus 3 ounces cream cheese, cut into small pieces, at room temperature**

**Finely grated zest of 1 orange**

**1 pound fresh ricotta cheese, drained overnight (see page 14)**

**1 cup sugar**

**½ vanilla bean, split lengthwise, seeds scraped out, bean and seeds reserved**

**2 teaspoons pure vanilla extract**

**½ teaspoon kosher salt**

**5 large eggs**

**FOR THE BURNT ORANGE SAUCE:** Using a mandoline or a sharp knife, slice the oranges crosswise, peel and all, as thin as possible; it is fine if the slices do not hold together. Remove any seeds. Put the orange slices and any juice in a mixing bowl, add ½ cup of the sugar, and mix well to combine. Then cover and refrigerate for at least 6 hours, or overnight.

In a small heavy-bottomed saucepan, stir the remaining ½ cup sugar with ¼ cup water so that all of the sugar is damp and none of it is coating the sides of the pan. Cook over high heat until the sugar is a golden caramel, about 8 minutes. Remove the pan from the heat and let the sugar continue to cook in the residual heat until the caramel is dark golden brown (drop a little onto a white plate to check), about 1 minute more.

Stir the orange mixture into the caramel. Return the saucepan to the stove and cook over low heat, stirring frequently, until the oranges are tender, about 7 minutes. Transfer the mixture to a blender and purée until the oranges are finely chopped. Then strain the sauce through a fine-mesh sieve into a bowl; discard the solids. (The sauce can be stored in an airtight container in the refrigerator for up to 2 weeks.)

**FOR THE GRAHAM CRACKER CRUST:** Preheat the oven to 350°F. Butter a 9-inch round springform pan and wrap the outside, including the bottom, in a double layer of aluminum foil.

In a large bowl, whisk together the graham cracker crumbs, brown sugar, flour, and salt, Add the butter and stir until the mixture is well combined. If the crumbs are not holding together when you press them against the sides of the bowl, add up to 1 tablespoon cold water and stir to combine.

Press the graham cracker mixture into the prepared pan, evenly covering the bottom and reaching 1 inch up the sides. Chill in the freezer for 10 minutes.

Place the springform pan on a baking sheet and bake, rotating the pan halfway through, until the crust is fragrant and set, about 14 minutes. Transfer the pan to a wire rack and let the crust cool completely.

Decrease the oven temperature to 300°F.

FOR THE CHEESECAKE: In the bowl of an electric mixer fitted with the paddle attachment, beat the cream cheese on medium speed until smooth, about 3 minutes. Add the orange zest and the ricotta, and continue mixing, scraping down the sides of the bowl as you go. Add the sugar, vanilla bean and seeds, vanilla extract, and salt; beat just to combine. Add the eggs, one at a time, letting each become incorporated before adding the next. Remove the vanilla bean from the batter, rinse, and save to reuse.

Pour the batter into the cooled crust. Drop teaspoonfuls of the burnt orange sauce on top of the batter. Using a wooden skewer or a toothpick, swirl the sauce into the batter. Place the pan in a roasting pan, and transfer it to the oven. Add enough hot water to the roasting pan to reach one-third up the sides of the springform pan, but not going over the foil wrapping the pan.

Bake, rotating the pan halfway through, until the cheesecake is set around the edges and slightly loose in the center, about 50 minutes. Remove the springform pan from the roasting pan and place it on a wire rack. Let the cheesecake cool completely. Then chill it in the refrigerator until it is cold and set, about 3 hours. Remove the sides of the springform and serve the cheesecake chilled or at room temperature.

The cake is best eaten the day it is baked but can be kept, loosely covered in plastic wrap, in the refrigerator for up to 3 days.

# BROWN SUGAR CAKE

This deconstructed upside-down cake is more than just a twist on a favorite technique. The brown sugar, butter, and cream bake into the cake, creating a deliciously crunchy caramel topping. Using almond flour along with all-purpose flour adds a nutty richness. I often serve seasonal roasted fruit or a fruit compote (which recalls the classic) and a scoop of homemade ice cream on the side, but the cake is just as good on its own.

**MAKES ONE 10-INCH CAKE**

**BROWN SUGAR TOPPING AND FILLING**

1 cup packed dark brown sugar

4 tablespoons (½ stick) unsalted butter

¼ cup heavy cream

**CAKE**

1 cup unbleached all-purpose flour

⅔ cup almond flour (see page 10)

1 teaspoon baking powder

½ teaspoon kosher salt

8 ounces (2 sticks) unsalted butter, very soft, plus more for the pan

½ cup granulated sugar

¼ cup packed dark brown sugar

¾ teaspoon pure vanilla extract

3 large eggs

**FOR THE BROWN SUGAR TOPPING AND FILLING:** Put the brown sugar in a medium bowl. In a small saucepan, bring the butter and heavy cream to a boil. Remove from the heat and pour over the brown sugar. Whisk until no lumps remain. Use immediately, or cover and refrigerate for up to 1 week.

**FOR THE CAKE:** Position a rack in the center of the oven and preheat the oven to 350°F. Butter a 10-inch round cake pan, and line the bottom with a round of parchment paper.

Cover the bottom of the prepared cake pan with three quarters of the brown sugar topping, spreading it out to make an even layer. Freeze for at least 5 minutes, or until ready to fill. Reserve the remaining mixture to use as a filling

In a medium bowl, sift together the all-purpose flour, almond flour, baking powder, and salt.

In the bowl of an electric mixer fitted with the paddle attachment, beat the butter, granulated sugar, brown sugar, and vanilla on medium-high speed until smooth, about 2 minutes. Add the eggs, one at a time, beating until each is well combined before adding the next. Scrape down the sides of the bowl as needed.

Remove the bowl from the mixer, and using a spatula, fold in the flour mixture. Pour the batter into the cake pan, over the topping, and smooth it out with a spatula. Put the pan on a baking sheet and bake until the cake begins to rise around the edges, about 30 minutes. Remove the pan from the oven and insert a scant teaspoon of the brown sugar filling in ten spots on the cake, sinking it down into the center.

Return the cake to the oven and bake until it is golden brown and firm to the touch, 15 to 20 minutes. Turn the cake out of the pan onto a plate and serve it immediately; or let it cool in the pan on a wire rack and then reheat it in a 350°F oven for 5 minutes before turning it out onto a plate and serving.

The cake is best eaten the day it is baked but can be kept at room temperature, loosely covered in plastic wrap, for up to 2 days.

## VARYING YOUR CRAFT
### CLASSIC UPSIDE-DOWN CAKE
Spread all of the topping in the cake pan. Add 2 cups sliced fruit (such as apple) or whole fruit (such as cranberries) of your choice, and then add the batter. Bake as directed above.

## COMBINING YOUR CRAFT
In the summer, serve this cake with scoops of Strawberry Ice Cream (page 212) and spoonfuls of Fresh Raspberry Compote (page 235). For fall and winter occasions, serve it with scoops of Saigon Cinnamon Ice Cream (page 205) and Rosé Poached Pears (page 232).

# RASPBERRY-PISTACHIO BROWN BUTTER CAKE

I love the play of both flavor and color in this *financier*-like tea cake. The pistachios contribute a pretty green tint and green flecks throughout. Raspberries contrast beautifully, with their sweet tang and brilliant pink tone. You can substitute blueberries or sliced plums or peaches for the raspberries. If you are making the cake ahead, warm it in a low oven before serving if desired.

MAKES ONE 9-INCH CAKE

8 ounces (2 sticks) unsalted butter, cut into small pieces, plus more for the pan

2¾ cups confectioners' sugar

1 cup pistachio flour (see Tip)

¾ cup cake flour

1 teaspoon kosher salt

7 large egg whites (¾ cup plus 2 tablespoons)

1 cup fresh raspberries

2 tablespoons Demerara sugar

Put the butter in a small heavy-bottomed saucepan and cook it over medium heat until it is light brown and smells nutty, about 6 minutes. Remove from the heat and strain through a fine-mesh sieve into a small bowl.

In a large bowl, sift together the confectioners' sugar, pistachio flour, cake flour, and salt. Whisk in the egg whites to combine. In a slow and steady stream, whisk in the strained butter. Cover the bowl of batter with plastic wrap and chill it in the refrigerator until thickened, about 1 hour. (This batter can be prepared up to 1 week in advance and stored, covered, in the refrigerator.)

Preheat the oven to 350°F. Generously butter a 9-inch tart pan with removable bottom.

Pour the chilled batter into the prepared tart pan. Sprinkle the berries over the top, keeping the fruit ½ inch in from the edge of the pan. Sprinkle the berries and cake with the Demerara sugar.

Place the tart pan on a baking sheet and bake until the edges of the cake are golden and the top is slightly springy to the touch, 35 to 40 minutes. Transfer the cake to a wire rack, removing the outer ring of the pan, and let it cool. Serve the cake warm or at room temperature.

The cake is best eaten the day it is baked but can be kept at room temperature, loosely covered in plastic wrap, for up to 2 days.

TIP Pistachio flour can be purchased in specialty stores or can be made at home: To make 1 cup pistachio flour, grind 1 cup unsalted pistachios and 1 tablespoon unbleached all-purpose flour in a food processor until fine.

## VARYING YOUR CRAFT

**BROWN BUTTER BABYCAKES**

Divide the batter among four buttered 4-inch springform pans or cake rings on a parchment-lined baking sheet. Bake for 20 to 25 minutes at 350°F, rotating the pan once, halfway through.

# BITTERSWEET
## CHOCOLATE CAKE

Even though flourless cake seems passé, I still return to this recipe time and again because no other cake produces the pure chocolate satisfaction that this one does. It is very rich and chocolaty and tastes great with a scoop of ice cream or with fresh berries tossed with fresh mint and a little sugar.

**MAKES ONE 9-INCH CAKE**

**3 tablespoons Demerara sugar**

**9 ounces bittersweet chocolate (65% to 72%), finely chopped**

**9 tablespoons unsalted butter, cut into small pieces, plus more for the pan**

**4 large eggs, separated**

**½ cup granulated sugar**

**¼ teaspoon kosher salt**

**TIP** This cake really show-cases the chocolate you use, so be sure to use a high-quality brand and a type of chocolate that you really love. When I want to take this over the top, I use Amedei Toscano Black 70% or Michel Cluizel 72%.

Preheat the oven to 350°F. Butter a 10-inch springform pan and dust it with the Demerara sugar.

Fill a large saucepan with about 2 inches of water and bring it to a simmer. Combine the chocolate and the butter in a large heat-proof bowl and set it over (but not touching) the simmering water. Stir frequently with a rubber spatula until melted and combined. Remove the bowl from the heat.

Beat the egg yolks in the bowl of an electric mixer fitted with the whisk attachment on medium speed for 1 minute. Add ¼ cup of the granulated sugar. Whisk on high speed until the mixture is pale and thickened, 7 to 10 minutes. Fold the yolk mixture into the warm chocolate mixture.

Clean and dry the bowl of the electric mixer well. Add the egg whites, and using the whisk attachment, beat the whites on medium-low speed until foamy. With the machine running, gradu-ally add the remaining ¼ cup sugar and the salt. Beat on medium-high speed until soft, glossy peaks form, about 5 minutes. In three additions, gently but thoroughly fold the whites into the chocolate mixture.

Pour the batter into the prepared pan and set the pan on a baking sheet. Bake, rotating the baking sheet halfway through, until the cake is cracked, the edges are firm, and a cake tester inserted into the center of the cake comes out clean, 20 to 25 minutes. Transfer the pan to a wire rack and let the cake cool for 30 min-utes. Then run a knife around the edges of the cake, release and remove the sides of the pan, and let the cake cool completely.

The cake is best eaten the day it is baked but can be kept at room temperature, loosely covered in plastic wrap, for up to 2 days.

# BANANA CUPCAKES WITH PEANUT BUTTER BUTTERCREAM

Serve these to little monkeys, and big ones too.

Preheat the oven to 350°F. Line a standard 12-cup muffin tin with paper liners.

In a medium bowl, whisk together the sugar and oil. Whisk in the banana, egg, egg yolk, buttermilk, and vanilla.

In another bowl, sift together the flour, baking soda, and salt. Using a whisk, mix the flour mixture into the banana mixture until just combined. Divide the batter evenly among the muffin cups, filling them three-quarters full. Bake, rotating the tin halfway through, until a cake tester inserted in the center of a cupcake comes out clean, about 20 minutes. Invert the cupcakes onto a wire rack, turn them top side up, and let them cool completely.

To make the buttercream, fill a medium saucepan with 2 inches of water and bring it to a simmer. In the bowl of an electric mixer, whisk together the egg whites and sugar. Set the bowl on top of the saucepan, and whisking constantly, heat the egg mixture until it is warm to the touch, about 3 minutes. Transfer the bowl to the mixer fitted with the whisk attachment, and whisk on medium speed until the whites become translucent and shiny and form a soft peak, about 5 minutes more.

With the machine running, add the butter, a cube at a time, and mix until combined. Increase the speed to medium-high and add the peanut butter, vanilla, and salt. Scraping down the sides of the bowl as necessary, beat until the buttercream becomes shiny and creamy, about 10 minutes. (The buttercream can be refrigerated for 1 week or frozen for up to 1 month. Before using, bring it to room temperature and beat it for a few minutes until smooth.) Spread the buttercream over the tops of the cupcakes, swirling it decoratively.

The cupcakes can be kept in an airtight container in the refrigerator for up to 3 days.

**MAKES 1 DOZEN**

### CUPCAKES

¾ cup sugar

⅓ cup plus 2 tablespoons grapeseed oil

¾ cup mashed banana (about 1½ medium bananas, mashed with a fork)

1 large egg

1 large egg yolk

⅓ cup plus 2 tablespoons buttermilk

¾ teaspoon pure vanilla extract

1 cup plus 2 tablespoons unbleached all-purpose flour

¾ teaspoon baking soda

½ teaspoon kosher salt

### BUTTERCREAM

2 large egg whites (¼ cup)

¼ cup sugar

8 tablespoons (1 stick) unsalted butter, cut into small pieces, at room temperature

¼ cup creamy peanut butter

¼ teaspoon pure vanilla extract

¼ teaspoon kosher salt

**TIP** The riper your bananas, the more intense the fruit flavor will be.

# CARROT CUPCAKES WITH MASCARPONE CREAM FROSTING

Demerara sugar—less sweet than granulated—allows the sweetness from the carrots to take the lead and produces a fine crumb.

MAKES 14

## CUPCAKES

**1 pound large carrots (about 5), peeled**

**1½ cups unbleached all-purpose flour**

**1½ teaspoons ground cinnamon**

**¼ teaspoon freshly grated nutmeg**

**1 teaspoon kosher salt**

**1 teaspoon baking powder**

**½ teaspoon baking soda**

**1 cup Demerara sugar**

**½ cup grapeseed oil**

**½ cup sour cream**

**1 teaspoon pure vanilla extract**

**1 large egg**

**1 large egg yolk**

## FROSTING

**1 cup mascarpone cheese**

**1 cup heavy cream**

**¼ cup crème fraîche or sour cream**

**2 tablespoons granulated sugar**

**½ teaspoon kosher salt**

**¼ teaspoon pure vanilla extract**

**Finely grated zest of 1 lemon**

For the cupcakes: Preheat the oven to 350°. Line a standard 12-cup muffin tin with paper liners, and line 2 more cups in a second muffin tin.

Using a food processor fitted with the shredding blade, or the medium holes of a box grater, grate the carrots. You will need a total of 2½ cups.

In a medium bowl, sift together the flour, cinnamon, nutmeg, salt, baking powder, and baking soda.

In a large bowl, whisk together the Demerara sugar, oil, sour cream, and vanilla. Add the egg and egg yolk, and whisk to combine. Add the flour mixture and whisk until just combined. Using a spatula, fold the carrots into the batter. Divide the batter evenly among the muffin cups, filling them about three-quarters full.

Bake, rotating the tins halfway through, until a cake tester inserted in the center of a cupcake comes out clean, 20 to 25 minutes. Invert the cupcakes onto a wire rack, turn them top side up, and let them cool completely.

To make the frosting, combine the mascarpone, cream, crème fraîche, sugar, salt, vanilla, and lemon zest in the bowl of an electric mixer fitted with the whisk attachment. Beat on medium speed until the mixture becomes thick, about 5 minutes. (The frosting can be kept in an airtight container in the refrigerator for up to 1 day. Let it come to room temperature and whisk it together if necessary before using.) Using a metal spatula or a butter knife, spread 2 to 3 tablespoons of the frosting over the top of each cupcake.

The cupcakes can be kept in an airtight container in the refrigerator for up to 3 days.

# GINGERBREAD CUPCAKES WITH CANDIED GINGER

These dark, rich beauties are packed with spicy ginger. Cocoa powder adds a hint of bittersweet chocolate to the coffee, beer, and molasses notes, making for a great combination of warming wintry flavors. They're even more robust the second day, so bake these ahead when you can.

To make the candied ginger, peel and thinly slice the knob of fresh ginger lengthwise. Cut each strip into thin sticks. Put the ginger in a small saucepan, cover with cold water, and bring to a boil over high heat. Strain out the ginger, return it to the pan, and repeat this process two more times. Drain the ginger and set it aside.

Combine 1 cup of the granulated sugar and 1 cup water in the same saucepan, stirring to make sure all of the sugar is damp. Bring to a boil, add the ginger, and simmer over medium-low heat until the ginger becomes translucent, about 10 minutes.

Strain out the ginger, discarding the syrup, and spread it out on a baking sheet. Toss it with the remaining 2 tablespoons sugar and leave it to dry for 2 hours, or overnight.

For the cupcakes, preheat the oven to 375°F. Line a standard 12-cup muffin tin with paper liners, and line 6 more cups in a second muffin tin.

In a large saucepan, bring the beer, coffee, and molasses to a boil; whisk together to combine. Remove from the heat and whisk in the baking soda. Be cautious; it will bubble up quite a bit. Let the mixture sit for 5 minutes to cool.

In a large bowl, whisk together the brown sugar, oil, Demerara sugar, and grated fresh ginger. Whisk in the egg. In a large bowl, sift together the flour, baking powder, cocoa powder, ground ginger, cinnamon, cardamom, nutmeg, white pepper, and salt. In three additions of each, alternately whisk the flour mixture and the beer mixture into the brown sugar mixture to combine.

MAKES 18 CUPCAKES

**CANDIED GINGER**

One 3-inch knob fresh ginger

1 cup plus 2 tablespoons granulated sugar

**CUPCAKES**

¾ cup stout beer, such as Guinness

¼ cup plus 2 tablespoons brewed coffee

¾ cup dark molasses, such as Grandma's

¾ teaspoon baking soda

1 cup packed dark brown sugar, or organic dark brown molasses sugar, such as Billington's

¼ cup plus 3 tablespoons grapeseed oil

3 tablespoons Demerara sugar

2½ tablespoons finely grated fresh ginger

1 large egg

1¾ cups plus 2 tablespoons all-purpose flour

2¼ teaspoons baking powder

2¼ teaspoons unsweetened cocoa powder

2¼ teaspoons ground ginger

1½ teaspoons ground cinnamon

RECIPE CONTINUES

Divide the batter evenly among the muffin cups, filling them about three-quarters of the way. Bake, without opening the oven, for 20 minutes. Then turn the tins and bake until the cupcakes spring back to the touch and a cake tester inserted in the center of a cupcake comes out clean, about 5 minutes more. Invert the cupcakes onto a wire rack, turn them top side up, and let them cool completely.

To make the icing, put the confectioners' sugar in a mixing bowl and whisk in the coffee, molasses, and vanilla. If the glaze is too thick for dipping, add another ½ tablespoon coffee.

Dip the top of each cupcake in the molasses icing and then top it with a couple of strands of candied ginger. Return the cupcakes to the wire rack to let the icing set up, at least 30 minutes.

The cupcakes can be kept in an airtight container at room temperature for a day or in the refrigerator for up to 3 days.

## VARYING YOUR CRAFT

### GINGERBREAD LOAF

Line the bottom of an 8½ x 4½-inch pan with parchment and grease well with butter. Pour in the batter and gently smooth the top with an offset spatula. Bake the loaf for about 1 hour at 375°F, turning the pan after 40 minutes.

### GINGERBREAD CROUTONS

Preheat the oven to 300°F. Cut the unfrosted gingerbread cupcakes or gingerbread loaf into ½-inch cubes. Spread the cubes in a single layer on a baking sheet. Bake for 20 minutes, rotating the baking sheet halfway through, until a cube is crunchy once cooled for a few minutes. Transfer the baking sheet to a wire rack and let the cubes cool. The croutons can be kept in an airtight container at room temperature for up to 2 weeks. Use over ice cream or sundaes.

### PUMPKIN ICE CREAM SUNDAE

Layer scoops of Pumpkin Ice Cream (page 209) with warm Spiced Caramel Sauce (page 246) and Gingerbread Croutons (see above).

1 teaspoon ground cardamom

⅛ teaspoon freshly grated nutmeg

⅛ teaspoon freshly ground white pepper

½ teaspoon kosher salt

## ICING

1½ cups confectioners' sugar

¼ cup brewed coffee, or more if needed, cooled

1 tablespoon dark molasses, such as Grandma's

¼ teaspoon pure vanilla extract

# DEVIL'S FOOD CUPCAKES WITH CREAM FILLING

A sophisticated play on a childhood favorite, these decadent cupcakes are packed with dense chocolate flavor surrounding a light creamy center.

## CUPCAKES

¾ cup plus 1½ teaspoons unsweetened cocoa powder

¾ cup cake flour

⅔ cup unbleached all-purpose flour

¾ teaspoon baking powder

¾ teaspoon baking soda

¼ teaspoon kosher salt

1¼ cups plus 2 tablespoons packed dark brown sugar

5 tablespoons unsalted butter, at room temperature

1 large egg

1 large egg yolk

½ cup plus 2 tablespoons buttermilk

¾ teaspoon pure vanilla extract

Preheat the oven to 350°F. Line a standard 12-cup muffin tin with paper liners.

In a medium mixing bowl, whisk the cocoa powder and ½ cup plus 2 tablespoons warm water together to form a paste; set it aside.

In another bowl, sift together the cake flour, all-purpose flour, baking powder, baking soda, and salt.

In the bowl of an electric mixer fitted with the paddle attachment, mix the brown sugar and the butter on medium speed until they are well combined, with no pieces of butter visible. Add the cocoa paste, making sure to use a spatula to get all of the cocoa paste into the mixer bowl. Once this is well combined, add the egg and egg yolk. Scrape down the sides of the bowl with a rubber spatula. In three additions each, add the buttermilk and the vanilla extract, alternating with the flour mixture.

Divide the batter evenly among the muffin cups, filling them three-quarters full. Bake, rotating the tin halfway through, until the cupcakes spring back to the touch and a tester inserted in the center of a cupcake comes out clean, 20 to 25 minutes. Invert the cupcakes onto a wire rack, turn them top side up, and let them cool completely.

To make the filling, combine the cream, confectioners' sugar, and vanilla extract in the bowl of an electric mixer fitted with the whisk attachment. Beat on medium speed to soft peaks, about 4 minutes. Put the whipped cream into a pastry bag fitted with a small piping tip. Using a paring knife, make a small cut in the bottom of each cupcake, through the paper, to insert the tip of the pastry bag. Insert the tip of the pastry bag about 1½ inches into a cupcake. Gently squeeze the bag while holding the fingers of your other hand over the top of the cupcake. When you feel a slight pressure on the top of the cupcake, stop filling. Repeat with each cupcake.

To make the glaze, put the chocolate in a small mixing bowl. Combine the cream and the corn syrup in a small saucepan and bring to a boil. Pour this over the chocolate, and stir slowly until all of the chocolate melts and the glaze is silky and shiny.

Dip the top of each cupcake in the ganache, tapping to remove any excess. Return the cupcakes to the wire rack to let the glaze set up, at least 30 minutes.

The cupcakes can be kept in an airtight container in the refrigerator for up to 3 days.

## CREAM FILLING

1 cup heavy cream

2 tablespoons confectioners' sugar

1 teaspoon pure vanilla extract

## CHOCOLATE GANACHE GLAZE

4 ounces semisweet chocolate, chopped

½ cup heavy cream

2 tablespoons light corn syrup

# LAMINGTON CUPCAKES

A fun twist on the classic Australian cake, these vanilla cakes are baked in muffin tins without paper liners so they can be dipped in a cocoa glaze and then rolled in toasted coconut.

**MAKES 1 DOZEN**

## COCONUT COATING

2 cups unsweetened shredded coconut

## CUPCAKES

1½ cups cake flour, plus more for the muffin tin

1 teaspoon baking powder

½ teaspoon kosher salt

8 ounces (2 sticks) unsalted butter, cut into small pieces, very soft, plus more for the muffin tin

1 cup granulated sugar

1 tablespoon pure vanilla extract

¼ vanilla bean, split lengthwise, seeds scraped out, bean and seeds reserved

½ cup whole milk

4 large egg whites

## CHOCOLATE GLAZE

¼ cup plus 3 tablespoons unsweetened cocoa powder

2 cups confectioners' sugar

¼ teaspoon kosher salt

½ teaspoon pure vanilla extract

Preheat the oven to 300°F.

Spread the coconut on a baking sheet and bake until it is lightly golden, about 5 minutes. Remove the baking sheet from the oven, let the coconut cool completely, and then transfer it to a wide, shallow bowl.

Increase the oven temperature to 350°F. Butter and flour a standard 12-cup muffin tin.

For the cupcakes, in a bowl, sift together the flour, baking powder, and salt.

In the bowl of an electric mixer fitted with the paddle attachment, beat the butter, granulated sugar, vanilla extract, and vanilla bean and seeds on medium-high speed until light and fluffy, about 5 minutes. Scrape down the sides of the bowl.

With the mixer on medium speed, add the milk and the flour mixture, alternating, in three additions each, scraping down the sides of the bowl as necessary to ensure that the mixture is well combined. Using a rubber spatula, scrape the batter into a large bowl. Remove the vanilla bean from the batter, and rinse and reserve it (see page 16).

Clean and dry the bowl of the electric mixer well. Add the egg whites, and using the whisk attachment on medium speed, beat to soft peaks, about 4 minutes. In three additions, fold the whites into the batter.

Divide the batter among the muffin cups, filling the cups about three-quarters full. Bake, rotating the tin halfway through, until the cupcakes are lightly golden and a tester inserted in the center of a cupcake comes out clean, about 20 minutes. Invert the cupcakes onto a wire rack, turn them top side up, and let them cool completely.

For the glaze, set a wire rack on a baking sheet.

In a medium bowl, sift together the cocoa powder, confectioners' sugar, and salt. Add ¼ cup plus 2 tablespoons water and the vanilla, and whisk to combine.

Dip 1 cupcake in the glaze, turning to coat the entire cupcake. Immediately roll the cupcake in the toasted coconut, covering the entire cupcake. Transfer the cupcake to the wire rack to let the glaze set up; this will take about 10 minutes. Repeat with the remaining cupcakes.

The cupcakes can be kept in an airtight container in the refrigerator for up to 3 days.

**TIP** The key to this recipe is to use very soft butter, which makes a thinner, more aerated batter and a lighter cake. Cut the butter into cubes while it is cold, and then leave it at room temperature for several hours or overnight.

# WHITE CHOCOLATE CUPCAKES WITH WHITE CHOCOLATE CREAM CHEESE BUTTERCREAM

Unsweetened coconut milk adds deep flavor to these tasty cupcakes, while also making them unbeatably moist. When you're in the mood to decorate, try a single fresh raspberry, white sprinkles, or silver dragées.

## CUPCAKES

**1¾ cups unbleached all-purpose flour**

**1 teaspoon baking powder**

**½ teaspoon kosher salt**

**12 tablespoons (1½ sticks) unsalted butter, very soft**

**1 cup sugar**

**1 tablespoon pure vanilla extract**

**8 ounces white chocolate, chopped**

**½ cup unsweetened coconut milk**

**5 large egg whites**

## WHITE CHOCOLATE CREAM CHEESE BUTTERCREAM

**6 ounces cream cheese, at room temperature**

**6 tablespoons (¾ stick) unsalted butter, at room temperature**

**½ teaspoon pure vanilla extract**

**¼ teaspoon kosher salt**

**4½ ounces white chocolate, chopped**

For the cupcakes, preheat the oven to 350°F. Line a standard 12-cup muffin tin with paper liners, and line 2 more cups in a second muffin tin.

In a medium bowl, sift together the flour, baking powder, and salt; set it aside.

In the bowl of an electric mixer fitted with the paddle attachment, beat together the butter, sugar, and vanilla on medium-high speed until light and smooth, about 3 minutes.

Bring about 2 inches of water to a simmer in a large saucepan. Place the white chocolate in a heatproof bowl, set it over the simmering water, and stir until it has melted. Add the warm melted chocolate to the butter mixture and stir to combine. Scrape down the sides of the bowl with a rubber spatula.

With the mixer on low speed, alternate adding the flour mixture and the coconut milk, adding one third of each at a time and letting them fully mix in before adding the next. Transfer the batter to a medium mixing bowl.

Clean and dry the bowl of the electric mixer well. Add the egg whites, and using the whisk attachment on medium speed, beat to soft peaks, about 4 minutes. In three additions, fold the whites into the batter.

Fill the muffin cups about three-quarters full with batter. Bake, rotating the tins halfway through, until the cupcakes spring back to the touch and a cake tester inserted in the center of a cupcake comes out clean, 15 to 20 minutes. Transfer the tin to a wire rack. Invert the cupcakes onto the rack, turn them top side up, and let them cool completely.

To make the buttercream, in the bowl of an electric mixer fitted with the paddle attachment, beat together the cream cheese, butter, vanilla, and salt on medium-high speed until light and smooth, about 3 minutes.

Bring about 2 inches of water to a simmer in a saucepan. Place the chocolate in a heatproof bowl, place the bowl over the pan, and stir until the chocolate is melted. Slowly add the melted chocolate to the cream cheese mixture and beat to combine, scraping down the sides of the bowl as necessary. If the buttercream is too soft to spread, cover the bowl and chill it for 20 minutes; then whip it in the mixer for 30 seconds before using. (The buttercream can be refrigerated for 1 week or frozen for up to 1 month. Before using, bring it to room temperature and beat it for a few minutes until smooth.) Spread the tops of the cupcakes with the frosting, swirling it decoratively.

The cupcakes can be kept in an airtight container in the refrigerator for up to 3 days.

# LEMON BEIGNETS WITH LEMON CREAM

Sweet-tart lemon cream dresses up these doughnutlike cakes a bit, making them more dessertlike than morning fare—though you can certainly serve them for brunch, if you like. Espresso or strong coffee is a must either way.

MAKES 12, SERVES 4 TO 6

### SPICED SUGAR

¾ cup sugar

1 teaspoon ground cinnamon

¼ teaspoon ground cardamom

⅛ teaspoon kosher salt

### FILLING

⅓ cup Lemon Curd (page 242)

### DOUGH

2 cups cake flour

½ cup sugar

1 teaspoon baking powder

¼ teaspoon baking soda

¾ teaspoon kosher salt

Finely grated zest of 1 lemon

⅓ cup buttermilk

1 large egg

1 large egg yolk

1½ tablespoons vegetable oil

Unbleached all-purpose flour, for dusting

Peanut or soy oil, for frying

### LEMON CREAM (OPTIONAL)

½ cup heavy cream

½ cup Lemon Curd (page 242)

**FOR THE SPICED SUGAR:** In a shallow bowl, whisk together the sugar, cinnamon, cardamom, and salt; set aside.

**FOR THE FILLING:** Cover a plate with a sheet of waxed paper or plastic wrap. Drop 12 separate heaping teaspoonfuls of the lemon curd onto the plate. Freeze until firm, at least 30 minutes, or up to 2 days.

**FOR THE DOUGH:** In a medium bowl, whisk together 1 cup of the cake flour, the sugar, baking powder, baking soda, salt, and lemon zest. In another bowl, whisk together the buttermilk, egg, egg yolk, and vegetable oil. Make a well in the center of the flour mixture, add the buttermilk mixture, and whisk together until well combined. Using a rubber spatula, gently fold in the remaining 1 cup cake flour. The dough will be very sticky.

Scrape the dough from the bowl onto a piece of waxed paper. Place a second piece of waxed paper on top and roll the dough into a 10 x 12-inch oval, about ¼ inch thick. Set the dough, still between the pieces of waxed paper, onto a baking sheet and freeze until it is firm enough to cut, about 30 minutes.

Remove the dough from the freezer and remove the top sheet of waxed paper. Dust the dough with all-purpose flour and replace the waxed paper. Flip the dough over; remove and discard the top sheet of waxed paper.

Using a floured 2-inch round cutter or inverted drinking glass, cut out 24 rounds of dough. Line the baking sheet with a clean piece of waxed paper, place the rounds on the baking sheet, and keep them in the refrigerator as you work.

Removing 4 rounds at a time to work with, sandwich 1 teaspoon of the frozen lemon curd between 2 rounds of dough and pinch the edges together to seal them. With lightly floured hands, roll each

beignet into a ball. Repeat until all of the beignets are complete. (The beignets can be kept, well wrapped, in the refrigerator for up to 1 day before frying.)

FOR THE LEMON CREAM: In a bowl, whip the cream to soft peaks. Fold the lemon curd into the whipped cream.

Fill a heavy medium saucepan with 2½ inches of peanut oil, and heat it over moderately high heat until a deep-frying thermometer registers 350°F. Fry the beignets in batches of three, gently turning them over once with a slotted spoon, until golden, about 3 minutes. Transfer them with the slotted spoon to paper towels to drain. While still warm, toss the beignets in the spiced sugar.

Spoon the lemon cream onto four to six plates. Arrange the warm beignets on top, and serve immediately.

# RICOTTA BEIGNETS

Like little ricotta cheesecakes, these lemon-kissed sweets incorporate the cheese in both the filling and the dough. I like honey along with sugar as the sweetener here. Its flavor pairs well with the taste of the cheese and adds an extra dimension to the cake. This is another treat that can be served as dessert for brunch, like a doughnut, if you like.

MAKES 15 BEIGNETS

**CINNAMON-SUGAR**

¾ cup sugar

1 teaspoon ground cinnamon

⅛ teaspoon kosher salt

**FILLING**

½ cup fresh ricotta cheese, drained overnight (see page 14)

1 tablespoon sugar

Finely grated zest of 1 lemon

**FOR THE CINNAMON-SUGAR:** In a shallow bowl, whisk together the sugar, cinnamon, and salt; set aside.

**FOR THE FILLING:** Whisk together the ricotta, sugar, and lemon zest. Cover a plate with a sheet of waxed paper or plastic wrap. Drop 15 separate heaping teaspoonfuls of the ricotta mixture onto the plate. Freeze until firm, at least 30 minutes, or up to 2 days.

**FOR THE DOUGH:** In a medium bowl, whisk together the flour, sugar, baking powder, nutmeg, lemon zest, and salt. In another bowl, whisk together the eggs, egg yolk, honey, butter, and vanilla. Make a well in the center of the flour mixture and pour the egg mixture into it. Using a rubber spatula, fold the two together. Then fold in the ricotta until well combined.

Transfer the dough to a 12 x 16-inch sheet of waxed paper. Place a second sheet of waxed paper on top, and roll out the dough into an 11 x 14-inch oval, about ¼ inch thick. Set the dough, still between the sheets of waxed paper, on a baking sheet and freeze until it is firm enough to cut, about 30 minutes.

Remove the dough from the freezer and remove the top sheet of waxed paper. Dust the dough with flour and replace the waxed paper. Flip the dough over; remove and discard the top sheet of waxed paper. Now the dough is loosened from the paper and is easy to cut.

Using a floured 2-inch round cutter or inverted drinking glass, cut out 30 rounds of dough. Line the baking sheet with a clean piece of waxed paper, place the rounds on the baking sheet, and put the sheet in the refrigerator to keep the dough cold as you work.

Removing 4 rounds at a time to work with, sandwich 1 teaspoon of the frozen ricotta mixture between 2 rounds of dough and pinch the edges together to seal them. With lightly floured hands, roll each beignet into a ball. Repeat until all of the beignets are complete. (The beignets can be kept, well wrapped, in the refrigerator for up to 1 day before frying.)

Fill a heavy medium saucepan with 2½ inches of oil and heat it over moderately high heat until a deep-frying thermometer registers 350°F. Fry the beignets in batches of three, gently turning them over once with a slotted spoon, until dark golden, about 3 minutes. Transfer them with the slotted spoon to paper towels to drain. Toss the warm beignets in the cinnamon-sugar and serve immediately.

**DOUGH**

1¾ cups unbleached all-purpose flour, plus more for dusting

¼ cup plus 1 tablespoon sugar

1 tablespoon baking powder

¼ teaspoon freshly grated nutmeg

Finely grated zest of 1 lemon

1 teaspoon kosher salt

3 large eggs

1 large egg yolk

¼ cup honey

2 tablespoons unsalted butter, melted

1 teaspoon pure vanilla extract

1 cup (8 ounces) fresh ricotta cheese, drained overnight (see page 14)

Peanut or soy oil, for frying

LEMON CREAM

# CUSTARDS & PUDDINGS

# MAPLE CUSTARD

Grade B maple syrup, darker and stronger in flavor than grade A, lends a hint of caramel taste to these creamy custards.

SERVES 6

2 cups grade B maple syrup (see Tip)

4 tablespoons (½ stick) unsalted butter, cut into small pieces

3 cups heavy cream

¾ teaspoon kosher salt

½ teaspoon pure vanilla extract

1 large egg

4 large egg yolks

☀ TIP Both grade A and grade B syrup can be found at most supermarkets, but if you don't have grade B on hand, you can use grade A with fine results.

☀ TIP The uncooked custard can be prepared up to a week in advance and kept in the refrigerator until ready to bake.

Preheat the oven to 275°F.

In a medium saucepan, bring the maple syrup to a boil and cook over medium heat until it is thickened and reduced by about half, about 15 minutes. Remove the pan from the heat and whisk in the butter. Add the cream, salt, and vanilla and whisk to combine.

In a mixing bowl, whisk together the egg and egg yolks. Whisk in about one third of the cream mixture. Return the egg mixture to the remaining cream mixture in the pan, and whisk well to combine. Strain through a fine-mesh strainer into a bowl.

Place six 4-ounce ramekins or custard cups in a deep baking dish or roasting pan, spacing them evenly. Divide the custard mixture among the ramekins. Cover the baking dish with aluminum foil, leaving the front side loose, and carefully place the dish in the oven. Fill the baking dish with warm water to reach halfway up the sides of the ramekins, then seal the pan tightly with the foil.

Bake for 20 minutes. Then rotate the baking dish and let the steam out by lifting the foil cover; replace the foil and seal it. Continue baking, letting the steam out every 15 to 20 minutes and resealing the foil well each time, until the custards are completely set around the edges and a little bit loose in the center, about 1 hour more (if the custards appear to need more time, continue cooking, checking them at 5-minute intervals).

Remove the foil from the dish.

Carefully transfer the baking dish from the oven to a wire rack, and let the custards cool to room temperature in the water bath. Then remove them from the water and refrigerate them, uncovered, until set, about 30 minutes.

Once set, the custards can be kept, loosely covered with plastic wrap, in the refrigerator for up to 2 days.

# BUILDING YOUR CRAFT
## CUSTARDS
## & PUDDINGS

Custards and puddings are generally made one of two ways: in a pot on the stovetop or in a sealed water bath in the oven. I prefer the latter. It's a gentler and more even technique. On a stovetop, the heat of the flame is most intense directly underneath the pot. To heat the custard or pudding evenly, you must constantly and thoroughly stir it. The process is pretty rough and tumble on the custard itself—imagine the difference between being continually pushed and swirled and being allowed to sit undisturbed in a steam environment.

When setting up custards for a water bath, I set my baking dish on a flat work surface as close to the oven as possible and then place the custard cups in the baking dish, spacing them evenly, before filling them with the custard or pudding base. This way I travel the shortest distance possible when transferring the pan to the oven, which limits my chances of spilling. I set the pan in the oven and then fill it with warm water. This helps ensure that the water will not splash into the custards, as I won't be moving the pan much once the water is in place.

As custards and puddings bake in the oven, steam builds up in the pan. You want a healthy dose of steam but not too much of it; other-wise the environment becomes so hot that the custards can curdle. This is why you release the steam every so often, resealing the dish tightly after each release, as the recipes indicate.

Once the custards are ready, you'll want to remove the foil from the pan before transferring the pan from the oven to a wire rack to cool the custards. This allows you to keep an eye on the contents of the pan while you move it, so that you can avoid splashing water onto your beautiful desserts.

# SWEET CORN CUSTARD

These silky-smooth custards combine one of the best duos in both sweet and savory cooking: fresh corn and cream.

Cut the kernels from the corncobs; reserve the cobs. In a large heavy-bottomed saucepan, stir together the kernels, cobs, cream, sugar, salt, and vanilla bean and seeds. Bring to a rolling boil and then remove from the heat. Transfer the mixture to a bowl, cover, and refrigerate it for at least 12 hours, and up to 2 days.

Preheat the oven to 275°F.

Whisk together the eggs and egg yolks in a medium bowl. Discard the corncobs and pour half of the cream mixture over the eggs; whisk together until combined. Whisk in the rest of the cream mixture. Strain through a fine-mesh sieve into a bowl.

Place eight 4-ounce ramekins or custard cups in a deep baking dish or roasting pan, spacing them evenly. Divide the custard mixture among the ramekins. Cover the baking dish with aluminum foil, leaving the front side loose, and carefully place the dish in the oven. Fill the baking dish with warm water to reach halfway up the sides of the ramekins, then seal the dish tightly with the foil.

Bake for 20 minutes. Then rotate the pan and let the steam out by lifting the foil cover; replace the foil and seal it. Continue baking, lifting the foil every 15 to 20 minutes to let the steam out and then resealing it well, until the edges of the custards are set and the centers are still slightly loose, about 1 hour (if more time is needed, check at 5-minute intervals).

Remove the foil. Transfer the dish to a wire rack. Let the custards cool to room temperature in the water bath. Remove from the water and refrigerate, uncovered, until set, about 1 hour.

Once set, the custards can be kept, loosely covered with plastic wrap, in the refrigerator for up to 2 days.

## COMBINING YOUR CRAFT

Top Sweet Corn Custards with Blueberry Compote (page 238) and serve with Cornmeal Shortbread Cookies (page 62).

SERVES 8

**2 medium ears fresh corn, shucked**

**1 quart heavy cream**

**¾ cup sugar**

**½ teaspoon kosher salt**

**¼ vanilla bean, split lengthwise, seeds scraped out, bean and seeds reserved**

**2 large eggs**

**6 large egg yolks**

**TIP** To get the most flavor and best sweetness from fresh corn, purchase it locally, preferably the day it was picked, and use it as soon as you can once you're back from the market. Corn's natural sugars quickly convert to starches once the cobs have been harvested.

# CREAM CHEESE PANNA COTTA

Cream cheese brings both flavor and texture to this dessert, which is a nice cross between classic cheesecake and panna cotta. In the summer I serve it with slices of juicy fresh peaches. Fresh berries are nice, too. In colder months, try a spoonful of fruit compote or a roasted fruit.

SERVES 4

¾ teaspoon powdered gelatin

¾ cup whole milk

⅓ cup plus 2 tablespoons heavy cream

3 tablespoons sugar

½ teaspoon pure vanilla extract

¼ teaspoon kosher salt

3 ounces cream cheese, cut into small pieces, at room temperature

Any ripe fresh fruit or fruit compote, for garnish

In a medium bowl, whisk together the gelatin and 2 tablespoons cold water.

In a saucepan, bring the milk, cream, sugar, vanilla, and salt to a boil. Remove the pan from the heat, and whisk about one third of the hot milk mixture into the gelatin mixture. Then pour the gelatin mixture back into the remaining milk mixture, and whisk to combine.

One cube at a time, whisk the cream cheese into the milk mixture, adding a new piece as the previous one dissolves. Strain the mixture through a fine-mesh sieve into a bowl, and then divide it among four ramekins, glasses, or cups. Refrigerate until set, about 3 hours. (Once set, the panna cotta can be kept, loosely covered with plastic wrap, in the refrigerator for up to 2 days.) Serve topped with fresh fruit or fruit compote, in ramekins, or dipped in hot water and unmolded onto a serving plate or bowl.

## COMBINING YOUR CRAFT

Serve these panna cottas with Sour Cherry Compote (page 235) and Crisp Honey Grahams (page 65) for a twist on cherry cheesecake. Or try spooning Spiced Red Wine Roasted Figs (page 228) over the top.

# SHEEP'S MILK YOGURT PANNA COTTA WITH HONEY

Sheep's milk yogurt lends a delicious tanginess to these panna cottas. Honey balances that tang with its warm, earthy sweetness. I have a preference for linden honey, which is a medium-bodied honey with delicate floral tones, but you can use any honey you like. You can also try any fruit compote or fresh or roasted fruit in place of the honey.

In a medium bowl, whisk together the gelatin and 3 tablespoons cold water.

In a saucepan, bring the cream, sugar, and salt to a boil. Remove the pan from the heat, and whisk about one third of the hot cream mixture into the gelatin mixture. Then pour the gelatin mixture back into the remaining cream, and whisk to combine. Whisk in the yogurt.

Strain the mixture through a fine-mesh sieve into a bowl, and then divide it among six ramekins, glasses, or cups. Refrigerate until set, about 2 hours. (Once set, the panna cotta can be kept, loosely covered with plastic wrap, in the refrigerator for up to 2 days.) Just before serving, drizzle with honey. These can be served in the ramekins, or dipped in hot water and unmolded onto a plate.

## COMBINING YOUR CRAFT

Serve the panna cotta with Apricot Compote (page 237) and Cherry Anise Biscotti (page 76).

---

### SERVES 6

1⅛ teaspoons powdered gelatin

1 cup heavy cream

⅓ cup plus 1 tablespoon sugar

¼ teaspoon kosher salt

2 cups (one 16-ounce container) sheep's milk yogurt

Honey, for drizzling

# MILK CHOCOLATE
# HAZELNUT PANNA COTTA

Nutella, a creamy chocolate-hazelnut spread, brings the richness of both flavors to a basic panna cotta in one simple step.

SERVES 8

**1⅛ teaspoons powdered gelatin**

**1 cup Nutella**

**½ teaspoon kosher salt**

**1½ cups heavy cream**

**½ teaspoon pure vanilla extract**

**1 cup whole milk**

In a medium mixing bowl, whisk together the gelatin and 3 table-spoons cold water.

Put the Nutella and salt into a medium mixing bowl and set it aside.

In a medium saucepan, bring the cream and vanilla to a boil. Pour one third of the hot cream mixture over the gelatin and whisk it well. Then pour the gelatin mixture back into the remaining cream.

Pour about one third of the cream mixture over the Nutella. Whisk well to form a smooth paste. Add the remaining cream mixture and whisk well to combine. Whisk in the milk.

Strain the mixture through a fine-mesh sieve into a bowl, and then divide it among eight ramekins, glasses, or cups. Refrigerate until set, about 3 hours. (Once set, the panna cotta can be kept, loosely covered with plastic wrap, in the refrigerator for up to 2 days.) They can be served in the ramekins, or dipped in hot water and unmolded onto a serving plate or bowl.

### COMBINING YOUR CRAFT

Top this panna cotta with slices of Rosé Poached Pears (page 232) and crushed Cacao Nib Brittle (page 100).

# TOFFEE STEAMED PUDDING

Made with dark, sweet dates, warming rum, and brown sugar, this is a comforting and very satisfying dessert, especially on chilly winter days. Demerara sugar—less sweet than granulated—tempers the sweetness of the dates and toffee sauce.

MAKES ONE 10-INCH CAKE

## SAUCE

½ cup heavy cream

1 cup packed brown sugar

2 tablespoons unsalted butter

½ teaspoon kosher salt

1 tablespoon dark rum, such as Myers's

## PUDDING

8 ounces dried dates

1 teaspoon pure vanilla extract

1 teaspoon baking soda

2 cups unbleached all-purpose flour

1 teaspoon baking powder

½ teaspoon kosher salt

4 tablespoons (½ stick) unsalted butter, at room temperature, plus more for the pan

1 cup Demerara sugar

1 large egg

Crème fraîche or unsweetened whipped cream, for serving (optional)

**FOR THE SAUCE:** In a saucepan, stir together the cream, brown sugar, butter, salt, and rum. Bring to a boil, and then reduce the heat to a simmer. Cook, stirring occasionally, until the sauce thickens, about 5 minutes. Remove from the heat.

**FOR THE CAKE:** Preheat the oven to 350°F. Butter a 10-inch round cake pan and line the bottom with parchment.

Bring a large saucepan of water to a boil. Add the dates and cook until the skins begin to come off, about 4 minutes. Drain; then peel and pit the dates while they are still warm.

In a blender, combine the pitted dates and 1 cup water. Purée until smooth, and then transfer the purée to a medium saucepan. Stir in the vanilla and bring to a boil, while whisking, over medium-high heat. Remove from the heat and stir in the baking soda.

In a bowl, whisk together the flour, baking powder, and salt.

In the bowl of an electric mixer fitted with the paddle attachment, beat the butter and Demerara sugar on medium speed until light and fluffy, about 4 minutes. Reduce the speed to low, and add the egg. Then alternate adding the flour mixture and the date purée, adding one third of each at a time and letting each fully mix in before adding the next. Turn the mixer speed to medium-high and mix for about 30 seconds to fully incorporate the ingredients and help to build the structure.

Pour the batter into the prepared cake pan. Set the pan in a roasting pan or a large wide pot, and fill the roasting pan with enough hot water to reach 2 inches up the sides of the cake pan. Cover the roasting pan tightly with aluminum foil.

Bake the pudding for 45 minutes. Then remove the foil and poke four evenly spaced holes into the top of the pudding. Pour 1 tablespoon of the toffee sauce into each hole; reserve the remaining sauce. Reseal the foil and continue to bake the pudding until it is dark brown and firm to the touch, about 15 minutes more. Remove the cake pan from the water bath and let it cool on a wire rack. Serve immediately, or rewarm in a 350°F oven for 5 minutes.

Run a knife around the edge of the pan and invert the pudding onto a serving plate. Warm the remaining toffee sauce and serve it with the pudding, topping each portion with a dollop of crème fraîche if desired.

## COMBINING YOUR CRAFT

Serve this cake with Coffee Crunch Ice Cream (page 205) or Caramel Ice Cream (page 207).

# LEMON STEAMED PUDDING

Steamed puddings are more like very moist cakes than creamy puddings. While they are traditionally rich and rather dense, this is a uniquely light version with a beautiful shiny layer of lemon curd on top. If you want to dress them up, serve the puddings with fresh berries and a spoonful of crème fraîche, plain yogurt, or vanilla ice cream.

Bring the eggs to room temperature by placing them in a bowl and covering them with warm water. Repeat two or three times if necessary, until the eggs no longer feel cool to the touch. Grease six 4-ounce ramekins or foil cups with the butter and coat them using the 2 tablespoons of sugar.

Preheat the oven to 325°F.

In a mixing bowl, whisk together the remaining ¾ cup sugar, the flour, salt, and lemon zest.

Separate the eggs, putting the yolks in a mixing bowl and reserving the whites in the bowl of a stand mixer. Add the buttermilk and lemon juice to the yolks, and whisk them together until the yolks are broken and everything is well combined.

Make a well in the center of the flour mixture and pour about one third of the buttermilk mixture into the center. Whisk together to form a smooth paste. Add the remaining buttermilk mixture and whisk until well mixed, about 30 seconds.

With the whisk attachment on the stand mixer, start whipping the egg whites on low speed. Once they become frothy, turn the mixer speed to medium. When the whites rise up and become opaque, turn the mixer to medium-high. Continue whipping to soft peaks. This whole process should take about 5 minutes.

Gently fold the egg whites into the batter in three additions, only really fully combining the whites with the last addition. The finished batter will look broken. Place the ramekins in a roasting pan. Ladle or pour the batter into the prepared ramekins, filling each all the way to the rim. Cover the pan with foil, leaving the

SERVES 6

4 large eggs

Unsalted butter, softened, for the ramekins

¾ cup plus 2 tablespoons sugar

¼ cup plus 1½ teaspoons unbleached all-purpose flour

¼ teaspoon kosher salt

Finely grated zest of 2 lemons

1 cup buttermilk

¼ cup strained fresh lemon juice (from 1½ lemons)

6 pieces Candied Lemon Slices (page 67), optional

**TIP** Don't be concerned about the batter looking broken when you make these little cakes; it's meant to be that way. As it bakes, the batter separates into two layers—one of cake and one of curd.

RECIPE CONTINUES

RECIPE CONTINUED

front side loose. Place the pan in the oven and pour enough hot water into the pan to reach halfway up the sides of the ramekins. Seal the foil over the pan.

Bake for 10 minutes. Then open the foil to release the steam; replace the foil and seal it. Rotate the pan and continue to bake until the puddings spring back and the tops feel dry to the touch, 10 to 15 minutes more, checking and releasing the steam after 10 minutes. Remove the foil from the pan. Carefully transfer the pan to a wire rack and let the puddings cool to room temperature in the water. Then remove them from the water and store them at room temperature until ready to serve.

Serve the puddings at room temperature, or reheat them gently by returning the ramekins to a water bath in a roasting pan and baking, uncovered, at 325°F for 10 minutes. Carefully turn the puddings out of the ramekins and onto dessert plates. Garnish each with a piece of candied lemon, if desired.

The puddings are best served on the day they are made.

# CHOCOLATE BREAD
## PUDDING

Here, a not-so-sweet chocolate bread is tossed and baked with a creamy, rich chocolate custard. The result is a dense, moist, bittersweet pudding/cake. Serving this warm with ice cream is a must. I go for Black Mint Milk Chocolate (page 211), but you can use any flavor you like.

Preheat the oven to 375°F.

Brush an 8-inch square baking dish with the butter, and sprinkle it with 1 tablespoon of the Demerara sugar.

Place the brioche cubes in a large bowl.

In a large heatproof bowl, whisk together the eggs, egg yolks, cocoa powder, and salt.

Combine the cream, milk, granulated sugar, and vanilla in a large saucepan. Heat over medium heat, stirring to dissolve the sugar, just to a bare simmer. Remove the pan from the heat and pour about one third of the cream mixture into the egg mixture. Whisk to combine well. Return the egg mixture to the remaining cream mixture, and whisk to combine. Strain the custard through a fine-mesh sieve directly into the bowl containing the bread cubes. Stir to coat all of the bread cubes with the custard.

Pour the bread and custard mixture into the prepared baking dish. Sprinkle with the remaining 1 tablespoon Demerara sugar, and cover the pan with aluminum foil. Bake, rotating the dish and removing the foil halfway through, until the top is crisp and toasted and the custard is set, about 45 minutes. Serve warm right from the oven, or cool to room temperature and then reheat in a 350°F oven for 10 minutes before serving.

### VARYING YOUR CRAFT
#### CHOCOLATE HAZELNUT BREAD PUDDING
Before transferring the bread and custard mixture to the baking dish, drizzle ¼ cup Nutella over the mixture and gently fold to combine. Before baking, sprinkle ¼ cup chopped hazelnuts, along with the Demerara sugar, over the top of the dish.

MAKES ONE 8-INCH
PUDDING/CAKE

1 tablespoon unsalted butter, at room temperature, for the pan

2 tablespoons Demerara sugar

1 loaf Chocolate Brioche (page 44), cut into 1½-inch cubes (6 cups)

2 large eggs

2 egg yolks

⅓ cup unsweetened cocoa powder

½ teaspoon kosher salt

1 cup heavy cream

1 cup whole milk

½ cup granulated sugar

1 teaspoon pure vanilla extract

# BERRY BRIOCHE
# BREAD PUDDING

This is a very flexible recipe. You can use one type of berry if you like, or substitute peaches or apricots for the berries, or even use bananas and chocolate chips. You can make your own brioche or purchase one from a good bakery.

MAKES ONE 8-INCH
PUDDING/CAKE

**1 tablespoon unsalted butter, at room temperature, for the pan**

**2 tablespoons Demerara sugar**

**1 Brioche Loaf (see page 40), cut into 1 ½-inch cubes (6 cups)**

**2 cups mixed fresh berries, such as blueberries, raspberries, blackberries, and strawberries**

**2 large eggs**

**2 large egg yolks**

**½ teaspoon kosher salt**

**1 cup heavy cream**

**1 cup whole milk**

**½ cup granulated sugar**

**¾ teaspoon pure vanilla extract**

Preheat the oven to 375°F. Brush an 8-inch square baking dish with the butter, and sprinkle it with 1 tablespoon of the Demerara sugar.

In a large bowl, toss the brioche cubes with the berries.

In a heatproof bowl, whisk together the eggs, egg yolks, and salt.

Combine the cream, milk, granulated sugar, and vanilla in a large saucepan. Heat over medium heat, stirring to dissolve the sugar, just to a bare simmer. Remove the pan from the heat and pour about one third of the cream mixture into the egg mixture. Whisk to combine well. Return the egg mixture to the remaining cream mixture, and whisk to combine. Strain the mixture through a fine-mesh sieve directly into the bowl containing the brioche and berries. Stir to coat all of the brioche cubes with the custard.

Pour the bread, berries, and custard mixture into the prepared baking dish. Sprinkle with the remaining 1 tablespoon Demerara sugar, and cover the dish with aluminum foil. Bake, rotating the dish and removing the foil halfway through, until the top is crisp and toasted and the custard is set, about 45 minutes. Serve warm right from the oven, or cool to room temperature and then reheat in a 350°F oven for 10 minutes before serving.

## VARYING YOUR CRAFT
### BANANA CARAMEL BREAD PUDDING
Substitute 2 ripe bananas, cut into ¼-inch slices, for the berries, and fold ½ cup Spiced Caramel Sauce (page 246) into the mixture right before baking.

# CHOCOLATE PUDDING

When you bake pudding in a water bath in the oven rather than cooking it in a pot on the stovetop, you can use egg yolks in lieu of cornstarch as a thickener. This technique produces a rich dessert with a deliciously creamy, silky-smooth texture. Top these with a dollop of crème fraîche or unsweetened whipped cream, if you like.

SERVES 6

3 ounces bittersweet chocolate (70%)

1 cup heavy cream

2 tablespoons sugar

¼ vanilla bean, split lengthwise, seeds scraped out, bean and seeds reserved

1 cup whole milk

⅛ teaspoon kosher salt

2 large egg yolks

Preheat the oven to 275°F.

Chop the chocolate into small pieces and place them in a medium bowl.

Combine the cream, sugar, and vanilla bean and seeds in a small saucepan, and bring to a boil. Pour half of the cream mixture over the chocolate and whisk well to combine. Add the remaining cream mixture and whisk well, making sure that all of the chocolate is melted. Remove the vanilla bean, rinse it, and reserve it for another use (see page 16). Whisk the milk and salt into the chocolate mixture.

Put the egg yolks in a large bowl. Add about half of the chocolate mixture and whisk to combine. Pour the chocolate-yolk mixture into the remaining chocolate mixture, and whisk to combine. Strain the mixture through a fine-mesh sieve into a bowl, and cool it in an ice bath or in the refrigerator.

Place six 4-ounce ramekins or custard cups in a deep baking dish or roasting pan, spacing them evenly. Divide the cooled chocolate mixture among the ramekins. Cover the baking dish with aluminum foil, leaving the front side loose. Carefully place the pan in the oven. Fill the baking dish with warm water to reach halfway up the sides of the ramekins, then seal the pan tightly with the foil.

Bake for 25 minutes. Then rotate the pan and let the steam out by lifting the foil; reseal the foil tightly. Continue baking, letting the steam out and resealing the foil every 10 minutes, until the edges of the puddings are darkened and set and the centers are lighter and slightly loose, about 20 minutes more (if the puddings appear to need more time, continue cooking, checking them at 5-minute intervals).

Remove the foil and carefully transfer the baking dish to a wire rack. Let the puddings cool to room temperature in the water bath. Then remove them from the water and refrigerate them, uncovered, for at least 1 hour before serving.

Once chilled, the puddings can be kept, loosely covered with plastic wrap, in the refrigerator for up to 2 days.

## VARYING YOUR CRAFT
### MINT CHOCOLATE PUDDING
Bring the bream to a boil. Remove from the heat and whisk in ¼ cup fresh peppermint leaves. Cover and let steep for 30 minutes. Strain. Use the flavored cream in place of the heavy cream in the recipe.

### MOCHA PUDDING
In place of the bittersweet chocolate, use 1½ ounces bittersweet chocolate and 1½ ounces milk chocolate. Combine the heavy cream with 2 tablespoons dark roast coffee beans in a small saucepan and bring to a boil. Remove from the heat. Cover and chill for at least 2 hours or overnight. Strain and use the flavored cream in place of the heavy cream in the recipe.

## COMBINING YOUR CRAFT
Chocolate Walnut Biscotti (page 78) are great alongside.

# JASMINE RICE PUDDING

Rice pudding is one of the easiest and most satisfying desserts. I like to use a risotto-style technique—stirring liquid into the rice little by little as it cooks over low heat—which makes for a very creamy pudding. As the rice pudding cools, it thickens. You can stir in more milk if you like a thinner consistency. Very comforting served warm on a chilly day, rice pudding is also delicious chilled in the summertime. Jasmine rice lends a nice floral note, though just about any rice can be used.

In a medium saucepan, combine the rice, cinnamon sticks, and lemon zest. Set the pan over medium-low heat and cook, stirring occasionally, until the rice has a nutty fragrance, about 5 minutes.

Add 1 cup water, increase the heat to medium, and cook, stirring occasionally, until most of the water has been absorbed, about 4 minutes. Add 1 cup of the milk and cook, stirring occasionally, until the rice kernels are visible and most of the milk has been absorbed, about 6 minutes. Add the remaining 1 cup milk and cook until the kernels are visible again and most of the milk has been absorbed, about 7 minutes.

Stir in the sugar and salt, and continue cooking until the liquid is mostly absorbed, about 3 minutes. Remove the pan from the heat and stir in the crème fraîche. Serve immediately, or chill over an ice bath and then refrigerate, covered, for up to 2 days. (The lemon zest and cinnamon sticks will continue to impart flavor. Remove just before serving.) Serve the rice pudding chilled, or reheat it gently in a saucepan, adding more milk as necessary to adjust the consistency.

## COMBINING YOUR CRAFT

Stir rum raisins (page 28) into warm rice pudding.

Serve chilled rice pudding with Chamomile Poached Apricots (page 234).

### SERVES 5

½ cup jasmine rice

2 cinnamon sticks, broken

Zest from ½ lemon, removed in strips with a vegetable peeler

2 cups whole milk

½ cup sugar

1 teaspoon kosher salt

½ cup crème fraîche

# BUTTERSCOTCH PUDDING

Just the right hint of salt balances the sweet and puts an adult twist on this rich childhood favorite.

SERVES 8

**2 cups heavy cream**

**1 cup whole milk**

**¼ cup packed brown sugar**

**¾ cup granulated sugar**

**3 tablespoons crème fraîche**

**1 teaspoon kosher salt**

**1 teaspoon pure vanilla extract**

**6 large egg yolks**

In a medium saucepan, combine the cream, milk, and brown sugar. Heat over medium-low heat, whisking, until the mixture is warm to the touch and the sugar is dissolved, about 7 minutes. Remove from the heat.

In a small saucepan, combine the granulated sugar and ¼ cup water, stirring to make sure all of the sugar is damp. Heat over high heat until the sugar becomes a yellow gold caramel, about 15 minutes. Remove the saucepan from the heat. Carefully whisk about ½ cup of the cream mixture into the caramel. Then add the caramel mixture to the remaining cream mixture, and whisk to combine. Whisk in the crème fraîche, salt, and vanilla.

Preheat the oven to 275°F.

Prepare an ice bath in a large bowl. Set the saucepan with the butterscotch mixture into the ice bath. Whisk until the mixture is chilled.

Put the egg yolks in a medium bowl. Add about 1 cup of the butterscotch mixture to the yolks and whisk well to combine. Add the yolk mixture to the remaining butterscotch mixture, and whisk well to combine. Strain through a fine-mesh sieve into a bowl.

Place eight 4-ounce ramekins or custard cups in a deep baking dish or roasting pan, spacing them evenly. Divide the mixture among the ramekins. Cover the baking dish with aluminum foil, leaving the front side loose. Carefully place the pan in the oven. Fill the baking dish with warm water to reach halfway up the sides of the ramekins, then seal the pan tightly with the foil.

Bake for 30 minutes. Then lift the foil to let the steam out and rotate the pan; tightly reseal the foil. Continue baking until the edges of the puddings are set and the centers are still slightly loose, 20 to 30 minutes more (if the puddings appear to need more time, continue cooking, checking them at 5-minute intervals).

Remove the foil and carefully transfer the baking dish from the oven to a wire rack. Let the puddings cool to room temperature in the water bath. Then remove them from the water and refrigerate them, uncovered, for at least 1 hour before serving.

Once chilled, the pudding can be kept in the refrigerator, loosely covered with plastic wrap, for up to 2 days.

## COMBINING YOUR CRAFT

Serve the puddings with a dollop of crème fraîche on top and Gingersnaps (page 63) on the side.

# ALMOND & SOUR CHERRY TRIFLE WITH LEMON CREAM

There's an elegance to trifles that even the fanciest cakes can't provide, yet they're so easy to put together. The curd, cake, and compote can be prepared two to three days ahead, leaving just the whipping of the cream and a quick assembly on the day of serving.

SERVES 8

**1 cup heavy cream**

**Lemon Curd (page 242)**

**Almond Pound Cake (page 144)**

**Sour Cherry Compote (page 235)**

In a bowl, whip the cream until it forms soft peaks. Fold about half of it into the lemon curd; then fold the remaining whipped cream into the curd.

Trim the crust off the pound cake, so that there is only yellow cake left. Cut the cake into 2½-inch-thick slices, and then cut each slice into 2½-inch cubes. Save any scraps to make smaller cubes to garnish the top of the trifle.

Into a 4-quart glass trifle dish or serving bowl, pour about one third of the lemon cream, spreading it to cover the bottom of the dish. Arrange 4 cake cubes on top, positioning some flat up against the glass and others with only an edge touching the glass. Spoon about half of the sour cherry compote over the cake, letting the cherries fall into the spaces around the cake. Add another third of the lemon cream, topping it with 3 or 4 cake cubes. Then top that layer with all but about 1 tablespoon of the remaining sour cherry compote. Finish with the remaining lemon cream, spreading it to cover the top of the trifle smoothly and evenly.

Just before serving, garnish the top with a few smaller cubes of pound cake and the remaining cherries.

The trifle is best when assembled 4 to 6 hours before eating and can be kept, loosely covered with plastic wrap, in the refrigerator for up to 2 days.

# LEMON RASPBERRY CRÈME BRÛLÉE

When you want something sweet but not heavy, these pretty brûlées are perfect. Tangy lemon and slightly sweet raspberries cleanse the palate and lighten up a classically rich dessert.

SERVES 6

2 cups heavy cream

¼ cup plus 2 tablespoons granulated sugar

½ teaspoon pure vanilla extract

Finely grated zest of 4 lemons

¼ cup strained fresh lemon juice (from 1½ lemons)

½ teaspoon kosher salt

4 large egg yolks

1 pint fresh raspberries

3 teaspoons Demerara sugar

Prepare an ice bath in a large bowl.

In a medium saucepan, bring the cream, granulated sugar, vanilla, and lemon zest just to a boil. Remove the pan from the heat and pour the mixture into a medium stainless-steel bowl. Set the bowl into the ice bath and stir until the mixture has cooled. Remove the bowl from the ice bath, and whisk in the lemon juice and salt. Cover, and refrigerate overnight.

Position a rack in the center of the oven and preheat the oven to 275°F.

In a large bowl, whisk the egg yolks together. Pour about one third of the chilled cream mixture into the yolks and whisk together well. Add the remaining cream mixture and whisk to combine. Strain the mixture through a fine-mesh sieve into a bowl.

Arrange six 4-ounce ramekins in a deep baking dish or roasting pan, spacing them evenly, and place 5 or 6 raspberries in a single layer in the bottom of each ramekin. Divide the custard among the ramekins, dunking the raspberries under with your finger. Cover the baking dish with aluminum foil, leaving the front side loose, and carefully place the dish in the oven. Fill the baking dish with warm water to reach halfway up the sides of the ramekins, then seal the pan tightly with the foil.

Bake for 20 minutes. Then lift the foil and release the steam; reseal the foil tightly and rotate the pan. Continue to bake until the edges of the custards are set but the centers are still quite loose, about 20 minutes more (if the custards appear to need more time, continue cooking, checking them and venting the steam at 5-minute intervals).

Remove the foil from the baking dish and carefully transfer the dish to a wire rack. Let the custards cool to room temperature in the water bath. Then remove them from the baking dish and refrigerate them, uncovered, for at least 30 minutes. (Once cold, the custards can be kept, loosely covered with plastic wrap, in the refrigerator for up to 2 days.)

To serve, remove the custards from the refrigerator, and using a paper towel, very gently blot any moisture from the surface.

Position a rack 8 inches from the heating element and preheat the oven to broil.

Sprinkle ½ teaspoon of the Demerara sugar evenly over each custard. Place the ramekins on a baking sheet and broil for 2 minutes. Rotate the sheet and continue broiling until the sugar is melted and caramelized, about 2 minutes more. Serve immediately.

COFFEE CRUNCH ICE CREAM, CACAO NIB BRITTLE,
AND HOT FUDGE SAUCE

# ICE CREAMS, SORBETS & FROZEN DESSERTS

# VANILLA BEAN
## ICE CREAM

If you think of vanilla as "plain," then you haven't yet tasted serious (and seriously yummy) vanilla ice cream. I make mine with both pure vanilla extract and vanilla beans, using two types of beans to create a complex flavor blend. Bourbon beans from Madagascar and the Comoros lend rich chocolaty flavors, while Tahitian beans offer floral notes and hints of tobacco and cherry. If you can't find both types, it's fine to use two of the same.

**MAKES ABOUT
1 ½ QUARTS**

**9 large egg yolks**

**1 cup sugar**

**2 cups whole milk**

**2 cups heavy cream**

**2 vanilla beans, preferably
1 Bourbon and 1 Tahitian, split
lengthwise, seeds scraped out,
beans and seeds reserved**

**½ teaspoon pure vanilla extract**

**½ teaspoon kosher salt**

In a large heatproof bowl, whisk together the egg yolks and ½ cup of the sugar until the mixture is pale yellow.

In a large saucepan, whisk together the remaining ½ cup sugar, the milk, cream, and vanilla beans and seeds. Bring the mixture to a full boil, and then, as soon as it begins to rise up the sides of the pan, remove the pan from the heat. In a slow and steady stream, pour about one third of the milk mixture into the egg yolk mixture and whisk to combine. Return the egg yolk mixture to the remaining milk mixture, and whisk to combine well. Whisk in the vanilla extract and salt.

Pour the hot custard into a bowl. Cover it with plastic wrap and refrigerate for at least 8 hours, or overnight.

Strain the custard through a fine-mesh sieve into a bowl. Recycle the vanilla beans (see page 16). Freeze the custard in an ice cream maker, following the manufacturer's directions.

Transfer the ice cream to an airtight container, and place plastic wrap directly over the surface of the ice cream to prevent ice crystals from forming. Cover the container and freeze until firm, about 2 hours. (The ice cream will keep up to 5 days.)

# COFFEE CRUNCH
# ICE CREAM

The "crunch" in this ice cream comes from the broken bits of Cacao Nib Brittle, which are stirred in just before freezing. I like a dollop of fresh whipped cream and an extra sprinkling of brittle on top.

In large heatproof bowl, whisk together the egg yolks and ½ cup of the sugar until the mixture is pale yellow.

In a large saucepan, whisk together the remaining ½ cup sugar, the milk, cream, coffee beans, and vanilla bean and seeds. Bring the mixture to a full boil, and then, as soon as it begins to rise up the sides of the pan, remove the pan from the heat.

Immediately pour about 1 cup of the hot milk mixture into the egg yolk mixture in a slow and steady stream and whisk to combine. Then return the egg yolk mixture to the remaining milk mixture. Whisk in the salt.

Pour the custard into a bowl, cover it with plastic wrap, and refrigerate until it is very cold, at least 8 hours, or overnight.

Strain the custard through a fine-mesh sieve into a bowl, and discard the coffee beans. Recycle the vanilla bean (see page 16). Freeze the custard in an ice cream maker, following the manufacturer's directions.

Fold the brittle into the ice cream with a rubber spatula. Transfer the ice cream to an airtight container, and place plastic wrap directly over the surface of the ice cream to prevent ice crystals from forming. Cover the container and freeze until firm, about 2 hours. (The ice cream will keep for up to 5 days.)

## VARYING YOUR CRAFT
### SAIGON CINNAMON ICE CREAM
Substitute ½ cup Saigon cinnamon bark or eight 3-inch cinnamon sticks (see Sources) for the coffee beans. Toast them in a sauté pan over medium heat until they become fragrant, about 5 minutes. Just as you do with the coffee beans, leave the cinnamon in the custard base until just before freezing.

MAKES ABOUT
1 ½ QUARTS

**9 large egg yolks**

**1 cup sugar**

**2 cups whole milk**

**2 cups heavy cream**

**½ cup whole coffee beans**

**½ vanilla bean, split lengthwise, seeds scraped out, bean and seeds reserved**

**½ teaspoon kosher salt**

**1 cup crushed Cacao Nib Brittle (page 100)**

**NOTE** If you don't have time to make the brittle, you can still use this recipe for a great coffee ice cream without the crunch.

# BANANA MALT
## ICE CREAM

Great on its own and even better with a generous swirl of hot fudge sauce on top, this ice cream is one of my favorites. Barley malt syrup can be found at most health food stores. Ovaltine or another malt powder, available in the supermarket, can be substituted in the same amount.

MAKES ABOUT
1½ QUARTS

**5 large egg yolks**

**1 cup barley malt syrup (see Sources)**

**½ cup plus 3 tablespoons sugar**

**1½ cups whole milk**

**1 cup heavy cream**

**½ vanilla bean, split lengthwise, seeds scraped out, bean and seeds reserved**

**½ teaspoon kosher salt**

**1 cup puréed ripe banana (about 2 medium bananas)**

In a large heatproof bowl, whisk together the egg yolks, barley malt syrup, and about half of the sugar until well combined.

In a medium saucepan, whisk together the remaining sugar, the milk, cream, and vanilla bean and seeds. Bring the mixture to a full boil, and then, as soon as it begins to rise up the sides of the pan, remove the pan from the heat. In a slow and steady stream, pour about one third of the milk mixture into the egg yolk mixture and whisk to combine. Return the egg yolk mixture to the remaining milk mixture, and whisk to combine well. Whisk in the salt. Pour the custard into a bowl, cover it with plastic wrap, and refrigerate for at least 8 hours, or overnight.

Whisk the banana purée into the cold custard. Then strain the custard through a fine-mesh sieve into a bowl. Recycle the vanilla bean (see page 16). Freeze the custard in an ice cream maker, following the manufacturer's directions.

Transfer the ice cream to an airtight container, and place plastic wrap directly over the surface of the ice cream to prevent ice crystals from forming. Cover the container and freeze until firm, about 2 hours. (The ice cream will keep for up to 5 days.)

### COMBINING YOUR CRAFT
Serve with Hot Fudge Sauce (page 245).

# CARAMEL
## ICE CREAM

I like to push sugar to its darkest reaches for this ice cream, creating a rich caramel with a slightly roasted flavor.

In a large heatproof bowl, whisk together the egg yolks and ¼ cup of the sugar until the mixture is pale yellow.

In a large saucepan, stir together the remaining 1 cup sugar, the vanilla bean and seeds, and ½ cup water. Heat the mixture over high heat, without stirring, until the sugar syrup turns a dark brown color and begins to smoke, about 5 minutes. Remove the pan from the heat, and in a slow and steady stream, carefully add the cream (the mixture will bubble vigorously), and then the milk. Return the pan to medium heat and stir until any caramel bits dissolve and the mixture comes to a rolling boil, 3 to 4 minutes. As soon as the mixture begins to rise up the sides of the pan, remove the pan from the heat. Immediately pour about 1 cup of the hot caramel mixture into the egg yolk mixture in a steady stream, and whisk to combine. Then return the egg yolk mixture to the remaining caramel mixture. Whisk in the vanilla extract and salt.

Pour the custard into a bowl. Cover it with plastic wrap and refrigerate until it is very cold, at least 8 hours, or overnight.

Strain the custard through a fine-mesh sieve into a bowl. Recycle the vanilla bean (see page 16). Freeze the custard in an ice cream maker, following the manufacturer's directions.

Transfer the ice cream to an airtight container, and place plastic wrap directly over the surface of the ice cream to prevent ice crystals from forming. Cover the container and freeze until firm, about 2 hours. (The ice cream will keep for up to 5 days.)

### VARYING YOUR CRAFT
**CARAMEL CRUNCH ICE CREAM**
Fold 1 cup crushed Honeycomb Brittle (page 100) into finished ice cream before freezing.

**MAKES ABOUT 1½ QUARTS**

**9 large egg yolks**

**1¼ cups sugar**

**½ vanilla bean, split lengthwise, seeds scraped out, bean and seeds reserved**

**2 cups heavy cream**

**2 cups whole milk**

**½ teaspoon pure vanilla extract**

**½ teaspoon kosher salt**

**TIP** The darker your caramel for this ice cream, the deeper the flavor. When the caramel turns a very dark brown, approaching black, it's ready (see page 20 for caramel tips).

# PUMPKIN ICE CREAM

Here, all of the flavors of a well-spiced pumpkin pie are churned into a creamy ice cream. A great fall dessert, especially festive at Thanksgiving.

In a large heatproof bowl, whisk together the egg yolks and granulated sugar until the mixture is pale yellow.

In a large saucepan, whisk together the milk, cream, brown sugar, vanilla bean and seeds, ginger, ground cinnamon, and the cinnamon stick. Bring the mixture to a full boil, and then, as soon as it begins to rise up the sides of the pan, remove the pan from the heat.

Immediately pour about 1 cup of the hot milk mixture into the egg yolk mixture in a slow and steady stream and whisk to combine. Then return the egg yolk mixture to the remaining milk mixture. Whisk in the nutmeg and the salt.

Pour the custard into a bowl. Cover it with plastic wrap and refrigerate until it is very cold, at least 8 hours, or overnight.

Whisk the pumpkin purée into the chilled custard, and strain it through a fine-mesh sieve into a bowl. Discard the cinnamon stick. Recycle the vanilla bean (see page 16). Freeze the custard in an ice cream maker, following the manufacturer's directions.

Transfer the ice cream to an airtight container, and place plastic wrap directly over the surface of the ice cream to prevent ice crystals from forming. Cover the container and freeze until firm, about 2 hours. (The ice cream will keep for up to 5 days.)

## COMBINING YOUR CRAFT

Make a Pumpkin Ice Cream Sundae with Spiced Caramel Sauce (page 246) and Gingerbread Croutons (page 163).

MAKES ABOUT
1 QUART

**5 large egg yolks**

**⅓ cup plus 2 tablespoons granulated sugar**

**1½ cups whole milk**

**1 cup heavy cream**

**¼ cup packed dark brown sugar, or organic dark brown molasses sugar, such as Billington's**

**½ vanilla bean, split lengthwise, seeds scraped out, bean and seeds reserved**

**1 teaspoon grated fresh ginger**

**½ teaspoon ground cinnamon**

**1 cinnamon stick**

**½ teaspoon freshly grated nutmeg**

**¼ teaspoon kosher salt**

**¾ cup canned pumpkin purée**

# BROWN BUTTER
# ICE CREAM

The fact that rich, toasty browned butter can be infused into milk and cream proves the nearly limitless possibilities of flavoring and making great ice creams. Delicious on its own, this ice cream is also good with baked apples or any apple dessert, pecan or any other nut pie, fresh berries, and even sectioned blood oranges.

**MAKES ABOUT
1½ QUARTS**

**8 ounces (2 sticks) unsalted butter, cut into small pieces**

**1 cup heavy cream**

**3 cups whole milk**

**9 large egg yolks**

**1 cup sugar**

**½ vanilla bean, split lengthwise, seeds scraped out, bean and seeds reserved**

**¾ teaspoon kosher salt**

**TIP** It's very important to let the butter cool adequately before whisking in the cream and milk. The mixture will bubble over the top of the saucepan if this is done too soon.

**NOTE** Once the flavor has been infused, the butter is discarded, so the recipe is not as rich as it might seem at first glance.

Put the butter in a large saucepan and cook it over medium-high heat until it is fragrant and dark brown (you will have some burned butter solids on the bottom of the pan; this is okay), 8 to 10 minutes. Remove the pan from the heat and let the butter cool for 5 minutes. Slowly whisk in the cream, then the milk. Pour the mixture into a bowl, cover it with plastic wrap, and refrigerate for at least 8 hours, or overnight.

In a large heatproof bowl, whisk together the egg yolks and ½ cup of the sugar until the mixture is pale yellow.

Whisk the chilled milk mixture well to break up any large hard pieces of brown butter. Strain it through a fine-mesh sieve into a saucepan, discarding any pieces of brown butter. Whisk in the remaining ½ cup sugar and the vanilla bean and seeds. Bring the mixture to a full boil, and then, as soon as it begins to rise up the sides of the pan, remove the pan from the heat.

Immediately pour about 1 cup of the hot milk mixture into the egg yolk mixture in a slow and steady stream and whisk to combine. Then return the egg yolk mixture to the remaining milk mixture. Whisk in the salt.

Pour the custard into a bowl. Cover it with plastic wrap, and refrigerate until it is very cold, at least 8 hours, or overnight.

Strain the custard through a fine-mesh sieve into a bowl. Recycle the vanilla bean (see page 16). Freeze the custard in an ice cream maker, following the manufacturer's directions.

Transfer the ice cream to an airtight container, and place plastic wrap directly over the surface of the ice cream to prevent ice crystals from forming. Cover the container and freeze until firm, about 2 hours. (The ice cream will keep for up to 5 days.)

# BLACK MINT MILK
## CHOCOLATE ICE CREAM

Black mint has a very dark green flat leaf and an intensely refreshing flavor. I find it at my local farmer's market in the summer and well through the fall. It's the only variety I use for this ice cream, which is very smooth, deeply chocolaty, and deliciously minty.

Put the chocolate in a large heatproof bowl and set aside.

In another large heatproof bowl, whisk together the egg yolks and ⅓ cup of the sugar until the mixture is pale yellow.

In a large saucepan, whisk together the milk, cream, the remaining ⅓ cup sugar, and the vanilla bean and seeds. Bring the mixture to a full boil, and then, as soon as it begins to rise up the sides of the pan, remove the pan from the heat.

Whisk about 1 cup of the hot milk mixture into the egg yolk mixture in a slow and steady stream. Then pour the egg yolk mixture back into the remaining milk mixture. Add the salt and whisk together to combine. Pour about one third of the custard over the chocolate and whisk until the chocolate is melted. Add the remaining custard and whisk to combine. Then add the mint and stir to combine.

Prepare an ice bath in a large bowl. Place the bowl of custard in the ice bath and let stand at room temperature for 1 hour. Then strain the cooled custard through a fine-mesh sieve into a bowl. Discard the mint. Recycle the vanilla bean (see page 16). Cover the bowl and refrigerate the custard for at least 8 hours, or overnight.

Freeze the custard in an ice cream maker, following the manufacturer's directions.

Transfer the ice cream to an airtight container, and place plastic wrap directly over the surface of the ice cream to prevent ice crystals from forming. Cover the container and freeze until firm, about 2 hours. (The ice cream will keep for up to 5 days.)

**MAKES ABOUT
1½ QUARTS**

**6 ounces milk chocolate, roughly chopped**

**9 large egg yolks**

**⅔ cup sugar**

**2 cups whole milk**

**2 cups heavy cream**

**½ vanilla bean, split lengthwise, seeds scraped out, bean and seeds reserved**

**½ teaspoon kosher salt**

**½ cup packed black mint leaves**

# STRAWBERRY ICE CREAM

My all-time-favorite ice cream! Make this one with the juiciest local strawberries you can find. It's not worth the time and effort with store-bought berries, which do not have the same quality of freshness or flavor. The fact that strawberry season is short makes it all the more special.

**MAKES ABOUT 1½ QUARTS**

1¼ cups plus 2 tablespoons sugar

1 pint fresh strawberries, hulled, large berries halved

9 large egg yolks

2 cups whole milk

2 cups heavy cream

½ vanilla bean, split lengthwise, seeds scraped out, bean and seeds reserved

½ teaspoon kosher salt

**NOTE** To make this ice cream, you prepare a quick fruit preserve. Cooking the fruit first, as opposed to just folding the fresh pieces into the ice cream before freezing it, produces a finished product that is filled with creamy fruit flavor and flavorful pieces of tender (not icy) fruit. You can use this method with any other berry or with stone fruits, like peaches or plums.

In a bowl, combine ½ cup plus 2 tablespoons of the sugar and the berries, stirring well to moisten all of the sugar. Cover the bowl with plastic wrap and let it sit at room temperature for 1 hour, or refrigerate it overnight.

Scrape the strawberries and their liquid into a small saucepan and bring to a boil. Reduce the heat to a simmer and cook until the strawberries are tender, about 5 minutes. Strain through a fine-mesh sieve into a bowl, and reserve the berries and the juice in separate containers. You should have about 1 cup juice and about ½ cup fruit. Refrigerate the containers for 1 hour, or overnight.

In a heatproof bowl, whisk the egg yolks with 6 tablespoons of the sugar until the mixture is pale yellow.

In a large saucepan, whisk together the milk, cream, the remaining 6 tablespoons sugar, and the vanilla bean and seeds. Bring the mixture to a full boil, and then, as soon as it begins to rise up the sides of the pan, remove the pan from the heat.

Immediately pour about 1 cup of the hot milk mixture into the egg yolk mixture in a slow and steady stream and whisk to combine. Then return the egg yolk mixture to the remaining milk mixture. Whisk in the salt.

Pour the custard into a bowl, cover it with plastic wrap, and refrigerate until it is very cold, at least 8 hours, or overnight.

Add the strawberry juice to the chilled custard and whisk to combine. Strain the custard through a fine-mesh sieve into a bowl. Recycle the vanilla bean (see page 16).

Freeze the custard in an ice cream maker, following the manufacturer's directions.

Fold the strawberries into the ice cream with a rubber spatula, making sure to distribute them evenly. Transfer the ice cream to an airtight container, and place plastic wrap directly over the surface of the ice cream to prevent ice crystals from forming. Cover the container and freeze until firm, about 2 hours. (The ice cream will keep for up to 5 days.)

### VARYING YOUR CRAFT

**PEACH ICE CREAM**

Pit and roughly chop 2 pounds of peaches, and use them in place of the strawberries.

**BLUEBERRY ICE CREAM**

Substitute 1 pint of blueberries for the strawberries.

## BUILDING YOUR CRAFT
# ICE CREAM

The base of all homemade ice creams is a sauce or custard called *anglaise*—a simple combination of milk, cream, and sugar thickened with egg yolks. Although it may not seem so, when you make an anglaise for ice cream, you are cooking the eggs. This process must be done with care so that the eggs cook but do not scramble. The key to success here is first to make sure that your milk mixture in the first step comes to a full and rising boil. Take the liquid to the point where it is rising up the sides of the saucepan and just before it boils over. This happens fast, so be sure to pay close attention and be ready to move your pot off the heat at just the right moment.

A small amount of the very hot milk mixture is then added to the egg yolks—just enough so that the heat of the mixture begins to cook the yolks, while not overwhelming and scrambling them. This process of slowly heating the yolks is called "tempering." The tempered yolk mixture is then added back to the remaining hot milk mixture, where it cooks further via the residual heat of the contents of the pot and, within a minute or two, thickens. The mixture is then cooled and later frozen to form ice cream.

# APRICOT
# SORBET

The natural pectin in apricots gives this sorbet a scrumptiously smooth and creamy texture. You can make a more rustic version, if you like, by leaving the puréed fruit unstrained. Vitamin C powder allows the fruit to retain its brilliant orange hue.

MAKES ABOUT
1 QUART

**1 pound firm-ripe apricots (about 10), pitted and cut into eighths**

**1¼ cups sugar**

**½ teaspoon vitamin C powder (see Sources)**

Combine the apricots, ¼ cup of the sugar, and the vitamin C powder in a bowl and stir together well. Cover the surface of the fruit mixture with plastic wrap to prevent browning, and seal the bowl well with a second sheet of plastic wrap. Refrigerate for at least 6 hours, or overnight.

In a small saucepan, bring the remaining 1 cup sugar and 2¾ cups water to a boil, whisking to dissolve the sugar. Transfer the sugar syrup to a bowl, and refrigerate until it is cold, about 1 hour.

Scrape the apricots and their juices into a blender, and purée until smooth. Strain the mixture through a fine-mesh sieve into a bowl, pressing well with a spatula to extract all of the liquid. You should have about 1½ cups of apricot purée. Discard the solids.

Add the chilled sugar syrup to the strained apricot purée, and whisk well to combine. Freeze in an ice cream maker, following the manufacturer's directions.

Transfer the sorbet to an airtight container, and place plastic wrap directly on the surface of the sorbet to prevent ice crystals from forming. Cover the container and freeze until firm, about 2 hours. (The sorbet will keep for up to 5 days.)

## VARYING YOUR CRAFT
### SOUR CHERRY SORBET

Luscious juicy sour cherries enjoy just a short season—about a month in early summer—but you can make this sorbet year round, using thawed good-quality frozen sour cherries. Substitute 3½ cups sour cherries, stemmed and pitted, for the apricots (you will have about 2 cups cherry purée) and use 2 cups of water instead of 2¾.

# TOASTED ALMOND MILK SORBET

An unexpected ingredient, olive oil, lends both a nice smooth texture and a subtle fruit flavor to this sorbet. Use a good-quality fruity-tasting oil rather than a grassy or peppery type.

MAKES ABOUT
1 QUART

**1 cup sliced blanched almonds**

**3 cups whole milk**

**¾ cup plus 1 tablespoon sugar**

**¼ teaspoon kosher salt**

**½ cup plus 2 tablespoons extra-virgin olive oil**

Preheat the oven to 350°F. Line a baking sheet with parchment paper.

Spread the almonds on the prepared baking sheet and toast in the oven until they are dark golden, about 10 minutes. Remove the baking sheet from the oven and transfer the almonds to a large saucepan. Add the milk and sugar and bring to a rolling boil over medium-high heat. Transfer the mixture to a blender, add the salt, and purée until smooth. With the machine running, slowly add the oil.

Refrigerate the almond milk mixture in a covered container for 8 hours, or overnight.

Strain the chilled almond milk through a fine-mesh sieve, pressing well with a spatula to extract all of the liquid. Freeze the mixture in an ice cream maker, following the manufacturer's directions.

Transfer the sorbet to an airtight container, and place plastic wrap directly over the surface of the sorbet to prevent ice crystals from forming. Cover the container and freeze until firm, about 2 hours. (The sorbet will keep for up to 5 days.)

# COCONUT SORBET

When I worked at Craft restaurant, we had a loyal customer who dined with us about twice a week. For dessert he'd start with up to six scoops of this sorbet, then often order three more. Every Christmas he sent me a bottle of Dom Pérignon with a note saying, "For the great desserts . . ." though he never once strayed from his dessert of choice! This is a very smooth sorbet—milky and fresh tasting. The lime juice adds a subtle brightness and enhances the coconut flavor.

In a large saucepan, combine the milk, coconut flakes, and sugar. Bring to a rolling boil. Remove the pan from the heat and whisk in the lime juice and salt. Pour the mixture into a bowl, cover it, and refrigerate for at least 8 hours, or up to 2 days.

Strain the chilled mixture through a fine-mesh sieve into a bowl and discard the coconut. Freeze the mixture in an ice cream maker, following the manufacturer's directions.

Transfer the sorbet to an airtight container, and place plastic wrap directly over the surface of the sorbet to prevent ice crystals from forming. Cover the container and freeze until the sorbet is firm, about 2 hours. (The sorbet will keep for up to 5 days.)

**MAKES ABOUT 1 QUART**

**6 cups whole milk**

**2 cups unsweetened coconut flakes**

**1½ cups sugar**

**1 tablespoon fresh lime juice**

**¼ teaspoon kosher salt**

# BLOOD ORANGE SORBET

This tangy brilliant crimson-colored sorbet brightens the cold winter months.

In a small saucepan, whisk together the sugar and 1 cup water. Bring to a boil, whisking to dissolve the sugar. Transfer the sugar syrup to a bowl and refrigerate it until it is cold, about 1 hour.

In a large bowl, mix the blood orange juice with the chilled sugar syrup. Freeze the mixture in an ice cream maker, following the manufacturer's directions.

Transfer the sorbet to an airtight container, and place plastic wrap directly on the surface of the sorbet to prevent ice crystals from forming. Cover the container and freeze until firm, about 2 hours. (The sorbet will keep for up to 5 days.)

**MAKES ABOUT 1½ QUARTS**

**1¼ cups sugar**

**1 quart fresh blood orange juice**

# RASPBERRY PROSECCO SORBET

Prosecco, a bubbly wine from Italy's Veneto region, makes a perfect pairing with fruit. Think "mimosa" and you get the idea. Both the effervescence and the flavors of the wine carry through in this sorbet. Some proseccos have a touch of melon flavor; others are a little lemony and floral, or have tropical notes or a touch of honey flavor. Some are drier than others. Any prosecco you enjoy drinking is a good one to use for this dessert.

In a bowl, gently mash together the raspberries and 3 tablespoons of the sugar so that the juice from the raspberries dampens the sugar. Cover and let stand at room temperature for 1 hour, or refrigerate overnight.

In a small saucepan, combine the remaining 1 cup sugar with ¾ cup water. Bring to a boil, whisking to dissolve the sugar. Transfer the sugar syrup to a bowl and refrigerate until it is cold, about 1 hour.

Scrape the raspberries and their juices into a blender, add 1½ cups cold water, and purée until smooth. Strain the purée through a fine-mesh sieve into a bowl, pressing the purée with a spatula to extract as much liquid as possible. There should be only dry seeds left in the sieve, and you should have about 3 cups of raspberry purée. Discard the seeds. Add the sugar syrup and the prosecco to the strained purée, and whisk together to combine.

Freeze the sorbet base in an ice cream maker, following the manufacturer's directions. (Because of the alcohol, this sorbet will still be slushy when it comes out of the machine.)

Transfer the sorbet to an airtight container, and place plastic wrap directly over the surface to prevent ice crystals from forming. Cover the container and freeze until firm, about 2 hours. (The sorbet will keep for up to 5 days.)

## VARYING YOUR CRAFT
**TANGERINE PROSECCO SORBET**
Use 3 cups strained fresh tangerine juice in place of the raspberries and the 3 tablespoons sugar.

**MAKES ABOUT 1 QUART**

1½ cups fresh raspberries
1 cup plus 3 tablespoons sugar
1½ cups prosecco

# CACAO NIB GRANITA

This granita is a lot like a fudgesicle—my favorite childhood frozen dessert—in both flavor and texture. Using a food processor to purée the frozen granita makes for small ice crystals, hence a smoother texture than you get from scraping with a fork (the more common technique). A few scoops in a bowl with whipped cream on top is divine.

**MAKES 1 QUART**

**3 cups whole milk**

**½ cup sugar**

**¼ cup cacao nibs (see page 15)**

**2 tablespoons unsweetened cocoa powder**

**½ teaspoon pure vanilla extract**

**¼ teaspoon kosher salt**

Whisk together the milk, sugar, cacao nibs, cocoa powder, vanilla, and salt in a large saucepan and bring to a boil. Remove the pan from the heat and pour the mixture into a bowl. Cover with plastic wrap and refrigerate until cold, about 1 hour.

Strain the granita mixture through a fine-mesh sieve into a shallow nonreactive baking pan. Freeze until solid, at least 2 hours, or overnight.

Transfer the frozen granita to a food processor, and purée it. Transfer the purée to an airtight container, and place plastic wrap directly over the surface of the granita to prevent ice crystals from forming. Cover the container and freeze until the granita is firm, about 1 hour, or up to 4 hours before serving. (The granita will keep for up to 5 days.)

# ALMOND FIG SEMIFREDDO

*Semifreddo* means "half-frozen" in Italian and refers to the smooth, mousse-like texture of this elegant dessert. Simple to make, this version is layered with a purée of fresh figs and a toasted almond crumb. Frozen in a loaf pan, its pretty layers are revealed when the loaf is cut into slices.

**FOR THE ALMOND CRUMB:** Preheat the oven to 350°F. Line a baking sheet with parchment paper.

Spread the almonds on the prepared baking sheet and toast in the oven until they are dark golden brown and fragrant, about 10 minutes. Remove from the oven and let cool to room temperature.

In the bowl of a food processor, combine the cooled toasted almonds, almond paste, sugar, and salt. Process until finely ground and well combined. Set the almond crumb aside.

**FOR THE FIG PURÉE:** Cut the figs in half lengthwise. Combine the honey, lemon juice, and vanilla bean and seeds in a skillet and bring to a boil over medium-high heat. Place the figs in the skillet, cut sides down, and cook until tender, 2 to 3 minutes. Remove the pan from the heat. Remove the vanilla bean and recycle it (see page 16). Transfer the mixture to a blender, and purée until finely chopped. Set the purée aside.

**FOR THE SEMIFREDDO:** Lightly coat the bottom and sides of an 8½ x 4½-inch loaf pan with nonstick cooking spray. Line the pan with plastic wrap, leaving a 2-inch overhang on all sides.

In the bowl of an electric mixer fitted with the whisk attachment, combine the eggs and egg yolk. Beat on medium speed.

Meanwhile, stir together the sugar and ¼ cup water in a small saucepan. Cook over medium heat until the sugar reaches the soft ball stage (240°F on a candy thermometer), or until the bubbles pop slowly and the sugar syrup appears thick but still has no color, about 5 minutes. With the mixer running, in a slow, steady stream, pouring along the inside of the bowl, add the sugar syrup to the eggs. Add the salt and vanilla extract. Increase the speed to high and beat until the mixture is cool, about 7 minutes. Transfer the mixture to a large bowl.

**ALMOND CRUMB**

¾ cup sliced blanched almonds

¼ cup plus 2 tablespoons almond paste (see Sources)

3 tablespoons sugar

¼ teaspoon kosher salt

**FIG PURÉE**

2 cups fresh black Mission figs, stemmed

¼ cup honey

1 tablespoon strained fresh lemon juice

½ vanilla bean, split lengthwise, seeds scraped out, bean and seeds reserved

**SEMIFREDDO**

Nonstick cooking spray

2 large eggs

1 large egg yolk

¼ cup pus 2 tablespoons sugar

¼ teaspoon kosher salt

½ teaspoon pure vanilla extract

1½ cups heavy cream

RECIPE CONTINUES

In a medium bowl, whip the cream to soft peaks.

Using a rubber spatula, in three additions, fold the whipped cream into the egg mixture. Fold in about half of the almond crumb. Pour about one third of this mixture into the prepared loaf pan, and spread it out evenly with a spatula.

Fold about ¼ cup of the remaining egg mixture into the remaining almond crumb (this ensures that the crumb and the mousse will bind together and not break apart when unmolded). Add the crumb mixture to the loaf pan and spread it out evenly. Top with the fig purée. Add the remaining egg mixture and spread it out evenly to create the top layer.

Tap the loaf pan on the counter a couple of times to eliminate any air bubbles. Cover the surface of the semifreddo with plastic wrap or waxed paper, gently pressing so it adheres. Wrap the pan in plastic wrap. Freeze until firm, at least 3 hours, or up to 5 days.

To serve, remove both the outer layer of plastic wrap and the layer covering the surface of the semifreddo. Pull on the over-hanging plastic lining to loosen the semifreddo, and invert it onto a serving platter. Unwrap it completely. Using a long serrated knife, cut the semifreddo into slices. Serve immediately.

## VARYING YOUR CRAFT
## ALMOND APRICOT SEMIFREDDO

Substitute 1 cup strained Apricot Compote (page 237) or 1 cup apricot preserves for the fig purée.

## ALMOND CHERRY SEMIFREDDO

½ cup sugar

1½ cups Bing cherries, stemmed and pitted

Combine the sugar and ½ cup water in a medium saucepan. Bring to a boil. Add the cherries, reduce to a gentle simmer, and cook for 10 minutes. Remove from the heat, and strain the cherries.

Substitute the cherries for the fig purée.

# ROASTED & POACHED FRUITS, FRUIT COMPOTES & SAUCES

# CARAMELIZED ROASTED PEACHES

A fresh, juicy, ripe peach makes for one of the most perfect desserts unto itself. That said, when you have great peaches and want to use them in a quick, unfussy dessert, this caramel-based sweet is just the thing. Apple juice thins out the caramel, making a nice light sauce.

**SERVES 6**

⅓ cup sugar

½ "recycled" vanilla bean (see page 16) or ¼ vanilla bean, split and scraped, bean and seeds reserved

3 large ripe peaches, halved and pitted

½ cup apple juice, or more if needed

Position a rack in the center of the oven and preheat the oven to 375°F.

In a large ovenproof skillet, mix together the sugar, ¼ cup water, and the vanilla bean (including seeds if using a fresh bean) and cook over high heat until the sugar becomes a dark golden caramel, about 7 minutes.

Place the peach halves in the skillet, cut side down, and reduce the heat to medium-high. Cook until the peaches are deep golden on the cut side and are starting to become tender, about 4 minutes. Flip the peaches over and carefully add the apple juice. Continue cooking just until the caramel and apple juice melt together to form a sauce, 2 to 3 minutes.

Transfer the skillet to the oven and roast, basting the peaches with the pan juices halfway through, until the peaches are tender to the touch and cooked through, about 10 minutes. You want a light, not too thick and sticky, caramel sauce. If the sauce thickens too much, thin it with up to ¼ cup additional apple juice.

Serve warm, straight from the oven. Or to serve the peaches up to 3 hours later, first cool them, still in the skillet, to room temperature; then reheat in a 375°F oven for 5 minutes just before serving.

# SPICED RED WINE ROASTED FIGS

Basting fresh figs in a cinnamon, black pepper, and clove–spiced wine syrup makes a sophisticated, not-too-sweet end to a meal—and one that's quick and easy.

3 cinnamon sticks

5 whole cloves

1 teaspoon whole black peppercorns

1½ cups full-bodied red wine, such as Cabernet or Shiraz

1½ cups sugar

Zest of 1 orange, removed in strips with a vegetable peeler

1 pint black Mission figs

Medium-coarse sea salt

NOTE These make a great spoon sweet on their own. They're also nice over creamy Greek yogurt, ice cream, simple cakes, or panna cottas.

In a large heavy saucepan, toast the cinnamon sticks, cloves, and peppercorns over medium heat, stirring occasionally, until fragrant, about 5 minutes. Whisk in the wine, sugar, and orange zest. Bring the mixture to a boil. Then reduce the heat and simmer until the liquid is reduced to about 1½ cups and bubbles up when stirred, about 15 minutes.

Remove the pan from the heat and strain the spiced wine syrup through a fine-mesh sieve into a medium bowl. Discard the spices and zest. (The spiced wine syrup can be cooled and then kept in a covered container in the refrigerator for up to 1 month.)

Cut the figs in half lengthwise, removing the stems. In a large skillet, bring ¾ cup of the spiced wine syrup to a boil over medium-high heat. Working in batches, arrange the figs, cut side down, in a single layer in the skillet. Cook the figs, basting them and gently turning them once with a spoon, until tender and softened, about 30 seconds per side. Transfer the figs to serving bowls, and when all figs are cooked, pour the wine from the pan over the top. Sprinkle each serving with a pinch or two of salt. Serve warm or at room temperature.

## VARYING YOUR CRAFT
### FIG AND SPICED WINE PRESERVES
Purée the roasted figs and the spiced wine syrup from the skillet in a food processor until smooth. Use extra syrup as needed to adjust the consistency. Makes 2 cups of preserves.

## COMBINING YOUR CRAFT
Serve these figs over Cream Cheese Panna Cotta (page 180) or Sheep's Milk Yogurt Panna Cotta (page 181), or with a slice of Almond Pound Cake (page 144) or Lemon Olive Oil Cake (page 148).

# RUM CARAMEL ROASTED BANANAS

I love the simple decadence of this warming dessert. The natural sugars really come forth from the bananas with just a simple roast in the rum-spiked caramel—a perfect melding of delicious tropical goodness.

Preheat the oven to 375°F.

Peel the bananas and cut them in half lengthwise.

In a large ovenproof skillet, stir together the sugar, vanilla bean (including seeds if using a fresh bean), and ¼ cup water. Cook over high heat until the mixture becomes a golden caramel, about 5 minutes. Arrange the bananas, cut side down, in one layer in the skillet and cook until they begin to caramelize and brown, about 3 minutes. Flip them over, add the rum, and cook until the sugar and rum melt together into a sauce, about 2 more minutes.

Transfer the skillet to the oven and roast until the juices in the pan are bubbling and the bananas are beginning to curl up around the edges, 5 to 7 minutes. Remove the skillet from the oven and serve immediately.

## COMBINING YOUR CRAFT

Serve these with Brioche Pain Perdu (page 48) and Caramel Ice Cream (page 207), with Bittersweet Chocolate Cake (page 158), or with Brown Butter Ice Cream (page 210) or Vanilla Bean Ice Cream (page 204).

### SERVES 4

**4 ripe bananas**

**¼ cup sugar**

**½ "recycled" vanilla bean (see page 16) or ¼ vanilla bean, split lengthwise and scraped, bean and seeds reserved**

**¼ cup dark rum, such as Myers's**

# MAPLE ROASTED PINEAPPLE

Whole green cardamom pods lend their distinctive citrus aroma and warm, slightly fruity flavor to these caramelized pineapple rings. The finished dessert is deceptively easy, beautiful, and delicious.

Position a rack in the center of the oven and preheat the oven to 375°F.

Peel the pineapple and cut it crosswise into 6 wheels. Using a 1-inch ring cutter or a sharp knife, cut out the center core from the pineapple wheels to form rings.

Combine the maple syrup, cardamom pods, and vanilla bean (including the seeds if using a fresh bean) in a large ovenproof skillet. Heat over high heat until the syrup begins to caramelize, about 10 minutes.

Arrange the pineapple rings in a single layer in the skillet. Reduce the heat to medium-high and cook until the pineapple rings are golden brown, about 4 minutes. Flip the rings over and carefully add the pineapple juice. Cook until the syrup and juice melt together to form a sauce, 2 to 3 minutes.

Transfer the pan to the oven and roast, basting the pineapple slices with the pan juices halfway through, until the slices are bright golden brown and have a beautiful shiny glaze, about 10 minutes. You want a light, not too thick and sticky, caramel sauce. If the sauce thickens too much, thin it with up to ¼ cup additional juice.

Serve warm, straight from the oven. Or, to serve the pineapple up to 3 hours later, first cool it, still in the skillet, to room temperature; then reheat in a 375°F oven for 5 minutes just before serving.

SERVES 6

1 ripe golden pineapple

¾ cup maple syrup

10 green cardamom pods

½ "recycled" vanilla bean (see page 16) or ¼ vanilla bean, split lengthwise and scraped, bean and seeds reserved

½ cup pineapple juice or apple juice, or more if needed

# ROSÉ POACHED PEARS

As they poach in rosé wine, pears take on a gorgeous pink hue. Such easy elegance!
I am partial to the smaller-sized Boscs and the tiny Seckel pears, which I find most
often at the farmer's market, but you can use any firm-ripe pear. Local pears tend
to be smaller and more beautiful than the ones you find at the supermarket. They
almost always taste better, too.

SERVES 6

3 ripe Bosc or Bartlett pears, or
6 Seckel pears

1½ cups sugar

1 (750 ml) bottle dry rosé wine

1 "recycled" vanilla bean (see
page 16) or ¼ vanilla bean, split
lengthwise and scraped, beans
and seeds reserved

Prepare an ice bath in a large bowl, and set it aside.

Peel and halve the pears. Scoop out the cores with a melon baller
or a ½-teaspoon measuring spoon. (If you are using Seckel or
other very small pears, peel them and remove the core from the
bottom with a tiny melon baller or a ⅛-teaspoon measuring spoon.)

In a large saucepan, whisk together the sugar, 1 cup water, the
wine, and the vanilla bean (including seeds if using a fresh bean),
and bring to a boil. Transfer about one third of this poaching liquid
to a metal bowl and set the bowl into the ice bath.

Add the pears to the saucepan, cut side up, in one layer, in batches
if necessary, and reduce the heat to a gentle simmer. Cut out a
round piece of parchment paper and place it over the surface of
the poaching liquid. Simmer until the pears become translucent and
tender (a knife should slide easily into a pear), about 15 minutes.

As they are done, use a slotted spoon to transfer the poached
pears to the cooled poaching liquid. When all of the pears have
been poached, pour the liquid from the saucepan over them and
let the mixture cool, adding more ice to the ice bath if necessary.
(The pears can be stored in their poaching liquid in a covered
container in the refrigerator for up to 1 week.) Serve the pears
cold or at room temperature, with a little bit of the poaching liquid.

## VARYING YOUR CRAFT
### GINGER POACHED PEARS
Use ginger beer in place of the wine, and add 10 whole coffee
beans to the poaching liquid before heating it.

## COMBINING YOUR CRAFT
Serve the pears alongside Milk Chocolate Hazelnut Panna Cotta
(page 182).

# CHAMOMILE POACHED APRICOTS

A sweet wine from Bordeaux, Sauternes is often used in cooking, probably because it offers such distinct and intense flavors. A lively mix of peach, citrus, melon, apple, and mango qualities from the wine mingles with the delicate floral notes from fresh apricots and chamomile here. This is a light dessert, perfect for fruit-lovers and the not-too-sweet set.

SERVES 6

2 cups Sauternes or other sweet white wine

2 cups sugar

¼ cup fresh unsprayed chamomile buds, or 2 tablespoons loose dried chamomile tea

1 "recycled" vanilla bean (see page 16), or ¼ vanilla bean, split lengthwise and scraped, bean and seeds reserved

1 strip lemon zest, removed with a vegetable peeler

9 ripe apricots, halved and pitted

TIP Fresh chamomile buds can be found at farmer's markets and in backyard gardens. When using dried loose chamomile tea in place of the fresh buds, tie the tea in an unbleached cheesecloth sachet or in a tea filter to keep the tiny leaves from sticking to the fruit.

Prepare an ice bath in a large bowl, and set it aside.

In a medium saucepan, combine the wine, 2 cups water, the sugar, chamomile, vanilla bean (including the seeds if using a fresh bean), and lemon zest. Bring to a boil over high heat. Transfer about one third of this poaching liquid to a metal bowl and set the bowl into the ice bath.

Add the apricots to the saucepan, cut side up, in one layer, taking care not to crowd the pan. Reduce the heat to a bare simmer. Cut out a round piece of parchment paper and place it over the surface of the poaching liquid. Simmer until the apricots feel tender to the touch and are bright orange in color, 7 to 10 minutes.

As they are done, use a slotted spoon to transfer the poached apricots to the cooled poaching liquid. When all of the apricots have been poached, pour the liquid from the saucepan over them and let the mixture cool, adding more ice to the ice bath if necessary. (The apricots can be stored in their poaching liquid in a covered container in the refrigerator for up to 3 days.) Serve the apricots cold or at room temperature, with a little bit of the poaching liquid.

COMBINING YOUR CRAFT

Serve these alongside Almond Pound Cake (page 144) or over chilled Jasmine Rice Pudding (page 195).

# FRESH RASPBERRY COMPOTE

This quick no-cook compote can be spooned onto biscuits, scones, or buttered toast, swirled into plain yogurt, or served over tea cakes. Since it does not keep well, make it on the day you want to use it. The recipe can be easily halved or doubled, so you can make only as much as you need.

Put 1½ cups of the raspberries in a mixing bowl. Stir in the sugar, and mash the berries with the back of a spoon. Let sit at room temperature for about 10 minutes to draw out the juices from the fruit.

Gently fold in the remaining 1½ cups whole berries. Serve immediately, or store, covered, in an airtight container in the refrigerator for up to 3 hours.

### COMBINING YOUR CRAFT
Serve the compote over slices of Bittersweet Chocolate Cake (page 158).

**MAKES 2 CUPS**

3 cups fresh raspberries

3 tablespoons sugar

# SOUR CHERRY COMPOTE

A perfect combination of sweet and tart. Dollop this brilliantly colored compote on top of pancakes, scones, or slices of cake.

Combine the cherries, sugar, and vitamin C powder in a bowl and stir together. Cover and refrigerate for at least 1 hour, or overnight.

Scrape the cherries and their juices into a small saucepan. Cook over medium-high heat until the juices increase and the mixture becomes foamy, about 7 minutes. Remove the pan from the heat and strain the syrup from the fruit, reserving both separately.

Place the cherries in a large bowl. Return the syrup to the saucepan and bring it to a boil. Then reduce the heat to a simmer and cook until the syrup is thickened and reduced by about one half, about 10 minutes. Pour the syrup over the cherries, and gently stir to combine. Chill in an ice bath or in the refrigerator. Serve chilled.

The sour cherry compote will keep, well covered, in the refrigerator, for up to 2 weeks.

**MAKES 2 CUPS**

4 cups (about 1 pound) fresh sour cherries, stemmed and pitted

¾ cup sugar

½ teaspoon vitamin C powder (see Sources)

# APRICOT COMPOTE

Apricot season is brief, and this compote should be made only with the best local apricots you can find, at their peak ripeness. Cherish them while they last!

MAKES 1 1/3 CUPS

**1 pound fresh firm-ripe apricots, pitted and cut into eighths**

**¾ cup sugar**

**½ teaspoon vitamin C powder (see Sources)**

Stir together the apricots, sugar, and vitamin C powder in a mixing bowl. Cover the fruit with plastic wrap, pressing the wrap against the surface to prevent browning, and then seal the bowl well with a second sheet of plastic wrap. Refrigerate for at least 8 hours, or overnight.

Scrape the apricots and their juices into a large saucepan. Cook over medium heat, stirring occasionally, until the fruit is tender, about 8 minutes. Remove the pan from the heat and strain the syrup from the fruit, reserving both separately.

Place the apricots in a large bowl. Return the syrup to the saucepan and bring to a boil. Cook until the syrup is thickened and reduced to about ¾ cup, about 10 minutes. Pour the syrup over the apricots and gently stir to combine. Chill in an ice bath or in the refrigerator. Serve chilled.

The apricot compote will keep, well covered, in the refrigerator for up to 2 weeks.

## COMBINING YOUR CRAFT

Serve Apricot Compote with Almond Pound Cake (page 144), or Brown Butter Waffles (page 38), or over Vanilla Bean Ice Cream (page 204).

# BLUEBERRY COMPOTE

Cooking half of the berries with sugar and lemon juice and then folding in the rest gives this simple compote a thickish jammy texture. I love the way the whole berries burst in your mouth when you bite into them. This is another instance where the freshest fruit produces the best results. Purchase locally grown blueberries, or pick your own when you can. If your berries are especially tart, use less lemon juice or leave it out entirely. This is great with buttered toast and baked breakfast treats, or as a sauce for ice creams and light cakes.

MAKES 2¾ CUPS

**4 cups fresh blueberries, any stems removed**

**½ cup plus 3 tablespoons sugar**

**1 tablespoon strained fresh lemon juice**

Put 2 cups of the berries in a large heatproof bowl, and set aside.

Combine the remaining 2 cups berries, the sugar, and the lemon juice in a medium saucepan. Bring to a simmer over medium-high heat and cook, stirring frequently, until the juices release, 8 to 10 minutes.

Increase the heat to high, bring the mixture to a boil, and cook, whisking frequently, until the compote has thickened, about 2 minutes. Pour it over the uncooked berries and, using a rubber spatula, gently fold together. Serve warm or chilled.

The blueberry compote will keep in a covered container in the refrigerator for up to 3 days.

# APPLE BUTTER

My favorite way to use this super-thick, rich, caramel-y apple sauce is as a spread for scones and muffins. It also makes a good side to a simple doughnut or slice of pound cake.

Peel and core the apples, and cut them into 1-inch pieces.

In a large saucepan with a lid, whisk together the sugar, cinnamon sticks, vanilla bean and seeds, and ½ cup water. Cook over high heat until the mixture becomes a dark golden caramel, about 10 minutes.

Add the apples and stir to coat them with the caramel. Reduce the heat to low and cook, covered, stirring frequently, until the apples are very soft and beginning to break down, about 45 minutes.

Remove the pan from the heat. Remove the cinnamon sticks and vanilla bean. Discard the cinnamon sticks, but reserve the vanilla to recycle for another use (see page 16).

In a blender, purée the apple mixture until smooth. Transfer the apple butter to a container, cover it, and refrigerate until ready to use. (The apple butter will keep for up to 2 weeks.)

## VARYING YOUR CRAFT
### QUINCE BUTTER
Replace the apples with 4 pounds of quince. Add 2 cups apple cider after stirring the quince into the caramelized sugar.

## COMBINING YOUR CRAFT
Spread Apple Butter or (Quince Butter) onto Pumpkin Spice Bread (page 33), or serve it alongside Apple Fritters (page 36).

MAKES 4½ CUPS

**10 McIntosh apples (about 4 pounds)**

**1½ cups sugar**

**2 cinnamon sticks**

**½ vanilla bean, split lengthwise, seeds scraped out, bean and seeds reserved**

# OLIVE OIL SABAYON

Sabayon is a light custard flavored with wine that is enjoyed as a dessert on its own or as a sauce. I love it over fresh fruit or pound cake. The character of the olive oil you choose really comes through in this sauce, without competing with the fruit and floral notes of the wine. Choose a good-quality, fruity-tasting oil, as opposed to a peppery one.

MAKES 1½ CUPS

**6 large egg yolks**

**¾ cup Sauternes or other sweet white wine**

**¼ cup plus 2 tablespoons sugar**

**Finely grated zest of 1 lemon**

**¼ teaspoon kosher salt**

**3 tablespoons good-quality extra-virgin olive oil**

**1 cup heavy cream**

**TIP** While preparing a sabayon, it's important to keep the water under the sauce at a bare simmer. If it's too hot, the sabayon will curdle.

Fill a large saucepan with about 2 inches of water and bring it to a gentle simmer.

In a medium nonreactive metal bowl, combine the yolks, wine, sugar, lemon zest, and salt. Place the bowl over the pan of barely simmering water and cook, whisking constantly, until the mixture changes in texture from light and fluffy to shiny and thick, about 15 minutes.

Remove the bowl from the heat. While whisking, slowly drizzle in the oil. If the sauce is at all lumpy, strain it through a fine-mesh sieve into a bowl, using a rubber spatula to push it through.

In a medium bowl, whip the cream to soft peaks. Gently fold half of the whipped cream into the yolk mixture, and then fold in the remaining half. Transfer the sabayon to an airtight container, and cover the surface directly with a piece of plastic wrap. Cover the container, and refrigerate for up to 4 hours.

## VARYING YOUR CRAFT
### LILLET SABAYON
Use white Lillet in place of the Sauternes. Omit the olive oil.

# LEMON CURD

Lemon curd is most often thought of as a tart filling. Reconsider it as more of an all-purpose ingredient, however, and the possibilities for enjoying this tangy topping quickly grow. Spread it on scones, muffins, toast, and pound cakes, or use it as a filling or frosting for cakes, cupcakes, and doughnuts on its own or folded into vanilla buttercream, meringue, or fresh whipped cream.

**MAKES 1¼ CUPS**

Finely grated zest of 3 lemons

½ cup fresh lemon juice (from 3 lemons)

½ cup sugar

3 large eggs

3 large egg yolks

½ teaspoon kosher salt

8 tablespoons (1 stick) unsalted butter, cut into small pieces, at room temperature

Bring about 2 inches of water to a gentle simmer in a large saucepan.

In a medium heatproof bowl, whisk together the lemon zest, lemon juice, sugar, eggs, egg yolks, and salt. Set the bowl over the saucepan of simmering water, and whisking constantly, cook until the mixture is thick enough that a trail can be pulled across the surface with the whisk without it immediately filling in, 10 to 12 minutes.

Remove the bowl from the heat and let the curd cool to warm room temperature, about 5 minutes. Then whisk in the butter, one cube at a time, until well combined and smooth.

Strain the curd through a fine-mesh sieve into an airtight container. Cover the curd with plastic wrap, pressing the wrap directly onto the surface to keep a skin from forming. Cover the container and refrigerate until ready to use. (The lemon curd will keep for up to 2 weeks.)

# MALTED CHOCOLATE SAUCE

This sauce brings an old-time soda fountain taste to ice creams and cakes. Blended with vanilla ice cream, it also makes a fantastic chocolate malted milkshake.

In a medium heatproof bowl, combine the two types of chocolate.

In a small saucepan, bring the cream, milk, and corn syrup to a boil. Remove the pan from the heat and whisk in the malt syrup. Pour about one fourth of this mixture over the chocolate, whisking well to melt as much as possible. Add a little more of the hot liquid and whisk to melt the remaining chocolate. Add the rest of the liquid to the chocolate and whisk together until smooth and well combined. Whisk in the vanilla and salt.

Use the sauce immediately, or transfer it to an airtight container and refrigerate for up to 2 weeks. Reheat the sauce in a double boiler or in a heatproof bowl set over a saucepan of simmering water.

**MAKES 2 CUPS**

4 ounces bittersweet chocolate (70%), roughly chopped

4 ounces semisweet chocolate (60%), roughly chopped

1 cup heavy cream

½ cup whole milk

¼ cup light corn syrup

½ cup barley malt syrup (see Sources)

1 teaspoon pure vanilla extract

½ teaspoon kosher salt

# PINEAPPLE CARDAMOM SAUCE

This tropical-tasting sauce is one of the easiest to make. Its base is maple syrup, making it great with pancakes or waffles, though it's also tasty drizzled over panna cottas and ice creams.

In a medium saucepan, toast the cardamom pods over high heat, shaking the pan occasionally, until they are lightly golden, about 2 minutes. Add the maple syrup and cook until the syrup begins to caramelize, about 3 minutes. Add the pineapple and continue cooking, stirring occasionally, until the pineapple is softened and golden, about 7 minutes.

Transfer the mixture to a blender and purée until smooth. Then strain the purée through a fine-mesh sieve into a bowl. Serve the sauce warm, or store it in a covered container in the refrigerator for up to 2 weeks. Reheat it in a saucepan over low heat.

**MAKES 1½ CUPS**

6 green cardamom pods

¾ cup maple syrup

½ large golden pineapple, peeled, cored, and cut into 1-inch pieces

# HOT FUDGE SAUCE

Drizzle this crowd-pleaser over ice cream and cakes, or use it like a fondue for dipping fruit.

In a large heavy-bottomed saucepan, bring the cream, milk, corn syrup, sugar, cocoa powder, and salt to a boil over medium-high heat. Whisk in 1 ounce (two-thirds) of the chocolate and the vinegar.

Reduce the heat to medium and cook until the mixture thickens and has a bit of a sticky elasticity to it, testing it as it gets close (see Tip), 12 to 15 minutes.

Remove the pan from the heat and whisk in the remaining chocolate, the butter, and the vanilla extract. Use the hot fudge immediately, or transfer it to an airtight container and refrigerate it for up to 2 weeks. Reheat the sauce in a small saucepan over low heat.

## MAKES 2 CUPS

**1 cup heavy cream**

**½ cup whole milk**

**1 cup light corn syrup**

**½ cup sugar**

**¼ cup unsweetened cocoa powder**

**1 teaspoon kosher salt**

**1½ ounces bittersweet chocolate (70%), roughly chopped**

**½ teaspoon cider vinegar or white vinegar**

**2 tablespoons unsalted butter**

**1 teaspoon pure vanilla extract**

**TIP** As the sauce begins to get close to being done, the best way to test it is to remove a few drops with a spoon, let it cool slightly, and then press it between your thumb and forefinger. When it feels tacky, it's ready.

# SPICED CARAMEL SAUCE

Combining sweet and spicy flavors works well in savory foods and sweets alike. Here exotic spices, like star anise, combine with pantry basics, like sweet cinnamon and nutmeg. Black pepper and ginger bring in the kick. The longer the spices steep in the sauce, the richer and more peppery your sauce will be.

**MAKES 3 CUPS**

**8 cinnamon sticks**

**3 whole star anise**

**1 teaspoon whole black peppercorns**

**5 green cardamom pods**

**2 cups sugar**

**¼ cup light corn syrup**

**½ vanilla bean, split lengthwise, seeds scraped out, bean and seeds reserved**

**Zest of 1 orange, removed in strips with a vegetable peeler**

**8 tablespoons (1 stick) unsalted butter, cut into small pieces**

**1 cup heavy cream**

**¼ cup crème fraîche**

**1 teaspoon ground ginger**

**½ teaspoon freshly grated nutmeg**

**¾ teaspoon kosher salt**

In a large heavy-bottomed saucepan over medium heat, toast the cinnamon sticks, star anise, black peppercorns, and green cardamom pods until they become fragrant, about 5 minutes. Add the sugar, corn syrup, vanilla bean and seeds, orange zest, and ½ cup water. Whisk gently together to make sure all of the sugar is damp, being careful not to get sugar on the sides of the pot.

Cook over high heat until the mixture turns a deep caramel color, about 8 minutes. Remove the pot from the heat and carefully whisk in the butter, cream, and crème fraîche. Whisk in the ginger, nutmeg, and salt.

Refrigerate the sauce, with all of the spices, in an airtight container for several hours, or up to 2 weeks. Just before serving, warm the sauce in a saucepan over low heat, and then strain it through a fine-mesh sieve into a bowl.

# APPLE CIDER
# CARAMEL SAUCE

In this version, fresh apples and apple cider replace the cream and butter used in a classic caramel, making for a lighter sauce with a clean, fruity flavor.

**2¼ cups sugar**

**½ cup light corn syrup**

**¼ vanilla bean, split lengthwise, seeds scraped out, bean and seeds reserved**

**2 small tart baking apples, such as Mutsu, Cortland, or Granny Smith, cored, and cut into 1-inch pieces**

**¾ cup apple cider**

**¼ teaspoon kosher salt**

Combine the sugar, corn syrup, ½ cup water, and the vanilla bean and seeds in a medium saucepan. Cook over high heat until the sugar becomes a medium golden caramel, about 15 minutes.

Add the apples and stir to combine. Reduce the heat to low and cook until the apples have softened, 2 to 3 minutes. Carefully add the cider and stir to combine. Continue to cook until the sauce is sticky, about 5 minutes more.

Remove the pan from the heat and remove the vanilla bean. Rinse and recycle the vanilla bean for another use (see page 16). Whisk the salt into the mixture.

Transfer the caramel mixture to a blender and purée until smooth. Strain it through a fine-mesh sieve into a bowl. Serve immediately, or store in an airtight container in the refrigerator for up to 2 weeks. Reheat the sauce in a saucepan over low heat.

## COMBINING YOUR CRAFT
Drizzle the sauce over Apple Fritters (page 36) and Caramel Ice Cream (page 207).

# SOURCES

## CHOCOLATES

Look for El Rey chocolates at fine supermarkets, including Whole Foods markets (www.wholefoods market.com). A listing of retail stores that sell El Rey is available at www.chocolateselrey.com.

For Chocovic chocolates, contact SOS Chefs (104 Avenue B, New York, NY 10009; 212-505-5813; www.sos-chefs.com).

Scharffen Berger chocolates and cacao nibs can be found at fine markets, including Whole Foods markets (www.wholefoodsmarket.com), or ordered from Scharffen Berger (800-930-4528; www.scharffenberger.com).

## CONDIMENTS

Rose petal jam is available at Kalustyan's (123 Lexington Avenue, New York, NY 10016; 212-685-3451; 800-352-3451; www.kalustyans.com).

## DAIRY PRODUCTS

Vermont Butter & Cheese crème fraîche is available at fine supermarkets, including Whole Foods markets (www.wholefoodsmarket.com), or at www.butterandcheese.net.

High-quality fresh whole-milk ricotta cheese can be purchased at fine supermarkets, including Whole Foods markets (www.wholefoodsmarket.com), and at specialty cheese shops, like Murray's Cheese (888-MY-CHEEZ; www.murrayscheese.com). Calabro's whole-milk ricotta is widely available in mainstream supermarkets.

Sheep's milk yogurt from 3-Corner Field Farm can be ordered at www.dairysheepfarm.com (County Route 64, Shushan, NY 12873; 518-854-9695). Old Chatham Sheep's Milk Yogurt is available at fine supermarkets, including Whole Foods markets (www.wholefoodsmarket.com), and at blacksheepcheese.com.

## FLAVORINGS

The absolute best vanilla beans and paste I've purchased can be ordered from Aaron Isaacson, aka Mr. Recipe (646-261-4460; www.mrrecipe .com; but note that Mr. Recipe has a $250 minimum order). Very high quality vanilla beans, vanilla paste, and pure vanilla extract are also available at King Arthur Flour (58 Billings Farm Road, White River Junction, VT 05001; 800-827-6836; www.kingarthurflour.com); at SOS Chefs (104 Avenue B, New York, NY 10009; 212-505-5813; www.sos-chefs.com); at Williams-Sonoma shops and online (www.williams-sonoma.com); and at Penzeys Spices (800-741-7787; www. penzeys.com).

For Trablit coffee extract, contact SOS Chefs (104 Avenue B, New York, NY 10009; 212-505-5813; www.sos-chefs.com).

## FLOURS

King Arthur flours, including nut flours, are widely available in supermarkets and can be ordered from King Arthur Flour (58 Billings Farm Road, White River Junction, VT 05001; 800-827-6836; www.kingarthurflour.com).

## FOIL RAMEKINS
Four-ounce foil ramekins can be purchased from the online kitchen store Kitchen Dance (866-638-3374; www.kitchendance.com).

## FRUIT
Fresh and frozen sour cherries are available at Friske Orchards (10743 N. U.S. 31, Ellsworth, MI 49729; 231-599-2604; www.apples-cherries.com).

## NUTS
Almond paste is available at Whole Foods (www.wholefoodsmarket.com) and other markets.

For Sicilian pistachios, contact SOS Chefs (104 Avenue B, New York, NY 10009; 212-505-5813; www.sos-chefs.com).

Marcona almonds can be purchased at fine supermarkets, including Whole Foods markets (www.wholefoodsmarket.com), and at specialty cheese shops, like Murray's Cheese (888-MY-CHEEZ; www.murrayscheese.com).

## POLENTA
Polenta from Anson Mills can be found at good supermarkets or ordered at www.ansonmills.com.

## POWDERED PECTIN
Pomona's Universal Pectin can be found in supermarkets or at www.amazon.com.

## SPICES
Green cardamom pods, pink peppercorns, and Saigon cinnamon can be ordered from Kalustyan's (123 Lexington Avenue, New York, NY 10016; 212-685-3451; www.kalustyans.com); from Penzeys Spices (800-741-7787; www.penzeys.com); and from the Spice House (847-328-3711; www.thespicehouse.com).

## SWEETENERS
Barley malt syrup, Demerara sugar, maple sugar, and grade B maple syrup can be purchased at health food stores, large fine supermarkets, or at King Arthur Flour (58 Billings Farm Road, White River Junction, VT 05001; 800-827-6836; www.kingarthurflour.com).

Natural granulated sugar, organic light brown sugar, organic dark brown sugar, organic molasses made by Wholesome Sweeteners, and organic dark brown molasses sugar made by Billington's can be purchased at fine supermarkets, including Whole Foods markets (www.wholefoodsmarket.com), and at www.amazon.com.

Honey from Tremblay Apiaries can be ordered from Tremblay (607-589-7638; www.tremblayapiaries.com). Many other fine honeys can be purchased at Whole Foods markets (www.wholefoodsmarket.com) and at fine supermarkets.

## VITAMIN C POWDER
Non-buffered vitamin C powder can be purchased at vitamin stores like GNC (www.gnc.com) and the Vitamin Shoppe (www.thevitaminshoppe.com), and at www.amazon.com.

## CREDITS
### OCHRE: 212-414-4332
Page 80: Plate and green linen throw,
Page 110: Forks and natural linen fabric,
Page 171: Plate, Page 199: Sheer linen,
Page 215: Bowl, glasses, and spoons,
Page 218: Plate and linen, Page 222: Cedar board,
Page 227: Sheer linen, Page 241: White bowl

### LA CAFETIERE: 646-486-0667
Page 194: Glass bowls, Page 208: Glasses,
Page 244: Glass bowl

# ACKNOWLEDGMENTS

A lot of talent and hard work went into this book. Thanks to my coauthor, Mindy Fox, whose meticulous attention to detail and perfection I admire and aspire to, and to Jocelyn Morse-Farmerie, our mutual friend who introduced us when the timing was right. To Ellen Silverman, our talented photographer, who from the day I met her treated this project as a labor of love, and to her talented assistants, Kevin Norris and Nick Duers. To Bette Blau, who shared our vision and made it a reality with the beautiful props she collected. Thanks to Marilyn Cadenbach for working so doggedly with us to make it possible for us to work with Ellen and Bette. Abby Swain, not only a great pastry cook—your keen eye (and hands) added so much to the success of our photo shoot. Thanks for making the trek from Atlanta. It has been exciting to work with such a talented group.

David Black—so much more than my agent—after many years, you have never lost your enthusiasm for this project. Thank you. Thanks also to David's great staff, especially Antonella Iannarino and David Larabell, for making everything run smoothly.

Thank you to everyone at Clarkson Potter: my editor, Rica Allannic, editorial assistant and passionate home baker Ashley Phillips, book designer Amy Sly, production editor Patty Shaw, and production manager Joan Denman.

Thanks to Tom Colicchio for years of guidance, trust, and support. Opening Craft, Craftbar, and 'wichcraft with you was an invaluable experience and one that helped make me the chef that I am today. Also thanks to the many great people I met there over the years: Damon Wise, Marco Canora, Akhtar Nawab, Sisha Ortuzar, Katie Greico, Victor Salazar, and so many others. Thanks to my former sous-chefs: Lauren Fortgang, Anya Regelin, and Laura Werts; along with all of the cooks who passed through my kitchen, most notably Erica Leahy, Gretchen Derov, Laura Morriss, Genevieve Meli, Nicole Carango Bengtson, Cristin Walsh, Carmen Perez, Aracelis Polonco, Elizabeth Flores, and Jessica Chien (who also helped so much with recipe testing). I have seen you all move on to great success, and I am so proud.

Thanks to Claudia Fleming, a friend and mentor, who taught me how to think about desserts, seasonality, the importance of making things fresh every day, and letting great products speak for themselves.

To Sam Hayward, Scott Bryan, Lisa Hershey, David and Karen Waltuck, Kevin Penner, John Schaffer, Andrew Carmellini—it has been such an honor working with you.

Thanks to the farmers and purveyors who have provided me with endless inspiration: Berried Treasures, Fantasy Fruit Farm, Phillips Farm, Samascott Farm, Stokes Farm, Tremblay Apiaries, Locust Grove Farm, and Red Jacket Orchards, Don Wagger, Steve and Sylvia Pryzant at Four Story Farm, Aaron Issacson of Mr. Recipe, and Atef Boulaabi at SOS Chefs.

Thanks to Robert Steinberg, who passed away in 2008. As a founder of Scharffen Berger Chocolate, he was a source of unending knowledge about chocolate as well as a good friend.

To my parents, David and Nancy Parham— for your unconditional love and support.

To Ena Barnett, thanks for the love and care you give to my daughters.

To the most important people in my life—my husband, Robert, and my daughters, Mary and Madeline—you bring me more happiness than all the sweets in the world.

—KAREN DEMASCO

Enormous thanks first and foremost to Karen DeMasco, for putting her trust in me as a coauthor and for being such a tireless, dedicated, and fun person to work with. My baking prowess has increased tenfold due to your generous sharing of the craft you know so well.

Thank you to the team at Clarkson Potter: our editor, Rica Allannic, who got us from "there to here" in one piece; designer Amy Sly, for her thoughtful and beautiful work; and editorial assistant Ashley Phillips, who quickly offered an answer to every question along the way.

To our photographer, Ellen Silverman, and our prop stylist, Bette Blau—amazing talents, incredible teammates, and now great friends— thank you for going the extra hundred miles and then some for this project. And to assistants Kevin Norris, Nick Duers, and Abby Swain.

Thank you to my close friends in the field whose creativity and cheering-on inspire me every day: Jennifer Aaronson, Lisa Amand, Josh Dake, Allison Fishman, G. Giraldo, Gabrielle Langholtz, Irene Hamburger, Linsey Herman, Marisa Huff, Robin Insley, Cameron Kane, Sumo Morrison, Jocelyn Morse-Farmerie, Corina Quinn, Gail Simmons, Meeghan

Truelove, Michael Wilson, and Amy Zavatto, among them.

To wonderful mentors Tina Ujlaki, Nancy Harmon Jenkins, and Dorothy Kalins—my gratitude for your continued support and guidance.

David Black—I am a lucky gal and a deeply appreciative one to have you as my agent. Thank you for bringing so much thought, sincerity, exuberance, and support to this and many other projects. Sincere thanks, as well, to your staff, especially David Larabell and Antonella Iannarino, for endless loads of help.

To my mom and dad, Phyllis and Neil Fox, thank you for your boundless enthusiasm for my path and for sharing so much of your good food and talent behind the stove with me. And to my brother, Jason Fox—a great chef, forager, and wine guy—it is so much fun sharing our parallel careers and love for all the good stuff we eat, drink, read, and think about.

And last, but far from least, deepest thanks to my husband, Stephen Hoffman, and our loving hound, Guinness, who make every day of my life a sweet one.

—MINDY FOX

# INDEX